Waterville

Augusta

Belfast

Rockland

Round
Pond

Owls Head

Spruce Head

Vinalhaven

Boothbay Harbor

South Bristol

Pemaquid Point

Muscongus Bay

Monhegan

Port Clyde

Tenants Harbor

Matinicus

Criehaven

Mi.
10   20

10   20   30

Km.

The Great LOBSTER Chase

FOR THE LOWES;
THEY ARE THE GREATEST

[signature]

The Great LOBSTER Chase

THE *REAL* STORY OF MAINE LOBSTERS AND THE MEN WHO CATCH THEM

Mike Brown

With illustrations by Jim Sollers

INTERNATIONAL MARINE
PUBLISHING COMPANY
Camden, Maine

©1985 by Mike Brown

Typeset by The Key Word, Inc., Belchertown, Massachusetts
Printed and bound by BookCrafters, Inc., Chelsea, Michigan

Second printing, 1986

Published by International Marine Publishing Company
21 Elm Street, Camden, Maine 04843
(207) 236-4342

Library of Congress Cataloging in Publication Data

Brown, Mike, 1929–
   The great lobster chase.

   Bibliography: p. 201
   Includes index.
   1. Lobster fisheries—Maine.   2. American lobster.
I. Title.
SH380.B76 1985   639'.541'09741   84-47847
ISBN 0-87742-174-9

 # Contents

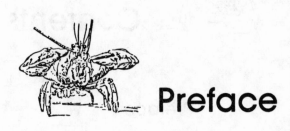

Preface

To purposefully sit down and try to write a book explaining the myriad nuances of lobsterfishing was a humbling experience. Perhaps the tasks and toils, rewards and hardships of lobstermen are better left as local, unrecorded knowledge passed down through generations like the unwritten dialects of ancient, forgotten peoples.

For, for every lobsterman there is an opinion. For every person, no matter how slightly associated with the harvest and trade of lobsters, there is pride and prejudice, success and defeat, joy and sorrow. But the most fascinating facet of lobstering is the overwhelming strain of independence that permeates an industry with few if any parallels in free commerce. Not to at least attempt to chronicle a part of this marine adventure would seem a shame.

I started lobsterfishing when I was about five years old at the hand and side of my father, who believed that all sons should learn the timetable of the oceans. Over half a century later, as I sit writing these words on the shore of Penobscot Bay where my lobster buoys are writhing in a cold northeast November snow squall, I have been completely captivated by the American lobster and his only true adversary, the lobsterman.

Over those decades, I have written thousands of stories about these two combatants. But it wasn't until the genesis of this book and the compilation of the seemingly inexhaustible supply of opinion and fact and fancy, that it all began to congeal and I began to understand what an incredible lifestyle is forged from predator and prey. One saying led to a story. One story to a chapter. One chapter to a book—a profile.

Happily, there is no definitive book of lobstering. To attempt one would be folly. But lest we all forget sometime, this is a small foray into one mystery of the sea. The makings of the book, the words, were born of frustration, laughter, pathos, wit, amazement, but most of all—enjoyment.

Mike Brown
Saturday Cove
Northport, Maine
November 15, 1984

ONE

The Lobsterman

It is cold, damn cold, one of those hanger-on late March teen-degree mornings when lobsterman Harold Martin slams the door of his pickup truck at the cooperative wharf. There is still snow on the ground, dirty gravel snow like butterscotch pudding that has been frozen and thawed too many times, finally to be left in the dog dish in the hope that it will disappear. Dirty snow, thinks Harold, as he walks down the planked dock to the co-op office. This is my fortieth year of dirty snow.

Already, at 5 o'clock in the morning, there are other lobstermen at the co-op. The double 55-gallon-drum wood stove is humping, as the co-op boy Stevie likes to say. The warmth spreads around the small office like flowing honey, and Harold turns his body rotisserie-fashion, making morning small talk. The starting price of lobsters. No-good wire traps. The $2-a-hundred increase in oak laths. Heading twine is up three bucks a ball. Jesus, Harold thinks, as he has thought every March morning for the past five years, this is my last year. Forty years of hauling. Forty years of stinking bait barrels, stinking boats, and leaky boots. Forty goddamn years of dirty snow.

Last night on high water Harold put 20 traps aboard his Jonesport lobsterboat, some new, some patched, some on their last voyage secretly riddled with yards of tunnels bored by invisible marine worms. Give me one more year, Harold silently muttered to the tender traps as he loaded them aboard *Bobby & Jean* under a cirrus sky. One more year, the story of my life.

The cleats on the gangway to the lobster float are clogged with ice. They fill with water and slush during the day and freeze at night, making a ladder of ice wedges. Twenty years ago Harold slid the whole length of the gangway breaking two fingers on his left hand. Forty years of ice wedges . . . .

His punt painter is on the bottom of the float as usual, and Harold has to uncleat four others before coming to his own. The ropes are semifrozen from salt vapor and water and wind. He thinks about when he was a kid and they chose up for scrub baseball. Somebody threw the bat and a kid grabbed it and everybody started piling fist upon fist. The top fist was up first. Harold was always up last. His fist on the bottom, like his punt painter.

There is only one oar in Harold's punt and it is lying in the white bottom slush. Just an old broken orange oar that Harold found floating one day. He has never rowed his punt. There are no oarlocks aboard. Harold, like all lobstermen, just stands up and paddles back and forth to his moorings. A warden stopped him one afternoon and gave him a warning because he didn't have a life preserver aboard. Now he carries one. It is frozen up under the stern seat of the punt. It has been that way since Thanksgiving. An iceball of kapok and straps and buckles. An official league ball to play the game with.

Harold thumps against *Bobby & Jean* and notices her short skirt of ice at the waterline. Tying the punt to the ringbolt on the stern, he climbs into the cockpit and walks forward and unlocks the sliding door to the pilothouse. Never locked it 20 years ago, never even thought about it. But lobstering ain't the same nowadays, for sure. Lifting the engine-box cover, Harold notices the bilge water is where it should be, the Rule automatic switch sitting high and dry like a fat, red bullfrog. He hits the starter switch and the Chevy growls its required seconds of protest, like a sleeping hound dog kicked out from under the kitchen table for a goodnight watering.

Harold is one to idle his engine. Warm her up slowly like a woman. They appreciate it and last longer is Harold's engine/woman philosophy. The bare stainless steel exhaust stack is giving out heat now, and Harold molds a pair of soggy blue dunker gloves around the pipe to dry them. They sizzle and sear and fall to the floor. Harold switches on his Radio Shack CB. Channel 14. Fifteen years ago when he installed the radio he set the dial at channel 14. It has never moved from that number. Harold has thought about getting a new CB, one of those 40-channel jobs. Everybody has them. But, what the hell, he's giving up lobstering this year.

Taking the mike from the overhead where it lives between two galvanized trap nails, Harold presses the talk button. "You on, Effiejean?"

He waits a couple seconds and then calls again. "You on there yet, Effiejean? C'mon back."

'I'm here, Harold."

"Christ, I've been calling you f'half an hour. Where the hell you been?"

"Just here. Where would I go, Harold?"

"Well, I'm on. Leaving the mooring now. Give you a call later on this morning. Ten, maybe half past."

Harold returns the mike to its double nail rest and climbs forward and lets go his mooring chain and ball after tying the punt painter through the chain loop.

"Take the day off, you little bastard," Harold says to his one-oared watchdog.

He clears the harbor buoy and heads sou'east. He'll set a 20-trap string south of Seal Island and then haul nor'west the 150 traps he set out last week.

"A little chop," Harold says to *Bobby & Jean*, "but a pretty good chance, old girl, considering March." He talks to his boat all day long. He is always calling her old girl.

"C'mon old girl, let's find that trap."

"C'mon old girl, what's a little fog."

"Well, old girl, let's eat lunch."

"That's it old girl, let's head f'the barn."

Running sou'west, Harold sees the other lobsterboats now. If he hadn't been an idler, he'd be hauling like the rest of them. Funny how they all look the same, haulers tugging on pot warp like a puppy on a rope—circling, tugging, and the trap jumping out of water to bite the rail. Yellow midgets throwing black specks back overboard. Splash and splash all day long. Tug, throw, splash. What damn fools we are, Harold thinks. I mean it, this is my last year.

Harold switches on his paper recorder, and the stylus offers him a soft, wide line at 30 fathoms. But he already knew he was on his grounds. The marks are there. Ledge, island spruce, water tower.

"Chore time, old girl."

For the next hour Harold does what 40 years of lobstering make him do. The ritual is pat. Harold likens lobstering to cowboying. All day in the saddle. Good horse under you knowing what to do. Roping in those doggies. He thinks he could go West and be cowboying in two days. Effiejean would like cowboys.

The twentieth trap buoy hits the water and Harold turns *Bobby & Jean* due north. The slanting morning sun shows Harold's track, his string of white and red buoys a mile long, straight as a string of popcorn, claiming that piece of ground he has claimed for 40 years. Rangeland for a cowboy, Harold thinks to himself, watching his colors dance in the chop.

"Not a bad chance out here this morning, old girl," he says as he picks up the mountain-range marks for his first string of traps.

Harold set out his first lobster trap when he was eight years old. His father was a lobsterman, and his two older brothers, in their teens, had been lobstering on their own since high school. Up until he was six, Harold was the gofer who ran a supply route from the trap shed to the house and store.

"Harold, how about getting me a sandwich?"

"Harold, my jackknife is upstairs in my pants pocket, you know the ones I wore yesterday."

"Harold, you run down t'the store f'three Cokes n' I'll give you a nickel."

Between gofer duties, Harold learned to build traps. He could set the bows on the jig, nail the laths, string the heads, and build a door by the time he was six. But the built trap was too heavy to lug outside.

3

At the co-op

His gofer chores became more rewarding and his father and brothers paid off his errands in trap stock so that by the end of the winter of the second year of his grade schooling, Harold Martin was a genuine lobsterman with three traps of his very own. When April came around he hitched a ride with his brother and set his first trap beside a huge underwater boulder at Little River Point. Harold remembers how it slid off the skiff rail, the splash it made of airy bubbles and gurgles and how the pot warp followed his trap to the bottom like a snake. Then silence as the warp went limp and he was holding his red and white buoy and his brother was standing there smiling at him. Harold threw the buoy high in the air and it went splat on the cove water and

4

Harold yelled and his brother laughed and at that moment he became a lobsterman.

Each year there were more traps. His small dory became a skiff, which got bigger every spring, which became too small every fall. The outboards became inboards. A piece of the open sky was challenged by a canvas dodger and then the sky was erased with a cabin roof, and before he graduated from high school Harold had 150 traps and a bank account.

His only detour was the Korean War and he has never been able to explain that to himself. His brothers had joined the service during World War II, and Harold remembered them coming home in sailor uniforms. He'd sit for hours listening to their stories of big ships and battles and going on liberty in Norfolk, and how there were places where for three dollars you could have a girl. Being a little brother staying home and hauling lobster traps was definitely a sacrifice, one that Harold collected on just about the time his brothers came home from the wars for good.

He joined the Marines. He couldn't explain this to his father and mother anymore than to himself, but the day came when he put his traps on the bank and his boat in the cradle and followed his orders to Parris Island, South Carolina. The days were long and the discipline rough, and many the night he lay under the USMC green wool blanket and longed for his boat, his traps, the splash and gurgle of oak laths hitting the water. He thought of them at Camp Lejeune, at Camp Pendleton, the maneuvers in the Caribbean at Vieques Island, and yes, once in a Norfolk whorehouse. His brothers were right, but the price was wrong. Harold waded ashore at Inchon and fought North Koreans to Seoul and stopped when the United Nations told him to. And he landed at Wonson and climbed the mountain road to the Chosin Reservoir and lay huddled in a fake down sleeping bag and told lobster stories to his buddies, and they laughed and wanted to know what in hell he was doing there. And the Chinese wanted to know also, and they kicked Harold and his Marine friends off the mountain. He thought more and more of red and white lobster buoys swinging in the tide until the day came, the orders to go home, the troopship sliding under the bridge at San Francisco, the Diego discharge, the drunken salute to four years and a Greyhound ride across the western plains, past smokestacks, neon, and people, and so finally to the New England air and home to salt surf and rocky ledges covered by pointed firs, like the lady said, and grinning, winking brothers and father and mother and what the hell did he ever join the Marines for?

He had been away in body only, and his boat and traps were waiting like puppy dogs for their master. With his discharge money and savings, Harold bought a new boat, a real Jonesport lobsterboat, and built 100 more traps. On the water, he found no strangers. The ledges, the rocks and buoys, the waves of whitecaps and rolling rhythms, the erasures by fog, they were as he had left them.

"Jesus, old girl, I been daydreaming," Harold says as he overruns his first buoy. Circling almost in its length, the boat spins like a reined quarter horse and settles alongside the missed buoy. Harold gaffs it and takes a turn around his hauler, and the sheave discs grab the pot warp and coil it counterclockwise onto the deck. The toggles pop to the surface and Harold guides them through the block and hauler, and the trap jumps out of the water and Harold sets it on the rail, opening the door. There are four keepers, three shorts, and half a pail of crabs.

"Four keepers, old girl, not bad."

Harold now becomes the professional man—Maine lobsterman. He is on his range and none in the whole world knows it better. Instinctively, he has timed his hauling against the tide so that he runs down his buoys spindle first. His father showed him that . . . my God, it was 40 years ago. The traps come assembly-line fashion and the routine begins to revive Harold. The gaff, the line through the hauler, the whine of the hydraulic motor retrieving 100 feet a minute, the idling engine in gear, and the wheel easy to starboard to swing the stern from the route of the ascending trap. And then it is there on the old girl's rail, a dripping, slatted prison covered with kelp and bottom slime. Harold squeezes the locking lath of his no-cleat door and looks inside. It is this moment, this one second in a lobsterman's life, that chains him to the sea forever, Harold once told Effiejean. It is the hunt, the uncertainty of prey, the skill of pursuit, the knowledge of lairs . . . . He really couldn't explain it. Effiejean understood.

"Three more keepers, old girl, finestkind of a day it's beginning to be."

Harold works up-tide along his popcorn string in small, precise circles, like those on the Palmer Method drawings above the blackboard when he was in the third grade. The gulls come now. They know Harold and *Bobby & Jean*. Harold is not only an idler of boat engines, he is also a gull feeder. Most lobstermen throw their old bait overboard or toss the bags in a pail and dump them ashore. Harold pulls the strings on his bait bags and heaves the bait on the stern deck. In a dungeon of fog, so thick the bow of *Bobby & Jean* disappears, the gulls will head straight for Harold. They know his engine as surely as Slicker his dog knows the sound of his Ford pickup. And the other lobstermen know where Harold is, too. See that flock of gulls, they'll say, Harold Martin is hauling down by the Fiddler.

"Well, old girl, let's eat lunch."

It is 10:15 A.M., and Harold has been up since 4 o'clock. Effiejean packed his lunch last night, as always, and Harold shuts off the engine, opens up his aluminum dinner pail, and sits down on the dry port rail. The sun is up now and the chop is down and the gulls all sit in the water like white toy boats, respecting Harold's lunchtime. Bologna sandwiches with lettuce and lots of mayonnaise. His favorite. And Effiejean has wrapped them in Cut-rite wax paper, the way he likes, rather than those god-awful plastic baggies. His battered old Stanley stainless thermos is full of Red Rose tea, too, and Effiejean has put a fat slab of chocolate cake under the wire that could hold the thermos but doesn't because Harold carries his Stanley separate. It is a pretty good day, considering. Harold looks in the crate and it is nearly full. Have a hundred pounds, for sure, by the time the old girl and me hit Flat Island, Harold thinks, throwing a ball of Cut-rite overboard. It is 10:30.

"You on, Effiejean?" Harold calls.

Harold visualizes his kitchen and can see the CB sitting on the shelf above the table, crackling out messages from Newfoundland to South America as they bounce off the stratosphere. But Harold knows that Effiejean will react to his voice among the multitudes as quickly as she hears it. She is probably in the bathroom, and he visualizes her slippered steps—eight, seven, six . . . .

"You on, Effiejean?" Harold repeats after counting down the steps to zero.

"I'm here, Harold."

"Checking in, Effiejean, pretty good chance out here, probably get the whole string in. Chop down, wind backing around."

"That's good, Harold. How you doing hauling." Effiejean puts it as a statement rather than a question. "Come back."

"Oh, gettin' a few, gettin' a few. They ain't movin' yet, be awhile. Come back."

"That's good, Harold."

"What you got on your list today?"

"Well, Laura called n' asked me t'go to Sears with her. I didn't think you'd care. Be back before Bobby gets home from school. We'll probably eat at McDonald's. Sure you don't mind, Harold? Come back."

Harold is thinking hard. Jesus Christ, if he'd known Effiejean was going to town and Sears today he could have made up a list. Oil filters are half the price at Sears. But Effiejean would probably get the numbers screwed up.

"Naw, have a good day Effiejean. *Bobby & Jean* out."

"We'll have some venison for supper, Harold. I'll take it out of the freezer right now. Base out."

Harold dumps the last dregs of cold tea over the side and rises with the gulls to finish hauling. Venison, he doesn't feel like venison tonight. More a lobster stew evening.

Noon passes and Harold notes the tide turning. The old girl will have to work harder, more circles, more Palmer Method circles. He is into his pair traps now. They take longer but save some warp. Two traps, two bait bags, two times two bricks for ballast, two times everything. Single traps are better, Harold thinks. Who the hell talked me into pairs, anyway? The sun, the March sun, is setting far south and early, as it has for 40 years. Dirty snow and fast sunsets and sloppy chop and 10 pairs to go for a first down across the Flat Island goal line, Harold old boy.

The gulls know exactly the last pair of traps, and they start home to their island before Harold has even gotten them aboard. Four keepers and a short pistol. Harold uses his banding pliers like a surgeon. The day is done.

"That's it, old girl. Let's head for the barn."

He comes into the co-op float and ties up to the float rail with a short piece of pot warp. Stevie slides down the gangway on his elbows, prompting Harold to think he should try that in the morning on his ass. The scales say 153 pounds, and Harold shoves the slip into his pocket along with six 50s, two 20s, one 10, one 5, and 90¢ in change. Stevie says the price will be going down 20¢ tomorrow. Stevie usually makes Harold's day.

He slips the rail hitch and idles the old girl to the middle of the harbor, coming up astern of his punt, gaffing the painter, climbing over the davit onto the foredeck, and securing the mooring chain to *Bobby & Jean*'s deck cleat. Harold opens the valve to the washdown pump and with a long-handled fiber brush scrubs the old girl down so shiny and clean she squeaks. Effiejean once, 20 years ago, asked why he never washed down the kitchen floor like he did his boat. "Ain't the same thing," he answered, and Effiejean never asked again. Harold pulls the tail of the punt's slip bowline and climbs in with his white plastic take-home bucket containing five lobsters.

Harold sees that the ice wedges in the co-op gangway have turned to water. He should speak to Stevie about drilling some holes in those cleats, but Stevie would never get around to it. He opens the co-op door and goes inside. The stove is out cold, like the bookkeeper, Harold thinks. He buys a bag of salt-and-vinegar potato chips and eats them all before climbing into his pickup. The store is right around the corner, and he pulls into the parking lot, waving to Junior Greenlaw, the town drunk, and goes inside. He buys a six-pack of Budweiser, as he has for 20 years, and a Slim Jim pepperoni stick. On the way out he gives Junior a couple of cans, gets in his truck, pops a pull tab on a Bud, and heads for home. Driving slow and down the Head Road, it's a two-can trip. Turning into his driveway, he sees that Effiejean is back from shopping. In the rear window of her Ford Pinto are assorted plastic boxes with yellow arches. Effiejean probably would have eaten the oil filters anyway, Harold chuckles to himself as the Budweiser tickles his biceps.

Slicker comes busting out through the screen door as the pickup drives in. Funny how Slicker opens that screen-door latch, goddamn funny, probably why I leave the thing on all year, just to see Slicker bust it open, Harold thinks, picking up the beer and the lobster pail. Inside, on the table, Effiejean has spread out some cloth she bought at Sears, and a round thermometer, and some Levi's for Bobby, and Eveready batteries for the flashlight, and white socks for Harold. She always buys Harold white socks. Effiejean gets the lobster kettle from the sink without a word about venison. Harold finishes another beer while washing up and changing to a clean set of green Dickies.

"Where's Bobby, Effiejean?"

"He's out in the trap shed, I guess, Harold."

Harold has nearly finished his last beer when Effiejean calls Bobby and puts the stew on the table. She sure as hell can make lobster stew, Harold thinks. But still, she'd eat an oil filter if it came with yellow arches. That oil filter thing is sure staying with me.

Bobby comes in and sits down, and Harold asks him how his day has been. "The same, Pop. What you been doing today?'' The kid can be a wiseass at times, but he's going to be good lobsterman. He has more traps and a bigger boat than when I was his age, Harold thinks. But then again lobstering ain't what it used to be.

"Hey, Pop,'' Bobby mouths between slurps of lobster stew, "I been thinking on what I'll do after graduation in June. Whatcha' think of me joining the Marines?''

"Oh, sweet Jesus,'' Harold says, lifting his eyes to the tin kitchen ceiling, "whatever made you decide that?''

"Well, I ain't decided, but you did, Pop. Remember you telling me about all those faraway places with the strange sounding names? La de da da. C'mon, Pop, remember last Fourth when we had the rum-plugged watermelon and you sang the titty ditty? How'd that go? She was a . . . .''

"You shush now, Bobby,'' Effiejean says, breaking another handful of Pilot crackers into her stew.

Harold smiles, but only from the Adam's apple down. He won't give in to Bobby quite yet. Wiseass new generation. How do you handle them? Harold thinks about his father and when he said shit the first time out loud. His father had laid a belt on his butt real good. Progress, maybe, Harold reflects. My dad rowed a peapod, I peaked out with an Evinrude 25 when I was a teen, and what's that thing Bobby has on his boat, a 125-horse Johnson?

"How's the trap building coming?''

"Pretty good. Got me another coil of wire. You should try them, Pop, it's real easy with that jig set-up.''

"Not me. No wire traps for me. Your grandfather would turn over in his grave if he saw you building wire traps.''

"C'mon, Pop, you know I outfish you.''

Harold smiles above the neck this time. Wiseass kid. Supper over, Effiejean clears the table and loads up her pride-and-joy Hotpoint dishwasher. For 10 years now it has leaked. Like a line of Scripture, every night after supper Effiejean will say, "Harold s'pose you could look at the dishwasher when you get time?'' And Harold will recite the line from his Book of Moses, "Take a look first thing in the mornin', Effiejean.'' The dishwasher leak has carved a yellow scar across the kitchen linoleum, and Harold has made a mental note that when the wound reaches the door, he will take a look at the washer. No hurry.

"Can I borrow the pickup, Pop?'' Bobby yells from somewhere upstairs.

"No gas and a quart low,'' Harold says, dropping into his birthday Lazyboy recliner.

Bobby rappels down the stairs three at a time pulling on a reindeer sweater. "No sweat, Pop old boy, I'll fill it and that's another two bushel of bait you owe me. Don't, I repeat, don't call the Coast Guard if I'm not home by 11 o'clock, they could not find the gravel pit anyway,'' he says, jumping over the sleeping Slicker and slamming the screen door.

Harold leans back in his recliner and closes his eyes, nodding on the hum-and-toil rhythm of the Hotpoint. The Budweiser and lobster stew feel warm in his beer belly. Effiejean has spread out the cloth on the table once again, and he can hear the snipping of her shears as she cuts by the patterns, humming while she works. He wonders how lobster stew and Big Macs are getting along in her little pot belly. Slicker leaves his linoleum spot and wanders over to Harold's side, collapsing with a thump after his 15-year routine of three turns to starboard. And then it is here, another Harold Martin sunset, 40 years of sunsets. Christ, Harold smiles as he drops behind the horizon, I can't give this up. Who'll carry the flag?

Just about every lobsterman in the State of Maine could step into Harold Martin's boots and walk down Main Street carrying the flag.

The evolution of the lobsterman, the breaking away and specialization from a wide-ranging fishing industry, was gradual. Pot fishing for lobsters was not everybody's cup of tea and still isn't. Of the 9,000 lobster licenses issued, only about a third are full-time-work-at-it-52-weeks-a-year fishermen like Harold Martin. Not all flyers are jet fighter pilots.

Maritime history suggests that the lobsterman as such emerged in the late 1700s, and his birthplace was Cape Cod, Massachusetts. That suggestion could probably be refuted. A lobster industry and a lobsterman are two different things. The early explorers of Maine all found lobsters and became instant lobstermen. Samuel de Champlain and Baron de Poutrincourt established a settlement at the mouth of the St. Croix River in 1604, and lobsters were mentioned. In 1605, Captain George Weymouth explored the coast of Maine and noted the abundance of lobsters around Monhegan Island. Captain Weymouth also captured five of the original lobstermen, Indians, and took them back to England, thereby instigating continual hostilities between the Indians and white men until peace in 1783, when Indians became state wards and lost control over their ancestral land.

When the Pilgrims arrived in America in 1620, they found thriving trading posts and fishing settlements in Pemaquid and Monhegan. The settlers were fishermen taking cod, haddock, and halibut from the cold North Atlantic waters and lobsters, crabs, oysters, and clams from the near and intertidal shores and flats. Lobsters were also caught by dragging fish nets over the bottoms of bays and coves. Cape Cod may claim the beginning of a lobster fishery, but the history books probably need some footnotes.

The Maine lobsterman was born when the demand for lobsters increased to a single voice in the fishmonger's song. Early Maine fishermen used their boats and homemade gear to harvest the sea and all that lived in it. Their crop was fish—all creatures from the ocean were fish. The necessity of fish for protein lessened as more affluence and the permanent settlements and structures of a society emerged. The diet changed, and palates, tastes, and desires created demands for particular foods. The lobster rose above his fodder-only seashore colleagues and became a special being. And so, to catch a taste, a unique harvester emerged.

Lobster fishing was an attractive occupation, considering some other tangents of fishing. A large boat was not needed, because the gear was small and a large harvest volume was not required to earn a respectable living. Deep, long, and expensive nets could be ignored. The lobstermen turned to the abundant woods, where all the materials for a lobster trap could be taken. Boats could even be rowed or sailed. And the work was nearshore and comparatively safe from the winds and waves and dangerous elements the offshore fishermen faced.

But perhaps the most compelling attraction of lobstering was the lonely independence of the life. The early lobstermen were not far from the traits and mores and instincts that had been needed by the early settlers to survive in a new country. Lobstering was not a new course but the sustaining of an old one. The lobsterman and the creature he pursued were remarkably alike in their different worlds. There was, and is, an uncanny compatibility in their coexistence. Just as the lobster has survived the aeons by his solitary habits and independent senses, so has the lobsterman. They were made for each other.

A lobsterman sitting on McLoon's dock at Rockland was asked by another what he was going to do that day.

"Take a tuck in my gumption, Junior, them lobsters are on t'me. Let 'em wait a day."

What he was saying was maybe he didn't feel like working that day. Maybe he didn't like the wind backing around to the east. Or he had had a fight with his wife. He had found out he needed a valve job on his old pickup. Whatever his attitude, he related it to lobsters—let 'em wait.

As the lobster profession progressed, the reasons for joining it became more varied. Demand, price, family, environment. The father-son heritage was especially strong. Perhaps no other profession, unless it is farming, retains such family bondage and values. A lobsterman's son is expected to assume the birthright of his father and his father before him, much as a monarchy needs heirs to survive. A majority of the lobstermen today come from family genes.

A visiting yachtsman anchored one late afternoon in a small Maine cove. The boats lay tethered to the tide, facing the strength. The from-away sailor knew the cove, he had been there before, and he knew the boy in the white cedar-planked skiff with the 35 h.p. Evinrude coming around the point. The boy was standing in the stern and steering with an extension handle. All Maine kids stand and steer, as though driving a chariot.

The skiff glided across the cove like a knife cutting paper and swung in alongside the yacht's stern quarter.

"Hi there, Mr. Johnson, it's nice t'see you back again this year. Your boat sure looks good."

"Hi yourself, Peter, been waiting all year for some of your lobsters. You remember Mrs. Johnson, don't you?"

"Afternoon ma'm. Thought you'd be this way soon. Been saving some nice ones. They're in my car. Be right back."

Peter idled over to his floating lobster crate and hauled it aboard. The 100 pounds of lobsters crawled and scraped and rustled and squirmed as the buoyancy left their senses. Peter sorted over nearly half the car before finding six lobsters so identical they could have been molded from the same clay. He made sure they were nice ones, because he had said they would be.

The lady of the yacht had the stainless steel kettle ready when Peter smiled alongside. She passed the kettle down and Peter put the lobsters carefully, one by one, face down and tail tucked, into the kettle.

"How much, Peter?" asked the captain.

"Same as last year, sir."

The skipper passed two $20 bills, and Peter made change as the captain had known he would. They had gone through the no-tipping explanation three years before; money over and above the fair price of lobsters was, well, not right, as Peter explained it. His father had told him that.

That night on deck as the yacht crew sipped drinks and waited for the gas-generated steam to claim the lives of the lobsters, the provider became the topic.

"I wonder what it is," said the captain to his guests in a flat but knowing statement, "that builds boys like Peter in a world that scorns their values. I look across the city lights at my financial world and I think often of this small Maine cove, seeing Peter come alongside in his totally adequate boat to say, 'Hi, Mr. Johnson, got some nice ones for ya,' and knowing very well he means it. And I know his father said that to another Mr. Johnson. It makes you feel, well, clean."

The dangers of the sea are inherent in its being there. The marine elements are forever challenging, luring, deceptive, subtle, and raging. And it seems quite paradoxical that a person surrounded by water has no fear of it. That is the strange case of lobstermen—and fishermen in general. The reason is the awesome respect fishermen have for the water, which completely inhabits any void for fear. They work a step away from death every day, and yet, there is no thought of drowning. There is a fatalistic demeanor acquired by fishermen over the centuries, but few believe that God or Neptune will spirit you away if you maintain one hand for the boat and one for yourself. Fatalism surrounds the few unexplained lost lobstermen. The rest were stupid, is the saying.

One key to his survival on a demanding sea is his self-sufficiency. The lobsterman often builds his own boat. He surely maintains it—changes the oil and filter, waters the batteries, paints the bottom, repacks the stuffing boxes, inspects the plugs and points. A hundred first steps into the drink are smothered by the inherent preventative maintenance schedule programed into the fisherman from birth. No calling for appointments; he alone is the beneficiary of the timely execution of his responsibilities. For better, or for dead.

But the best of lobstermen are lost at sea. By far the most common cause of accidental drowning is being hauled overboard in a tangle of pot warp as the lobster trap descends to the bottom. The combination of the weight of trap and warp and the forward speed of the boat means that a misplaced foot in a turn of rope will result in an overboard situation, or a maiming, or both. The breaking strength of today's nylon pot warp is about 2,600 pounds. Even if a lobsterman manages to untangle himself from a clinging mass of rope before being dragged under, the boat is probably in gear and moving away. Rubber boots, a set of oilskins, and 40-degree water are no comfort. If the boat happened to be in neutral and the lobsterman could reach it, he probably could not get aboard. Few lobsterboats have side ladders, and the rail is a forever 3½ feet away. And all this assumes the lobsterman can swim—which he often cannot.

There are sad stories and funny sad stories and tragic stories of drownings and near drownings. They are usually taken in the context of their severity. Nobody talks of the young fisherman lost and of the tearful wife and two small children who must overcome last images of their dad and husband every time they watch a lobsterboat leave the harbor. But let a lobsterman fall overboard from his punt while paddling ashore and then porpoise the rest of the distance with a half-learned dog paddle, and the whole town talks for years about the time old Charlie walked ashore from his mooring because he drank the harbor dry.

There are full- and part-time lobstermen. The part-time handle is probably not deserved. Many lobstermen, because of finances or other reasons, cannot afford to acquire the necessary traps, large boat, and gear to fish year-round. Most full-time Maine lobstermen do not fish year-round, either. They put gear overboard in March or April, fish through November or December, then haul out and spend the rest of the winter building new gear.

The part-timer could be a lobsterman and a clam digger, a lobsterman-scalloper, lobsterman-gillnetter, or lobsterman-pulpwood cutter. Money is needed to support the partial income from lobstering. Because lobsters leave the inshore in winter, the part-timer will turn to whatever source is available to fill the hiatus. Full-timers resent part-timers, but the latter often work many more hours of the year than their colleagues, who often take three- and four-week winter vacations to southern climes. What the full-timers really object to is the summer-weekend lobstermen who, they shout in legislative halls, "come on down here every goddamn summer, slap five softwood traps in the water, and haul everybody's gear from Small Point to 'Tit Manan."

There have been some successful campaigns to get this guy. In June, July, and August, for instance, lobstering is prohibited on Sundays. Conservation, said the full-timers, but obviously this cuts the summer-cottage-resident lobstering opportunity right in half. But there are Saturdays and weekdays after work, say the full-timers while successfully pushing through a law that makes hauling traps illegal from June 1 to August 31 from a half hour after sunset to a half hour before sunrise. Moonlighting, literally, is outlawed quite effectively. The part-timers do hold their own fairly well. They have a rather loose association that operates covertly, lobbying colleagues at Rotary and Lions Clubs and at hospital staff meetings. In Maine, lobster catchers are found in the damndest places.

Probably because of the reticent, reserved nature of the lobsterman, there is no comparable Paul Bunyon. Legends and myths, for sure, but no superfisher. There is the statue. In 1939, sculptor Victor Kahill completed a large plaster statue of lobsterman Elroy Johnson of Bailey Island, shown kneeling down to plug a lobster. The statue eventually ended up with the State of Maine and was stored in a warehouse for years. In the 1970s, three bronze casts of Elroy were made from the original. One was erected at Harpswell, next door to Bailey Island; one stands in Portland; and one is on Maine Avenue in Washington, D.C. The original, somewhat damaged from the casting, is back in storage at the Maine State Museum in Augusta. Kahill's work is dedicated to the generic Maine lobsterman, and only those who are in the know know that the model was Elroy Johnson.

Every port and fishing community has its favorite.

There was Bert. He was a skiff fisherman who went about his business happy as a sand peep eating shrimp along a tide line. Everybody sort of kept an eye on Bert, because, as the natives whispered, Bert only had one oar in the water. But Bert was a competent lobsterman. He had 50 traps, fished nearshore and on the harbor fringes. Only when Bert came ashore was he, well, rather queer, as the folks quietly said. One late April day, the Bert-watchers realized that he was not on his mooring at 4 P.M., a most unusual event. The query went out almost instantaneously. The lobster industry may be one of the few in the world with instant communications via their radio network. Lobstermen returned to their boats and started a search. His aluminum 16-foot skiff would be easy to spot, they thought. Probably a motor problem, and he had drifted ashore someplace. The search continued for two hours and no Bert. The Coast Guard was called. Darkness was approaching and the late afternoon offshore westerly began to beat its daily whitecap ritual. The searchers ran down his string of traps; hell, he only had fifty. They swung close to islands and circled them for any conceivable glimmer of a boat. By now, the sun long set, the permanent darkness settled on the water, and there was grave and desperate concern for friend Bert, somewhere drifting in an open boat. It was too late to call in aircraft from Cape Cod. But the radar-and-eyeball futile search continued throughout the night.

The helicopter and fixed-wing Coast Guard planes were in the air at first light. Flying their learned grid patterns, the searchers crisscrossed all conceivable drift possibilities. An observer in one aircraft remarked to his pilot that a small aluminum boat would be hard to spot among the whitecaps. By 10 A.M. the village began to apprehend a tragedy. The fishing families knew the bitter, unforgiving nature of a sea given time. Bert, poor Bert.

The boatswain of the CG 44-footer, tied up at the village co-op wharf for fuel, was the first to get the word.

"They've spotted a boat south of Seal Island!" he shouted to the fishermen sitting by the diesel pump.

The CB and marine radios became beehives. People ran to the waterfront. Could it be Bert? Could he have drifted all night in his open skiff in the cold and wind and harsh wavetops that nibble away at senses until the will is shattered? Word from the helicopter. It was Bert. He was alive. The crew had hoisted him aboard and were on their way to the hospital. Good old Bert.

Bert returned to his island a week later. A little frostbite, that was all. He was welcomed home.

"Hiya Bert, how's she going?"

"Whatcha' say Bert, how's the toes?"

"Hey Bert, the boys hauled your gear and put it on the bank."

How, why, and what was not asked of Bert. It wouldn't be the thing to do. But the Coast Guard doesn't send boats and planes all over the ocean and write no comment in its cost-effectiveness logs. An inquiry was held, and Bert dutifully took the ferry to the mainland and the bus to Portland with a couple of island shepherds. The hearing lasted all morning and then Bert was told he could go home. The Coast Guard was pleased that he had been found alive and well. Bert and his friends caught the last ferryboat. The shepherds decided it was time to cash in their guidance chips.

"Bert," one said over the steady din of the ferry diesels, "it ain't really none of my business, but what the hell happened out there? I mean, the Coast Guard said your oars were in the boat n' everything."

Bert was about three-quarters through a double bag of barbecued potato chips and sort of mumbled between handfuls. The bag finally empty, Bert wiped his paprika hands on his best khaki pants and told his bookends his version.

He was on his last trap outside the harbor and the motor stopped and he pulled eleventy-seventy times and there was no noise and he took off the top thing and took his plug wrench thing like he'd been showed and unscrewed the plug and knew that was the trouble because he'd been showed up at the co-op about the black stuff on the plug and that could make the motor not go and he dropped the plug with the black stuff and the wrench and everything all overboard and that was a bad sign.

"Whatcha' do then, Bert?"

He put the top thing back on so the motor wouldn't get wet like he learned up at the co-op and sat down to think. Bert said he thought a long time and when he got done thinking it was dark and he was pretty cold and he didn't stand up because it was too dark to stand up in a boat because he couldn't see the water good and didn't know where to fall if he had to fall. Bert said he could see the island and the lights when he drifted by in the dark because dark on the water isn't really dark like in the cellar and he bet he could throw a rock and hit the island.

"Jeez, Bert, you mean you drifted right by the island and didn't row ashore?"

Bert said he was afraid because it was a strange island and some islands have Indians and cannibals and pirates and he was afraid and he sat right in the middle seat and didn't move around because you ain't supposed to when the motor isn't running like they said up at the co-op. And he sat all night and didn't make any noise because he was afraid and the morning came and the sun was kinda warm and he couldn't see any land, not even the cannibal island, and then there was the airplane and he felt better because it had a stripe and planes and boats with stripes help people like they said up at the co-op.

The shepherds were silent for a very long time as the ferryboat Jimmy diesel whined past the homeward channel markers. The pilothouse throttle suddenly released the power and pitch and the cabin passengers reached for their mainland shopping paper bags from Sears and Western Auto and J.C. Penny. The ferry scraped her starboard dock bumpers, as always, and drivers started their engines.

The first shepherd spoke. "Bert, ya' know, you're one hell of a guy." And the second shepherd carried Bert's two boxes of Dunkin' Donuts all the way to the co-op, where Bert stopped to buy each a can of Coke from the machine.

Partnerships are a tough alliance in the lobster business. Two-owner boats, a sternman fishing on shares, brothers gone sour. They all hone the knife edge of friendship in a business where solitude is happiness.

Two lobstermen in New Harbor shared ownership of a boat. An accumulation of divisive factors from bitchy wives to wiseass kids to paint colors finally resulted in them not speaking to one another. Amazingly, they didn't need to. They each knew exactly what to do. They swapped captain and mate jobs on alternating days. Neither responsibility had language as a prerequisite. When a third person entered their domain they used a system of nods, flinches, eye rolls, grunts, and groans to convey quite explicit meanings. Of course, everyone knew that neither spoke to anyone in the presence of the other, and small talk was adjusted around that particular boat.

Drunks are woven through lobster stories like shards of blue mussel shells in shore sand. The public's conception of hard-drinking fishermen, however, is grossly over-rated. Drink they do, but a daily hangover is not an enjoyable mate all day long on a bouncing boat engulfed in continual roar from an eight-cylinder mechanical bull. Lobstermen use the spirits as a topic, a theme subject, a class assignment. In a provincial, narrow social life, there are acceptable subjects for gossip and others that are better left untouched. Booze can be bandied about. The spouses of lobstermen rarely engage in drunk stories, and there is a sort of neutral truce concerning alcohol and the family. Wives are generally adamant about exposed liquor, and although knowing full well of the widespread use, they prohibit it in their houses in most cases. The lobsterman condescends and uses subterfuge, which gives birth to booze stories by the mile. It is said Demon Rum, for openers, built 85 percent of the churches in coastal Maine. Lore and historical fact are not too far apart on this one. The merchants who owned and sent vessels loaded with lumber and ice and northern-clime cargoes around the world often brought them back with equatorial molasses in the distilled form. Shipping merchants were the pillars of their communities. When the temperance movement, of which Maine was a born leader, came about in the 1930s, the individual wharf-rat entrepreneur saw his opportunity for a slice of the pie. Revenue agents were tied in granny knots attempting to catch rumrunning boats with crafty, shoal-wise, night-cat-eyed lobstermen at the wheel. Like grabbing a handful of fart, one agent told his boss.

For every mission there was a tale. Embellished, tailored to individual style, these stories persist to this day, and there is not a fishing community in Maine where one cannot be directed to "Old Bill on the Hill" or "Chicken-Eyed Charlie" for intimate details of their rumrunning days.

When a fishing community member is forced to explain a genuine town drunk, there is always a disclaimer so that the inquisitor knows that the man is not a derelict, or a bum, or in the same league with the common stupor. He simply has his gear on the bank. Old Bill, they will explain, used to be a highliner, had the biggest, fastest boat in the harbor, fine wife. He, errrr, put his gear on the bank 10 years ago.

Squirt Carter had stacked his gear on the bank 20 years ago. He did odd jobs, changed oil in boats at the co-op, lived in a trailer, and talked incessantly about the good old days. There was not a man in the village who would not trust Squirt with anything he owned. Except a can of beer. Sitting around on the wharf drinking a six-pack after coming in from hauling, the lobstermen would see Squirt coming down the road and say, "Oh, oh, Squirt-alert, Squirt-alert." The beer would go under a bait bucket. When Squirt joined the group they would give him two bucks to go to the store for a quart of Narragansett beer for the group. Squirt would leave, the fishermen would leave, and Squirt knew that when he returned the lobstermen would not and he and the quart would go home to his trailer and watch a soap opera through a tall sudsy glass. The lobstermen treat their community life with dignity for all.

The matter of territorial imperative is important. Lobster wars, gear disappearing, shots in the night, boat rammings—all are true. They have persisted since the beginning of lobstering. The water is a public body, and once a person has purchased a state license he should be able to set his lobster traps anyplace he desires, but in the real lobster world, it doesn't work that way. Lobster grounds and fishing rights are a ball of string wound with various-length pieces of family, integrity, geography, and fear. Territories are staked between communities as well as fishermen. There is, for instance, an imaginary line drawn down eastern Penobscot Bay, with Saddleback

Ledge and Eagle Island the landmarks. The Deer Isle-Stonington-Isle au Haut fishermen lobster on the eastern side, and the North Haven-Vinalhaven lobstermen set and haul their gear on the western side. First-time trespassers will be warned in the traditional way, a half hitch around the buoy spindle. Sometimes a second warning of two half hitches is issued, sometimes not. If the foreign trap is still over the line in a week, the trap is cut off. There is usually retaliation by the loser even if this means a raid into enemy territory. A few skirmishes of this magnitude and a full-scale lobster war can erupt.

Lobster wars involve all the tactics of general battle from Biblical times, from the relatively mundane warning shot across the bow to actual cases of bottling up an enemy lobsterboat fleet in harbor with armed marine picket boats. A single blockaded lobsterman, pinned in a cove, unable to use his radio because of jamming, and the light and tide falling, has one of two choices. He can either try to ram one of the pickets and risk losing either his boat or life, and maybe both, or he can repent in a truce raft-up whereby he is released from bondage with the promise that before God, Jesus Christ, Mother's honor, Neptune, and suicide, in no particular order, his line-jumping days are over.

Territories within communities are more subtle. The dimensions diminish in scale and relate to particular sides of the harbor, ledges, coves, west and east ends of islands, a channel, or certain compass courses. If the Smith family lobstermen have fished Herring Cove for centuries, the family name is branded upon that lobster ground as surely as granite monoliths at the Roman Colosseum. It is in trust, however, a life tenancy, and Smith family fishermen must work their heritage. It cannot be sustained by marital infusion. A brother-in-law has no more right to Herring Cove than the next guy. If the island queens do not conceive boy heirs, the lobster throne begins to crumble.

Territorial imperative is above judicial law, and in-community violators are rarely turned over to uniformed marine law enforcement people. Brothers-in-law, maybe. But a neighbor trap molester is reckoned with much differently than the foreign-fleet pirates. Warnings start with anonymous phone calls. Then there is the Citizens Band weapon. Everybody, just everybody, listens to CB, and subtle innuendo messages dart around the waterfront ether like arrows shot into the air, and they know where, just where, they will fall. Ignored prescriptions and continual lobster trap illness will bring on more drastic medicine. Morning sunrises have revealed white lobsterboats with "Trap Thief" spray-painted from stem to stern. The silent treatment at the store, the co-op, and basketball games sometimes gets a point home. Violence is the last refuge. Boats, pickups, and even trailers and houses have been flamed by irate vigilantes.

In a small community near Deer Isle there was a rash of thefts from lobsterboats moored in the harbor. Eventually, the fishermen traced the stolen gear to a young lobsterman who lived in a trailer with his wife and two small children. Six fishermen drove up to the trailer one night, knocked on the door, and walked right past the startled young man. He was given a trial right there in front of the 6 o'clock TV news with wife huddled on the turf-bare sofa holding two frightened children. Confronted by the prosecutor, judge, and jury, the young man confessed and admitted he had stolen and sold the gear. The fishermen laid ten $100 bills on the dirty Formica kitchen table—full payment, they said, for the young fisherman's fiberglass skiff, outboard, and 50 traps. The family was to load all their trailer belongings in their pickup and be out of town by the next day noon. They had no choice. The laws of the open range.

Not all incidents end in such dire family consequences.

Dicky Bridges didn't dislike Floyd Drinkwater, he just found him a pain in the ass. They fished from the same cove and were cordial enough ashore and afloat, but Dicky knew that Floyd never went out of his way to miss one of his lobster buoys. He had seen Floyd run over three that summer alone, cutting them off. Dicky found the top toggles and saved his traps, but nevertheless, the sonofabitch couldn't be trusted. Like the time Floyd borrowed his skiff. How did the bastard tie it back up? With a slipknot, naturally. And Floyd was always going aboard his boat and borrowing a handful of lobster bands. Sure, he'd pay Dicky back, whenever he felt like it. At least once a summer Dicky towed Floyd home because he never would drain the crap out of his engine's sediment bulb. Dicky knew damn well that Floyd had something to do with the time he lost 200 pounds of lobsters from his lobster car. Floyd was too anxious to help track down the thieves. Floyd saying everybody was involved from Aunt Bea to Richard Nixon. Floyd suggesting this. Floyd with the new clues. Floyd, what a pain in the ass.

Floyd was always grinning. Never trust a perpetual grin or gold teeth, Dicky remembered his father saying. Up at the store, Floyd would always try to buy Dicky a bottle of Moxie and a bag of chips. Grinning bastard.

Floyd had a beautiful skiff. It was 16 feet in length, a dory model, cedar planked with four solid thwarts. Floyd had had it built in South Bristol, and he loved that boat. Kept it painted Woolsey bright with varnished seats, and everybody agreed that Floyd Drinkwater had the best skiff in the cove. Floyd had turned down some attractive offers from summer people who admired his skiff. He scorned them all, keeping his boat for a personal showpiece and for going back and forth to his lobsterboat mooring.

It was a late April day, and the cove was full-bore setting out traps. Dicky was a little late getting going, having spent the evening at the American Legion hall watching rented girlie movies, sipping Bud, and smoking three packs of unfiltered Camels. But, by trusting in some saltwater instinct, he cleared the cove and started down the shore along the high bluff. The water dropped off to 60 feet where the granite chunks had calved from their mother lode over the aeons. You could run a lobsterboat right up to the rocks and jump ashore. About 50 yards downrange, Dicky saw something on the rocks that shouldn't be there. It didn't fit his brain program. He eased his boat closer, closer, and the bow gently touched. And there, laying splayed on the granite croppings, was a deer, obviously dead. Dicky knew without asking himself what had happened. Dogs had chased the deer and it had run off the cliff, falling to the rocks and breaking its back and neck. He kicked the boat's stern around, came alongside a large granite table, and stepped ashore, securing his boat to a rock with a piece of pot warp. The deer was still warm. The fatal leap must have just happened. Dicky pushed the large doe with his rubber boot, and it quivered like a large bowl of brown Jello.

The plan hit Dicky right between the eyes with absolutely no warning. Like miscounting the last stair step in the dark. Oh, sweet Jesus, sweet Jesus; Dicky was beside himself. It took five minutes to get the deer aboard his boat. Each limp leg wanted to go in a different direction. The head flopped and the guts in the belly felt like a glob of mercury rolling back and forth. Dicky was sweating when he cast off from the fatal scene, but he was grinning, as his daddy used to say, like a tomcat shitting canary beaks.

Returning to the cove, Dicky idled in alongside Floyd's most proud possession. It glistened in the morning sun like a gilded $40 menu in a honky-tonk diner.

Dicky lashed Floyd's skiff along his rail, and for the next 10 minutes he labored in sweat and laughing tears, stuffing the deer down under the skiff's four thwarts. He spread hair and skin and head and feet and legs underneath and around the seats and risers and Woolsey-clean floorboards of Floyd Drinkwater's famous cedar lady. Then Dicky stood up and gave her a long, long look. His mission fulfilled, Dicky Bridges whistled down the bay to just another day in the life of a Maine lobsterman.

It was late afternoon when the lobstermen returned to the cove with white neutron clumps of seagulls in pursuit, diving and swirling after old bait thrown overboard. One by later one the fishermen picked up their mooring buoys, and after cleaning and hosing down the day's debris, sculled ashore for peace before supper. Floyd was one of the last in. Even Dicky was ashore, of course he was ashore, as Floyd patiently throttled up to his skiff. He had never as much as taken a scratch of paint off her rails since owning her. As each fisherman tied his punt to the float and walked up the gangway, Dicky would meet him with a few chosen words. Soon, there was a whole pod of fishermen standing on the wharf watching Floyd.

Floyd saw the cargo but didn't believe it. At first it looked as though somebody had thrown a tub of old bait in the bottom of his beautiful skiff. But coming closer, he saw hair and head and hooves. Floyd gaffed his skiff and made it fast alongside. He looked down and suddenly realized not only what that thing was, but the problem it presented. The deer, by this time, was laced with rigor mortis and had set up in the bottom of the skiff like a cement footing. Just as Dicky had imagined when the revenge thunderbolt hit him about eight hours ago. Floyd glanced at the wharf and saw the gallery.

"Those bastards."

Floyd was on the horns of a dilemma called "a doe out of season." He couldn't very well tow the skiff ashore and try to get the deer out. Those Christless jerks had probably already called a warden. And how would he get that goddamned deer separated from his skiff anyway? He decided to do nothing. He'd go ashore, have supper, go to bed, and maybe when he woke up in the morning the dream would have taken care of itself. Sitting on the middle thwart just above a very cold heart, Floyd rowed ashore, pulled the skiff out on his pull-off line, and walked past the dock where 20 pairs of red eyeballs peeked out a grimy fish-house window.

When Floyd left the harbor the next morning with his skiff in tow, he had company. The whole cove. They followed him to Flat Island, where Floyd loaded knives, an ax, a saw, and a crowbar aboard his little raped girl and rowed ashore. With all eyes on his efforts, Floyd first tried cutting the deer in pieces. The gases had expanded and bloated the body cavity during the night, and when Floyd stuck his knife through the hide a hissing noise like a flat tire could be heard by the vulturous offshore spectators. Those downwind said the smell was worse than the bushel of pogies someone had discovered behind the furnace in the church cellar one July.

There was little else Floyd could do. One can't operate on meat in the round when it's three-sided. He started ripping his skiff apart. Thwart by thwart, riser by riser, plank by plank. When he finished and a cheer went up from the wave bleachers, there was no more skiff, just one oversized stinky deer surrounded by half a cord of Bristol-fashion cedar kindling wood.

With tears emerging from angry eyes, Floyd shook his fist at the flotilla and yelled across the silent bay, "You fuckers."

The Maine lobsterman is a unique creature in an animal world. He possesses instincts for survival much like those of the chosen adversary he pursues. But the lobsterman has learned the parameters of life and death and does not dwell on either. The middleground of life to him is his house of cards, and he builds it with as many aces as he can muster. He will convert tragedy to humor, abstract to reality, stars to kitchen matches, and his goal, which he will not discuss candidly with anyone, is something he calls the simple good life.

TWO

The Gear

Once upon a time, so goes the tale, if people wanted lobsters they merely walked down to the shore, kicked aside the seaweed, and picked them up. The evolution from fetching to catching has taken over 300 years of trial and error with assorted paraphernalia known by lobstermen as simply—gear.

Gear can be anything from pot warp (rope) to bait (cuttings, brim) to the officially sanctioned brass gauge, which the lobsterman, in his homely way, calls a measure.

Aside from the boat, which gives him access to the water, the most important piece of gear is the lobster trap. The history of the trap began with European fishermen taking lobsters from the intertidal shore using crooked staffs. (The European lobster is close kin to the American lobster.) Norse tales, particularly, tell of "hooking" lobsters from beneath large shore boulders where the lobsters crawled to hide between tides. It was a logical step for the fishermen to next use boats to reach lobsters lurking below the tide line. The same shepherd staff device was used, however, until crude tongs came into use in England and Ireland. Passive catching devices probably were used in Europe in the 17th century. The ritual and sophistication of baited traps were not needed because of lobster abundance, but enterprising fishermen undoubtedly used mazes of tree limbs and shrub brush to entangle lobsters roaming between the high and low tide lines.

The trapping of fish was commonplace in Europe at the beginning of the 18th century, and lobsters were a bycatch. The Dutch eel pot was a particularly efficient lobster catcher and was probably the ancient predecessor of today's lobster trap.

Precolonial American history is vague on the relationship between the Indians and lobsters. The 2,000-year-old shell heaps or "middens" of Blue Hill Bay, Ellsworth, and the Ogunquit River in Wells—where Colonial records indicate that the Maine Abenaki Indians camped and ate shellfish—show little sign that the Indians feasted upon lobsters. During the 19th century, the largest of these shell heaps, named the Whaleback and located in Damariscotta, was removed for commercial purposes. The contents were mussel, oyster, quahog, and clam shells. No lobster shells. A logical answer would lie in chemistry. Lobster shells are composed of chitin, somewhat short-lived, whereas oysters and their like have shells made primarily of calcium, a long-lasting element.

It's just possible that lobsters were a taboo food with the Indians. There is evidence in the journals of early explorers of the Maine coast that mussels were generally shunned by the Indians, and even today, centuries later, Maine natives do not consider the blue mussel in the gourmet class that other people do. There is a reason. Recent marine research clearly indicates that blue mussels, which were and are plentiful along the coast, feed on and thereby concentrate small organisms called dinoflagellates, one species of which *(Gonyaulax tamarensis)* causes paralytic shellfish poisoning to any unlucky soul who ingests it in a large enough dose. Periodic population explosions of this microscopic organism are termed "red tide." In Maine, the Department of Marine Resources maintains a continual monitoring program, and when shellfish from a given region accumulate dangerous levels of the toxin, their gathering is prohibited until the red tide passes and the shellfish "cleanse" themselves. The Indians had no monitoring program, and very likely many got sick from eating contaminated mussels. Although the lobster is not a carrier of the poison, he is a formidable-looking creature of the ogre class, with an appearance to indicate he just might be up to all sorts of evil.

The Indians, however, were ingenious in trapping fish with brush weirs on the tidal shores, and they were experts with spears and snares. It's doubtful that they would pass up lobsters if the crustaceans were as plentiful as history seems to tell us. Taboo or not, the Maine Indian very likely used traps to catch lobsters, and the good old *Homarus americanus* was probably a part of man's diet long before the white man landed on the rocky coast of Maine.

Probably the first trap designed especially for lobsters was the hoop net, in the first quarter of the 19th century. The construction and method of fishing was simple, but it was the first lure, or baited, lobster-catching device. Early hoop nets were crude. They consisted of a hoop made of supple, small-diameter wood such as alders or even birch limbs. Attached loosely all around the inside circumference of the hoop circle was loosely gathered netting. A four-legged bridle was tied to the rim, and a piece of line and a buoy were made off to the bridle. Bait, usually fish, was attached or sewn into the middle of the netting, and the hoop was lowered into shallow areas of known lobster habitat.

Lobsters scavenging along the bottom would smell the bait, cross the hoop rim, and proceed with a free lunch. The hoop nets had to be hauled quite frequently—say, on a half-hour basis—because the lobsters made short work of the bait. However, early lobstermen working a string of hoop nets had surprisingly good results.

Hoop nets are still in use. Illegally, of course. They do not meet the test of Maine statutes defining a "conventional" lobster trap. They are used illegally because they are quite effective. Modern-day hoop-net fishermen, called "hoopers" among their brethren, have invented ingenious hoop nets that have trip hinges on the rim so that hauling tension on the pot warp will snap the net shut. Other inventions involve trammel or entangling twine for the inside of the nets. Lobsters get caught even before they get to the bait.

One hooper off Islesboro in Penobscot Bay was so successful that he ignored all but a dozen of his conventional traps and concentrated on his hoops. Until apprehended by the wardens, his yield per trap was about 10 pounds per day. He also hooped by night, which compounded his criminality. He told the judge, who gave him a rather reasonable fine of $50, that he came from a long line of hoopers and it was a tough gene to expel from his system.

The Maine lobsterman today uses two styles of pots or traps. (The words "pot" and "trap" are interchangeable, but generally the fishermen west of Penobscot Bay say pot and the eastern fishermen use the term trap.) The two types are known as square and round. Neither is the case. The lobsterman sees no purpose in being superfluous in word or description. For the record, the round trap is half-round and the square trap is rectangular. In the beginning, about 1800, American wooden traps were almost always round style, probably from the heritage of the European creel, inkwell, or eel pots. Square traps gradually replaced round traps in Massachusetts and then showed up in the southern and western areas of Maine. The Bay State coast, like western Maine, is an exposed fishery ground with vast areas of sandy bottom. Strong tides and storms raise hell with lobster gear, and the square trap does not have the tendency to roll along the bottom in heavy weather that the round trap has. With increasing use of larger boats, the square trap stacked much better. Amazing numbers of square traps, up to 100, are carried on 32-foot lobsterboats when fishermen transfer traps at the beginning and closing of the season.

The standard wooden parlor trap is constructed of oak laths, bows, sills, and runners. Trap mills are specialty sawmills dealing only with trap stock. Not only do they saw the laths and other straight stock, but they also steam-bend the bows. Probably 90 percent of wooden-trap fishermen build their own after buying trap stock. There are, however, a number of increasingly "big" fishermen, full-time types, who fish up to 4,000 traps and have them factory made because they simply do not have the time to build them.

The wooden parlor trap is a relatively simple box divided into two sections—kitchen and parlor. There are three knit heads shaped like funnels. Two of the heads, one either side of the kitchen, allow the lobsters to enter the trap to get bait, which is positioned in the middle of the trap at the inner end of the kitchen. Once the lobster has eaten or ripped off a piece of bait, he tries to escape. The most convenient egress is up the apron of the third head, which opens into the parlor section. Of course, some of the smart-ass lobsters refuse to accept this cunning route and crawl, no room to swim, back out the ring openings of the side heads. But, considering that the trap design has been around and little changed for two centuries, something about the catchability must be right.

The heads, as mentioned, are knit of nylon twine from two-pound "balls" purchased at marine-supply stores and fishery cooperatives. It's fair to assume that almost all lobster-trap heads are hand-knit at home. The lobsterman knits in the evening by the black iron kitchen stove where he has conveniently screwed a hook into the wall to function as a holdfast for his knitting. The wife knits. Grampa and Grandma knit. And head knitting, along with making bait bags, is one of the first teachings of children in lobster families.

Lobster trap design and effectiveness have been much studied by scientists, who generally conclude that a better mousetrap would be hard to build. The rings or head openings, however, have received little attention. There has been an increasing usage in the last few years of larger rings, allowing larger sizes to be caught. The traditional ring varies from 4 to 6 inches. In Maine, few fishermen use rings over 6 inches because of the maximum-size regulation, but in Canada, ring size has reached 7 inches in some areas. Retention of smaller lobsters decreases with such a large opening, however. Researchers are now looking into ring-size selectivity. Interestingly, many Canadian lobstermen and a few Maine lobstermen do not use rings at all. Ringless fishermen claim that an all-twine head, usually of a "hake-mouth" design, catches as many lobsters and certainly retains far more once they are inside the trap. As a bonus, hake-mouth openings prevent large fish from entering the trap and devouring the bait.

In recent years, increasing numbers of wooden traps have their ends closed with knit pieces rather than laths. The trap offers less resistance to being hauled back through the water when fitted with these ends. Also, the trap is more open, allowing the bait scent to disperse more quickly. If lobsters can see farther than the experts claim, obviously a more open trap has advantages. A Beals Island fisherman said he put twine ends on his traps because he wanted to see any skunks that climbed into his traps when they were stored ashore in the winter. Good a reason as any.

There are many variations on the standard wooden parlor trap. Size is one. The old faithful measured 36 inches long, 26 inches wide, and 18 inches high. Traps just naturally got bigger with bigger boats, hydraulic haulers, and offshore winter fishing. Double-headers have two parlors with two sets of heads to better hold the catch when traps aren't hauled as frequently. There are center-headed traps, which have their entrances in the middle with parlors on each end. Some traps have entrances on each end with one parlor in the middle.

It seems every fishing community also has quirks and traditions in trap building.

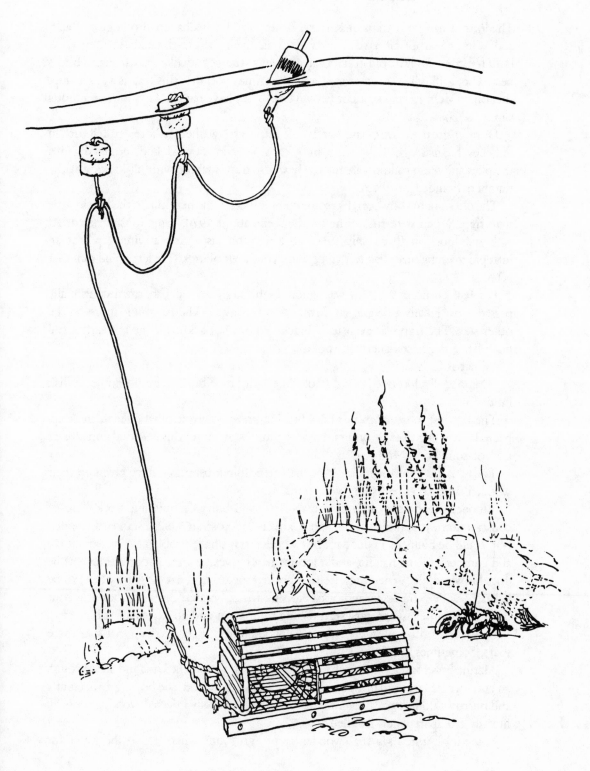

The lobsterman-built traps of Kittery, Bailey Island, Vinalhaven, Stonington, Beals, and Winter Harbor all have slight variations. Even the big-timers have their traps built to order. And the old-timers will go over a strange trap like a cat around a bird's nest. They will tell you sometimes, and sometimes not, that this trap is a Dyer trap, that one a McInnis trap or a Lot Brown trap. They have names. They are patented as surely as Coca-Cola.

During great storms, thousands of traps are washed ashore, balled up in unbelievable masses of laths, warp, buoys, toggles, and seaweed. Lobstermen dig into the piles and seem to know instinctively whose trap is whose without looking at the numbers branded on them.

The old standby, however, has some competition in the new kid on the block—the wire trap. When wire first came on the scene about 1970, some lobstermen at Al Roberts's dock in Friendship spent an afternoon inspecting a wire trap that an intrepid manufacturer had left alongside a couple of pilings. (He left it and ran, that is.)

For half an hour the trap was ignored, although several fishermen continually passed it by. Finally a couple sat down a few feet away. Then a couple more on the other side. The trap was eventually bracketed but not acknowledged. Nearly a full hour later, the first fisherman spoke.

"What is it, Alfie?"

"Damned if'n I know, Junior. Looks like a bird cage but there ain't no water dish inside."

The farthest lobsterman put his whittling knife down, strolled over to the trap, peered down like an eagle on a rabbit, and said, "Boys, either this is a goddamn lobster trap or somebody's funning us."

Today, Alfie, Junior, and most of the Friendship lobstermen have given up their wooden ways and are fishing wire traps.

Wooden traps have their assets, such as availability of building stock, ease of construction with familiar tools, and relatively low cost. In 1982, a standard wooden trap could be built for under $15. But wooden traps have problems. They are heavy and cumbersome to handle, and a lobsterman moves his gear about as much as he does his woodpile. When they are first put overboard in the spring, they have to be ballasted with extra rocks and bricks to sink them, because the wood has dried out during the winter. Wire traps start fishing right away, and no extra ballast is needed. Wooden traps also have a predator—the wood borer. It's a rare trap that lasts three years. Sometimes, one year.

Marine borers attach themselves to the wood and enter the laths and sills through an entrance no larger than a pinhead. Once inside the wood, the borer grows rapidly and burrows along by rasping away at the wood. A heavily infested wooden trap will literally fall apart when handled.

Some lobstermen say that wooden traps "go sour" when left in the water for extended periods. Slime, in the form of algae, adheres to the traps, and in this condition the traps will not fish, say the detractors. Traps that go overboard in early spring are candidates for hauling in June, July, and August to "dry out" and kill the algae and worms. Of course, there is another reason. These are shedder months, and the lobstering is hardly worth it for the Maine fisherman. Landings are way down, and an influx of Canadian lobsters meets most of the summer tourist and restaurant demand. The fishing year for most Maine lobstermen is made or broken in the fall months.

Trap preservatives are in limited use. These chemical compounds are brushed or sprayed on, or traps are dipped in barrels of the stuff. The main ingredient of the original trap dip was copper, and this killed lobsters like crazy. It was also expensive. Later formulas used creosote bases; although these are somewhat effective, trap preservatives are not widely used.

The advantages of wire traps are many, and the number of these in use grows each year. But wire traps had, and have, their problems. The first is human resistance to them. Lobstermen accept the new about as quickly as they speculate on the stock market. The common excuse for not using wire traps is that "they don't fish." That's usually about the sum of the explanation, and persistent questioning will be futile.

The no-fish argument has some merit, or did at one time. The first wire traps were built of dissimilar metals such as aluminum mesh wire and iron hog rings, or poorly plastic-coated iron wire and aluminum rings. The two metals immersed in salt water caused electrolysis, which not only corroded the trap to pieces in a very short time, but also set up an electrical field to which the lobsters were quite sensitive. The original wire traps sold in Maine had a poor reputation. In fact, one company went bankrupt when thousands of its wire traps fell apart after one year's use.

Today, the wire traps are constructed of plastic-coated wire that stays put and has a rather long life. That's a far cry from that aborigine once lurking on the Friendship lobster wharf.

A couple of other styles have invaded Maine but had a brief stay. One was an "igloo"-type trap, like the Cornish pot but made of plastic. This beehive design came from Canada. Not only didn't the thing fish for beans, but the Maine distributor for the pot was caught hauling traps from his pleasure boat, taken to court, found guilty, and fined. Well, now, even if the igloo were the best lobster pot in the world, no Maine lobsterman would ever buy one.

A trap of conventional design came on the market a few years ago. Trouble was, it went together with plastic laths, frames, and other assorted pieces. Something like Lincoln Logs or an Erector Set. Didn't get off the shore.

The line running from the trap to the surface is called pot warp, sometimes trap warp. When the word "warp" was first substituted for rope or line is a good question, but it is a short, terse, rather elegant word, perfectly suited to the lobsterman's vocabulary.

The original pot warp was sisal. This hairy rope, an import made from the fiber of the Yucatan agave plant, really didn't impress the fisherman, but it was the only available inexpensive line until the synthetics such as nylon and Dacron came along after World War II. A few showboats might have used Manila, but sisal was king for many decades.

The lobsterman refers to his pot warp not in size but threads. The commonly used warps are ¼-inch and ⁵⁄₁₆-inch diameter—six-thread and nine-thread, respectively. Warp line is cable-laid, twisted, or braided, although most all warp in use today is cable-laid. Also, warp is hard lay or soft lay—stiff or limber.

Today, Maine coast pot warps are almost exclusively nylon and Dacron. Fortunately, these tough synthetics were born about the same time as other changes in gear technology. Traps were once hand-hauled, gnarled fist over fist, miles and miles a day. Mechanical haulers, starting with capstans called niggerheads and evolving into hydraulic sheaves, would have torn apart natural-fiber warps in less than a season. The old faithful sisal could not have withstood the rigors of trawl-style lobsterfishing, with more than one trap on a pot warp. Even the Cadillac of natural fibers, Manila, would have been strained hauling a string of double-parlor traps. Nine-thread Manila has a breaking strength of about 500 pounds, versus about triple that for the newer synthetics. Synthetics, as the pitchman says, cost a little more but they do so much more.

Nylon and nylon-blended line is the most expensive, and the frugal fisherman, always looking for a bargain, found blended Dacron, or what is known the length of the coast as "rag warp." This fuzzy rope is recycled Dacron sweaters, panty hose, shirts, skirts, and stockings. Anything the Salvation Army can't use. It's not unusual for a lobsterman to find a few zippers when cutting up a coil of warp for his traps.

Some fishermen use split-warps comprised of a few fathoms of polypropylene at the trap end and nylon or Dacron at the buoy end. The reason for this is that polypropylene floats, and the other synthetics sink. Poly on the bottom keeps the warp off the rocks, preventing hang-downs. Lobstermen who use poly on the surface are called spaghetti fishermen, or farmers, or worse. Trying to navigate around a mine field of floating rope is impossible, and those traps usually, mysteriously, disappear on the first foggy day.

Pot warp of any kind is sold to lobstermen by coils, which weigh about 25 pounds each. Depending on the synthetic, there are between 50 and 70 feet of warp in a pound. Panty-hose warp starts at $35 a coil. Some ship chandlers push quality, and the venerable Harris Company in Portland sold a prestige nylon warp named after one of its well-known salesmen, Winnie Doane. That's making it in life, having a pot warp named after you.

Pot warp has been the principal character in a few shady smuggling operations. Most Canadian fishing gear is less expensive than comparable equipment in the States. The problem is getting it here. First, there is the duty, or tariff, which slaps about a third of the value on top of the price. And second, the transportation cost. Together, they bring the price of imported Canadian fishing gear above that of the domestic equivalent.

Pot warp wholesalers and dealers often discover that their sales have plummeted to zero in specific fishing ports, usually those small Washington County places where trade secrets have been kept for generations. No change in the number of fishermen. Same community routine. But *nobody* is buying pot warp.

Well, probably a fisherman has "taken a trip." It happens like this: The steaming time across the Bay of Fundy is not that long—a few hours. The Maine boat makes port in one of those heel-print Nova Scotia coves and takes on a "few" coils of Bluenose warp. Few, meaning a few thousand pounds. Timing the return trip to arrive home in the dark, moonless hours, the pot warp–runner ties his contraband in 5- to 10-coil strings or bunches and throws it overboard in the harbor. Just heaves it over the side. Come the dawn, thousands of pounds of tariff-free rope is lying in U.S. waters. Not a trace, a fingerprint, or buoy shows as a telltale. The word permeates the community in the fog-way of coastal communications, and by midmorning everybody knows about the warp caper. Sales are simple. When a fisherman wants warp, he cruises over the loot area, throws out his grapple, and hauls aboard as many coils as he desires. Payment is on the trust system.

Warps are cut in length according to the depths a lobsterman fishes. Nearshore fishing is done during the summer months when the lobsters are "in the rocks" and shedding, and inshore warps are about 12 fathoms or 72 feet. Warp is often doubled up or tripled so that it can be used for fall lobstering in deeper water. Inshore warp is made about a third longer than the depth fished, while offshore the warp is often twice the depth because the tides will "run under" the buoys. Still, on a hard-running tide such as a moon tide, lobstermen will have to wait for the currents to slacken before the buoys pop to the surface.

The warp is made fast to the trap by means of a small (about 4-foot) bridle half-hitched from corner sill to corner sill on the kitchen end of the trap. The bridle arrangement is used so that the warp can be easily removed from the trap when it is brought ashore for winter storage or when the warp needs replacement. The bridle also gives two contact points in case one end chafes away. Positioning the bridle on the kitchen end is an interesting practice. Presumably, because the entrance heads are on either side at the kitchen end, the trap is hauled from that end so that any lobsters will be thrown backward, away from the entrances. Also, when the trap comes aboard kitchen end first, it is swung forward onto the boat's washrail with the trap door facing inboard. But, as we should have learned by now, lobstermen are individuals, and some fish left-handed boats—that is, with steering and hauling gear on the port side. They are called queer fishermen by others. Well, anyway, queer fishermen have the doors made on the opposite side of the traps.

Both straight and queer fishermen occasionally tie their trap bridles on the parlor end. Ass backwards, they call it. As an explanation they usually say, "always have" or "like it that way." How about "none of your goddamn business." All responses are valid, but very likely these lobstermen feel that the pot warp moving around in the tide in front of the head entrances has a tendency to spook lobsters. They tie the spooker on the other end. Why not?

Buoys are the visible brands of the range. Cutting, stealing, or molesting a lobster buoy is worse than cattle rustling. Bullets have been fired in anger, and boats of known buoy rustlers have settled slowly to the bottom under a no-telling starry northern smile from the heavens.

The buoys of yesteryear were simply pieces of wood—usually pine or cedar, but anything would do. As time passed, fishermen became more fanciful and began to shape their buoys so that they torpedoed into the tide. The pieces of wood were shaped to individual likes and whims. Names or initials were carved into the buoys when some started to look alike. When the licensing system came into being, the individual fisherman's numbers were carved or branded into his buoys. Today it's the law, and each trap, crate, car, or lobster holding device must also be branded.

The plastic era knew no bounds of decency, and it entered the lobster-buoy field in the mid-1960s. Pressed beads of Styrofoam were shaped into buoys by the thousands. Hugo Marconi of Badger's Island in Kittery was a pioneer in these plastics. Acceptance was fairly rapid (the seagulls ate up the first ones thinking the new thing was a bonanza) because it was no simple chore to shape out a hundred or so buoys a year. To be sure, there were a few (and still are) small wooden-buoy makers who had ancient jigs, but the price began to creep up past plastic as cedar came into demand for other uses.

Today, wooden lobster buoys are rare-ish. Plastic prevails, so much so that in 1981 a bill was introduced into the Maine legislature to ban wooden buoys. The explanation of the statute was that wooden buoys get tangled in the propellers of boats and cause considerable damage, not the least being broken drive shafts.

Then a funny thing happened on the way to the forum. The hearing was held before the Marine Resources Committee in Augusta. The chairman read the bill and asked for comment.

A lobsterman rose and said, "Now, whose idea is this anyway?"

The chairman named the representative who had sponsored the proposal. He explained that "many, many" boatmen had requested the document be drafted.

The lobsterman: "Well, the way I see it, this is just another one of those goddamn foolish things where the state ain't got no right into. I fish 400 traps with plastic buoys but I carved a mess of wooden ones in my time. I think we got a skunk in the woodpile here. This here bill was put up by a bunch of pleasure boaters who couldn't steer 'round Monhegan at high noon. Christly, I been fishing f'forty years 'round wood, plastic, n'some things I didn't figure out what the hell they were, but I ain't never got nothing in my wheel without on purpose.''

"I appreciate your comments, sir," said the chairman, "but there is quite a lot of evidence that wooden buoys are hazards." He eyed the few assorted Coast Guard Auxiliary types hunched down in the last row.

"Goddamn it," said the lobsterman, jumping to his feet, "I think we got us a plastic committee.''

"There will be order at this hearing," gaveled the chairman.

Well, it was like turning a pack of wolves loose on a litter of rabbits. Every lobsterman in the room jumped to be heard. The confusion was coastal royalty at the highest. The fishermen had sensed a preconceived committee bias against wooden buoys, and they shot the whole works right out of the water. Probably they were about divided at the beginning. Anyway, the committee vote was 12-0 against compulsory plastic lobster pot buoys.

By law, buoys also have individual colors. With 8,500 lobstermen and half a dozen basic colors, there can be a few duplications. But again, individuality and originality prevail. Such combinations as hot pink and cool green, Jonesport yellow and North Haven red show up on application forms. They are dutifully recorded by state department clerks in the serious vein in which they were conceived.

The lobsterman's buoy colors must also be displayed on his boat, a rather recent law. The instigator was the warden service. Wardens in the 1960s suddenly found out they had difficulty matching the boat with the gear from a distance. Old-time wardens had the right connections. When the boat-color bill went to hearing, there was the usual confrontation. The sum of the opposition argument was that wardens should "get off their asses, stop peeking out from behind shore trees, and get the hell out on the water where any idiot could see who was hauling what." Proponents, mostly wardens in civilian clothes, said it was another needed enforcement tool. This prompted a back-row lobsterman to remark about the overflowing tool box the wardens already had. Nevertheless, the committee gave the ought-to-pass nod, and a man's boat and buoys were impregnated forever by the same hue and cry.

Colors can be displayed in two ways. One, as a panel painted on a boat hull in color strips 4 inches high by 18 inches long. Or, as a lobster buoy stuck up in the rigging. At least 99 and 99/100ths percent of lobstermen stick it.

Lobstermen select their colors in strange ways. Inquiries will reap a non-answer harvest. Yellow is the favorite color, and red is next, both because of logical visibility reasons. Old-timers usually have single colors. Why go to all that trouble of a combination paint job? As other fishermen came along they found all the good, visible, single colors taken and had to double up, sometimes triple up, on a paint scheme. So, it's somewhat safe to assume that a solid yellow buoy floating in a maze of confetti buoys belongs to a harbor mentor.

Eccentricity in hues is known. Yellow buoys with black polka dots obviously belong to a part-timer who has nothing better to do than paint buoys. Solid black is an interesting color, if you can call black a color. One skiff lobsterman fishing black said he rarely gets hauled after dark with his midnight shade. Ocean blue and sea green are beautiful colors but don't survive too well in traffic. One fledgling fisherman started out with pearly white buoys, and on his first haul-back the wind was blowing and the waves were cresting. He chased down 40 miles of whitecaps before finding his first trap. Those Day-glo colors are definitely in. They can be seen for miles. A little gaudy, but visible.

One veteran all-yellow fisherman in Penobscot Bay always advises newcomers to paint their buoys like his—all yellow. "So's I can keep an eye on 'em," he says. The "old yellars" don't get that way letting Irish moss grow on their thinking.

One of the strictest marine laws is that governing the molesting of lobster gear, which includes buoys. Fines up to $500 are applicable. But if there is one souvenir that each Maine tourist covets, it's a lobster buoy. Most of them are authentic, once-fished, genuine buoys. And legally, they are still the property of those individual fishermen. Perhaps a million pilfered Maine lobster buoys adorn recreation rooms, bar walls, and dens all over the world. Bringing these out-of-state thieves to justice would wipe out the Maine debt.

There are a couple of other small pieces of gear between the buoy and the lobster trap. They are called toggles. They, like the buoys, were originally small pieces of cork or wood, and their purpose was to keep the warp from fouling on the bottom. Two toggles are used, one about three fathoms from the trap and the other about the same distance from the buoy. Sometimes the lower toggle is replaced by floating polypropylene split-warp. With the introduction of motorboats into the industry, the top toggle became quite important. Propellers foul buoys and cut them off, but with the upper toggle still visible at low tide, the trap can be saved.

The cork or wood toggle evolved into bottle toggles. Before the days of returnables, the most popular toggle was the Narragansett pint beer bottle. Picwik Ale was a close second. These two brands carried more line than the United States Navy. Solid rubber stoppers sealed the bottles, and they were made onto the warps by a couple of half hitches. Sometimes short gangions were used.

Toggles had other uses. Lobstermen who enjoyed a small nip of the spirits at intervals during the course of the long fishing day were known to keep toggles half full of lovely, constantly chilled, 40-degree port wine. Rum toggles on the last trap of the day made the homeward-bound a little more cheerful.

A Harvard professor who comes to Maine every year and "goes out" with a lobsterman a few times said, "Never, ever, have I had anything that tasted any better than a slug from a toggle of New England Pilgrim Rum which has been silently rocking to smoothness in a cradle of seawater tides on the coast of Maine. My God, I salivate at the mere thought of it as I walk across Harvard Square in the dead of a winter's night."

As anyone who has purchased a live lobster can attest, the business ends of the creature have been neutralized. The claws are made inoperative by either plugging or banding. This practice involves another piece of lobster gear.

The "plugging" of lobsters is not for the benefit of the consumer, really. The lobsterman could care less if the buyer gets nipped. And this might be the time to digress a moment from plugs, bands, and the sort, to explain how to pick up a lobster. Orienting a lobster into automobile terminology, the creature should be picked up by the body, from the rear, with thumb and forefinger on either side close behind the right and left front tires (claws, of course). Disregard those numerous little walking legs with pincer ends, they merely tickle. It's important to hold the lobster firmly and close behind his claws because the reflex action of the lobster is to swim away. In the water, which he still thinks he is, this is accomplished by vigorously snapping his tail, which has a very strong muscle. This is a rather violent movement, and if the grasp is loose, the lobster will end up on the floor. Another reason for holding the lobster high on the body is that when the lobster flexes his tail shut, the sharp, pointy ends of the tail sections, called somites by experts, will pierce the fingers like needles if they are not out of the way.

A few souls perform with lobsters and could care less about danger. Ed Muskie, Maine's longtime senator and Jimmy Carter's onetime secretary of state, was one of the more famous lobster ringmasters. Secretary Muskie spends summers at Kennebunk and is a close acquaintance of lobsters. With only the slightest of suggestions at a clambake or other lobster function (it's rumored that he has performed for presidents), Muskie will hypnotize a lobster or a whole chorus of them. Thusly. Placing a lobster head down on a flat surface and folding the claws under the head to make a three-point contact with the nose and two claw knuckles, he arches the tail backward and spreads the tail flippers fanlike. The smiling secretary holds this mass in this position for a minute or so, which is time enough to mutter some black-magic Maine mumbo jumbo. The lobster, once released, remains riveted and mysteriously statuesque to admiring guests. Ed Muskie says it's harder to train a Maine lobster than a Russian bear.

Bands and plugs are used by lobstermen who don't have time for mystical applications. The reason for the plugging is to prevent lobsters from harming each other in the confinement of lobster pounds.

In Maine, the plugging of lobsters began with string tying but quickly evolved to small wooden pegs hand-whittled from woods such as pine and cedar. Inserted in the claw joint, these keep the claw from opening. The industrial age gave Maine lobstermen a machine-made plug from basswood. Plastic, naturally, entered the scene in the 1950s, mimicking the wooden plugs, and for a period of several years these plugs were the accepted method of immobilizing lobsters.

There is an interesting reason for the birth of the plastic plug, although plastic will imitate anything just for the hell of it. When a plug is inserted into the claw joint, an infection usually results. The longer the plug is kept in the lobster, the more

1½"

Plugging a claw

widespread the infection. When a lobster that has wooden plugs is cooked, there is a section of dark meat surrounding the area where the plug has been removed prior to eating. This was not aesthetically pleasing to nice couples from St. Louis and other parts who had shelled out $20 apiece for an authentic Maine clambake.

Well, in one of those fortuitous discoveries, it was found that plastic plugs, like their wooden counterparts, also caused black meat, but when the plastic was removed the unsightly colored meat came with it. Ergo, chefs presenting the famous gourmet Maine critter could throw out the bad baby without heaving the bathwater. Plastic plugs were in—for a while.

Gimmickry was tried with plugs—cute tricks such as stamping them with "Maine" and manufacturing them in pads like book matches. But the lobstermen had little truck with the hype and refused to pay the extra cost of branded plugs or to separate them from pads with wet, cold, bait-slimy gloves.

In 1951, rubber bands were introduced. Wholesalers and retailers were getting consumer flak about discolored claw meat despite plastic plugs. Also, a couple of other potential problems with plugging were worrying the wholesalers and pound keepers. One was the bleeding to death of lobsters through the punctures in their external skeletons. The other was a blood disease caused by the same wound. It's unlikely that lobsters bled to death, although the belief still exists today. They routinely "throw" (or discard) their claws when excited, stressed, or when fighting. The fresh wound is quickly covered with a crust of coagulated blood, which prevents further bleeding until a skin is formed. But blood disease is another matter. This infection from a bacterium classified as *Gaffkya homari* exists in the natural environment, and when lobsters are confined closely in holding pounds, the disease can spread rapidly and fatally, causing losses of thousands of pounds of lobsters. The disease, commonly called "redtail," is transmitted in several ways. Healthy lobsters feeding on dead, diseased lobsters is one way. Scientific data and common sense both indicate that redtail can more easily infect a lobster through any break in its exoskeleton. Plugging a lobster claw creates a most decided wound.

For a decade, Maine lobstermen avoided rubber bands like a split oar. Trying to slip slippery, stretchy, snappy rubber bands on lobster claws aboard a pitching, broaching sea platform in a nasty November breeze was just another burr of progress under the fisherman's saddle of lifestyle.

The original rubber bands had tabs, completely useless, as an aid to stretching the band over the claw. L-shaped hooks strung with bands helped, but hardly. The savior of the rubber band was the invention of rubber band pliers, the action of which is opposite that of regular pliers. A band is placed on the plier end tabs. Closing the handles then stretches the band, which is inserted over the claw quite neatly. A simple device. The plier invention and some real hardball pressure from dealers has brought

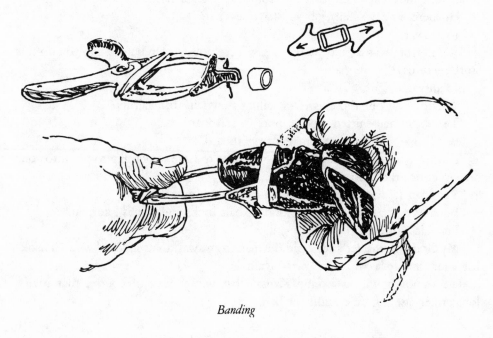

Banding

banding into general acceptance. Many dealers will not even accept lobsters with plugs. Bills to prohibit plugging, heretofore rejected by the legislature, may succeed one of these sessions. However, any legislation must face the problem of Canadian lobsters, upon which the Maine dealers rely to a great extent. Almost all Canadian lobsters are plugged.

Plugging and banding is not always done when lobsters are taken from the traps, especially if the lobsterman is fishing alone, without a sternman. Unplugged lobsters thrown in crates and baskets rarely have room to injure one another, and the fisherman may wait to plug them after he returns to port, treating it as another of his end-of-the-day chores. A few lobster pounds have employees who do the banding when the lobsters are bought. And in most banding practices, only the larger crusher claw is plugged.

In late 1982, the state marine resources marketing specialists suggested that a "new, innovative" way to promote lobsters and the state of Maine was to have the rubber bands on lobsters impregnated with "Maine." Sometimes, the lobstermen wonder if there is really anything new under the capitol dome.

Lobster bait is a science, no doubt about it. Fish heads and fish guts are not thrown haphazardly into traps and lobsters come running. The annals of lobstering are replete with the myth and lore of lobster bait. Consider the conversation between a nice touristy couple and two fishermen that took place on the Stonington Cooperative wharf.

The tourists, camera-shrouded, lime-green clad, curious, and friendly, approached the men, who were sitting on two overturned trawl tubs stuffing bait bags with fish heads that were two minutes away from the state of rancid.

"Hi there. Pretty smelly job you have, isn't it?"

No answer.

"We're from Kansas and we never saw a real lobsterman before. Do you do this stuff every day?"

No answer.

"Why do you put those awful-smelling things in that hairnet?"

The lobstermen shifted moons, port to starboard.

"Bait," one said, flicking a maggot overboard.

"Bait, you say? Oh, I see, of course, you have to have something to put into your box to entice the lobsters."

"Yep, bait it 'tis," answered one in profuse response.

"But my word, what on earth kind of bait looks and smells like that?"

"Pig shit," offered the bait-bag fillers.

"My God, Martha, let's go," said the man from away to his shocked wife. "Thanks for your time fellas, hope we meet again."

The rumor bouncing around Kansas that winter was, of course, that Maine lobstermen use pig defecation for bait.

Pigs do play a role, incidentally, in lobstering off Great Britain's eastern coast. R.C. O'Farrell, an inshore jack-tar fisherman of everything, claims that one of his finest baits is bones, bacon bones he calls them, straight from the butcher shop. But the very best bait, says R.C., is the oily-fleshed cormorant that abounds in England as well as Maine. The English blow them out of the sky with shotguns, lop off their wings, drive a nail through their head into a plank, make a cut clear around the neck, and haul the skin and feathers off like a glove. Alas, the laws in the Colonies are not so liberal. Shooting a cormorant in America, where they are lovingly called shags, is a federal offense for some obscure reason that lobstermen can't quite fathom. But in the bulging genealogy of baits, the shag will hardly be missed. Fish are the staple bait. But a fish is not a fish is a fish.

Herring. The bread and butter of lobster bait. More herring and parts thereof are used than all other fish combined. The reasons are availability, price, and good catching qualities. Herring and sardines are the same thing, although to be Maine proper, sardines are made from herring and never the other way around. The last sardine plants in the United States are in Maine. The procedure of making a sardine from a herring is quite exact and simple. Cut the head off and stick it in a can. Herring are individually hand-trimmed to can size, one at a time, by experienced ladies wielding sharp scissors. One herring head may be snipped right behind the ears and the next halfway down its belly. It's the fit that counts, not the fish.

Anyway, the headless fish travel their pathways to eventual saltine snacks and the heads are sloshed down a chute into an offal or bait truck parked outside the sardine factory and underneath endless conveyor belts. Lobstermen in sawed-off 1956 Buick sedan pickups fitted with rough-sawn wood platforms pull up to these bait trucks every day "fish are in." Coal-like chutes divert the herring heads, which at this point assume the name "cuttings," into wooden bait tubs, plastic garbage cans, 55-gallon oil drums, and every other kind of container, including the bare hermaphrodite pickup body itself. The price is interesting. The factory pays about $2.50 a bushel for the whole fish, snips off the heads, sells the sardines for $30 and then the heads to lobstermen for $3.50 a bushel. This has to be Yankee business ingenuity at its apex. The factory also sells the lobsterman a couple of 80-pound bags of salt for $4 each, so each 200-trap fisherman baiting up at the factory every week drops 50 bucks into the plant till for the privilege of hauling away its offal and gurry.

Whole herring are hard to come by on the mainland. Sometimes a boat load of fish is condemned because of softness or "red feed," which causes the herring stomachs to "blow" when cooked in huge retorts. These condemned fish are sluiced to the same waiting gurry trucks and are eagerly sought for bait. Also, there are a few weirs left in Washington County, and small catches are sold to lobstermen. This practice is more common in the Canadian Maritimes, where bait seasons and quotas are especially set aside for weirmen.

The off-islanders get their fish from bait boats. These are old sardine carriers usually run by owners and one-man crews. They purchase fish from herring stop seiners, who fish at night and tie up by early morning in lobster harbors. Fishermen come alongside and take on whatever they need for that day's lobstering. It's a fine arrangement because a fisherman doesn't have to salt, store, and transport bait from home to harbor to boat. Bait boats like Joe Upton's *Amaretto* and Pete Collins's *Maine* have serviced large island communities such as Vinalhaven and Stonington in the summer months. The islanders also store bait for rainy days or when the herring aren't running. Fishery cooperatives buy cuttings and redfish racks or brim in hundreds-of-bushel lots for use by members.

On Vinalhaven, there was a lobsterboat "seining fleet" at one time. Fishermen made up a mini–purse seine from old stop twine and whatever else was handy. It was about 200 fathoms long, give or take a few rim-racks. Two lobsterboats full of fishermen would take off about dusk. The Fox Island Thorofare near the Sugar Loaves was a favorite spot. The seine boat would cruise the area using only a simple flasher-type depth sounder. When the flashes became a solid line between bottom and top, it meant the boat was over a school of herring. With a guess which way the school was headed, the seine was set and pursed together. Sometimes they hit them,

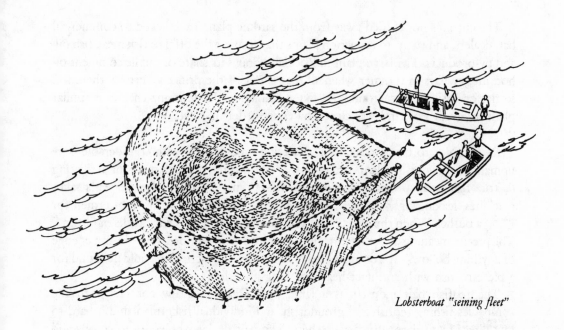

Lobsterboat "seining fleet"

sometimes not. The seine was pursed through the hydraulic lobster hauler, both purse lines, and if fish were caught, they would be bull-netted into the second lobsterboat, which had scuppers plugged with rags and lobster-crate boards plugging the companionway to the fo'c's'le and engine compartment. The fish were divided among the entrepreneurs, and any surplus was sold back at Carver's Harbor for beer money.

These nightly pursing expeditions were fun. A few jugs of spirits fueled the enthusiasm, and on several occasions the two-boat explorers stopped at islands where summer belles would come down to their docks with rubber boots and baskets of fine French wine to join as nonpaid but appreciated crew members the horniest band of sailors since the whalers left New Bedford on two-year cruises.

The practice of scaling herring doesn't sit too well with lobstermen. All herring caught along the North Atlantic coast, not only in Maine, are run through pumping apparatuses that descale the fish. The scales are then sold for various uses including paint manufacture and fire extinguisher contents. According to veteran fishermen, the scales make a difference in catching lobsters. There is the usual reticent reply to the question why, but a few cite the light reflections caused by the iridescence of the herring scale. "It 'tracts 'em," they say. Some studies on artificial bait and lights by a company called Loblure in the late 1950s seem to somewhat support this light-attraction theory. This might also have some bearing on the popularity of alewives. This river herring is regarded as excellent bait, and alewives are not scaled when sold.

The cuttings not carried away from the sardine plant are trucked to commercial bait dealers, and lastly, to reduction plants that convert the offal to fish meal, fish oil, and by-products. The large plant in Rockland draws its share of public comment on hot, muggy days in summer when all that is left of the princely herring, the odor, settles on residential surroundings like a blanket of Liederkranz cheese. A similar plant in South Portland was closed by court order in 1984.

Redfish. Not to be outdone by the herring canners, and with considerable one-upmanship, the redfish plants run their rosy ocean perch through mechanical filleting (a true fisherman pronounces fillet as "fill-it," not "fill-lay," for heaven's sake) machines, leaving only the head and backbone, which they sell to lobstermen for $7.50 a bushel. When the remains hit the bait truck they are called racks or "brim." The precise meaning of the latter term, taken from a fat dictionary, is "the upper edge of anything hollow." It's doubtful that a more precise description could be found for a piece of fish with an intact head and long-gone loins.

The redfish bait industry is a large one. Dealers usually contract with the companies fishing redfish and groundfish, and individual fishermen find it hard to buy direct from those primary catchers. The bait dealer wholesales to co-ops and lobster buyers, who supply those lobstermen selling to them. Brim is also stored in frozen blocks, which negates the need for expensive salting at the wholesale level. Redfish stored for any length of time must be preserved with salt or frozen or it will rot most magnificently.

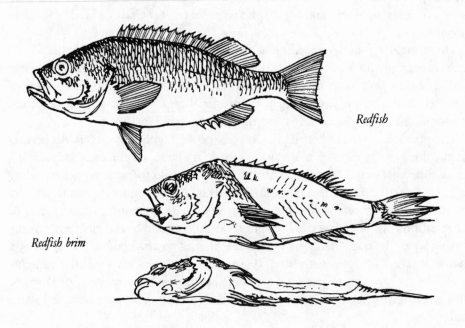

Redfish

Redfish brim

FROM

JESSIE & DAWN

The Vinalhaven Fisherman's Cooperative, a heady band of independent fishermen, once had a new manager who spared the salt and ruined his life. A bait shed is no rose garden, and Tommy Hildings had seen bait come and go with the best of noses. But one day Tommy was sitting in the office munching on a Hershey bar, without nuts, when his ears heard a strange thing.

"What's that chirping noise?" asks Tom.

"Ain't nothing I hear," answers brother Dicky.

"Jesus Christ, I know a strange sound when I hear it, Dicky."

"Probably the wind or somebody's fartin' down on the dock."

Tom got up and went into the bait shed, which had about the same decor as the office, except for the telephone. Then he saw it. The noise. The top layer of redfish was rising up and down like a bellows. Tom hauled back a layer of brim and then jumped like he'd been stabbed. The bait was a solid mass of black, munching, clicking maggots. A couple of co-op meetings later a secret landsite was selected, a convoy of pickups was loosely collected into a passive posse, and maggots et al were given a midnight pauper's burial.

Fishing brim has its advantages. First of all, the lobsterman doesn't have to fill "those goddamn bait bags." Brim is "strung on" with a baiting iron. The redfish racks last longer than bait bags, and brim fishermen will tell all to a man that lobsters crawl to bones. But redfish is not an oily fish like herring and menhaden, so the popularity of the bait is more in the ease of handling than the chemical attraction of the carcass.

Mackerel. This summer visiting fish would seem to have all the characteristics of fine lobster bait. Quite abundant through the season from June on. An oily fish. Easy to handle. But a lot of fishermen shun this itinerant *scomber* of the seas. Those opposed to its use for bait will unhesitantly (remarkable in itself) tell you that mackerel "physics" the lobsters.

The state operated an experimental floating fish trap in Penobscot Bay in the mid-1970s. The purpose was to determine trap performance in strong tides and currents. Another objective was to inventory different species of area fish with an eye to utilization for lobster bait. The catch was distributed free to area lobstermen, who showed up at the trap just about every day it was hauled. The fishermen would take anything offered, anything including dogfish. But never mackerel unless it was "for a few t'eat."

"Nope, don't want any mackerel, they physics the lobsters."

"Guess I won't take any them herring, too many mackerel mixed in with 'em."

"If'n you split that bunch of mackerel off, I'll take the kyacks."

The bad rap on mackerel is rooted in the oiliness of the fish. It is quite perishable and turns soft more quickly than other fish baits. Mackerel also do not salt down very

43

well. When sardine carriers arrive at the factories, usually several bushel of mackerel are mixed in with the herring. These are discarded at the factory and sluiced through to the bait trucks. Mixed in with the cuttings, they are bought by fishermen (the factory will not pick out) and taken home to salt down. When the bait is used a few days later the mackerel are always in a very sad state of preservation. Real slimy, in fact. A very long time ago, it is conceivable that a lobsterman holding a soft, slimy, oily mackerel imagined the correlation between that mess and the doses of castor oil used in the relief of his own malfunctions.

Lobstermen have no aversion to eating fresh mackerel themselves. They eat them fried, broiled, canned, crocked in spices, and nowadays from Japanese cans containing boneless fillets marinated in sild and olive oils. What is not good for the goose is fine for the gander.

Of course, the shyness from mackerel bait is not unanimous. In fact, with the occasional scarcity of bait in the summer when herring aren't running and brim is $10 a bushel, the fishermen will use most anything to stay out on the water. Then, they welcome mackerel, which at such times may not be available because it's an excellent food fish. Fish traps, seiners, and weirs take hundreds of thousands of bushels and ship them to ready markets out of state. Lobstermen cannot pay the price that mackerel bring at the fresh food outlet. Fish trappers in 1982 were getting over 40¢ a pound.

Menhaden. This is the pogy, the mossbunker, the fat back. In Maine everybody calls them pogies. This pelagic fish feeds chiefly on microscopic plankton, primarily diatoms, and migrates to Maine waters in the summer months. Surface schools acres wide infiltrate shallow-water bays and travel far up the estuaries and rivers. In recent years they have been very abundant in July, August, and September. There is evidence that pogies may winter along the Maine coast, because small pogies (6 inches) have been taken on the Northport shore in upper Penobscot Bay in gillnets as early as April. These fish did not contain spawn. The larger pogies (10 to 12 inches) arrived in July and were ripe with spawn. It's doubtful that the early, small pogies had migrated from their traditional southern waters, such as Chesapeake Bay. It is more likely that there are resident populations in Maine rivers like the Penobscot, Georges, Kennebec, and Saco.

Pogy boats from as far away as Virginia come to the Maine coast in summer. The pogies are caught by large purse seines and pumped aboard vessels that transport them to reduction plants in Rockland, Maine, and Gloucester, Massachusetts. And talk about an oily fish! Almost 20 gallons of oil can be pressed from 1,000 pogies. The menhaden was once one of the most commercially important fish swimming on the Atlantic Coast of the United States. They were used not only for oil but also for fertilizer and increasingly, post-World War II, for fish meal, which is an important ingredient in animal feed.

In Maine, pogies have always been used for lobster bait, the oil factor, in this case, being viewed as a decided asset. But the saturated pogy, like the sophisticated lady, may have outdone itself. Pogies are one huge dilemma to hold in a bait stage for any length of time. If they are salted down whole, the entrapped gases bloat the fish, and one of the eight wonders of the fishing world is the odor from a punctured pogy that is a few weeks old. "T'would gag a maggot" is an apt description. Pogies are cut up in pieces to prevent this happening, but whole or cut, the profuse oil gets on, over, under, and into everything it touches. When pogies are used as bait in cold weather,

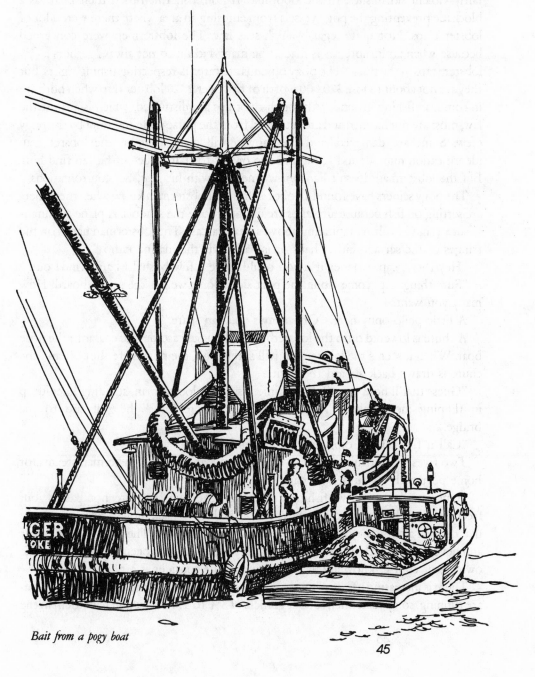

Bait from a pogy boat

the oil congeals and hands and gloves look as though they have been dipped in a Crisco can.

Crews aboard pogy boats meticulously hose down their vessels. Still, a berth aboard a mossbunker is two years before the smell.

Lobstermen get their pogies from the seiners. These large vessels trespass on lobstering grounds quite frequently in chasing this fish, and there have been some fairly violent skirmishes. In the Boothbay region, fishermen used their boats as a blockade preventing the pogy vessels from entering an area where there were a lot of lobster traps. Not quite legal by high-seas law. The lobstermen were concerned because when an inshore set is made, the many-fathomed net always gathers a few lobster traps in the purse. The pogy captains are careful, respecting fishing rights, but they are not about to lose $20,000 worth of fish over a $20 lobster trap when both are in common fishing grounds. Although the traps are disturbed, which is against the law, most are not harmed and are retrieved from the purse seine and reset by the pogy crew. Some are damaged, and the captain will make note of the lobster trap identification number and reimburse the owner for fair value—if he can find him. But the lobsterman doesn't like *anybody* messing with his gear. So, confrontations.

The pogy seiners have found a politic solution. Lobstermen know when the seiners are setting on fish because airplanes are used to locate the schools. A plane circling is as sure a sign as vultures spiraling above a dead carcass. The lobsterman hangs on the fringes of the set and either hails or is hailed via the marine radio.

"Hey there, cap, wonder if'n you could spare a few bushel f'bait. Kinda out."

"Sure thing, cap, come along the port side soon's we get the seine aboard. How many you want?"

A little philosophy here. "Oh, many's you can spare."

A chute is lowered onto the lobsterboat and pogies cascade like coal into the little boat. When it seems the lobsterman will surely sink, the pogies are shut off and the chute is drawn back aboard the seiner.

"Guess that'll hold me 'til dinnertime," says the lobsterman, standing knee-deep in flipping mossbunkers. "How many I got here, cap?" he yells up to the bridge.

"Call it five bushel, cap, give me ten bucks."

Two fives are dutifully passed to a pogy crewman, and the lobsterman steams for home port with 50 bushels of bait.

Sometimes, in sensitive fishing areas, even the two fives are not passed, but freebees are rather rare because the coin for the bait is shack money. Shack money is that divided among the crewmen for extracurricular activity. The owners never see it and never have. Shack money is a fishing way of life and has been for centuries. The owners, of course, know about shack money but consider it a perk.

There is increasing use of gillnets, or rather a resurgence of them. When the pogies are running, some fishermen set out gillnets of 3⅛ to 3¾ inches and haul them in the afternoons, when lobstering is over. With a 100-foot net a fisherman can catch 10 to 15 bushels of pogies on an overnight set.

Alewives. The alewife is a fish similar to the herring, but it has a greater depth of body. Other names heaped upon this fish are sawbelly and kyack. The sawbelly moniker comes naturally, for the fish has a decidedly sharp midline down its belly, and the way to handle alewives is carefully. The label of "kyack" is one of those fisherman metaphors that is hard to argue with because of its primitive accuracy. An alewife looks like a kayack (same pronunciation, less efficient spelling).

Alewives are anadromous. They are born in fresh water, go to sea for growth, and return to the exact rivers of their birth to spawn. Like the salmon. The arrival of the alewives in the spring of the year has been the salvation of early lobstering. In April, the first schools of herring are lurking far offshore. Winter-stored bait is sparse. The pickup truck line for brim is long and discouraging. Scurrying for any kind of bait is time-consuming.

In the beginning, the fishing Bible tells us, alewives ran up about every respectable river, brook, and stream on the coast. Lobstering families traveled to these streams and netted alewives as they ascended the rapids and shoals to spawn. In the latter part of the 19th century, almost all the catch was salt-brined and smoked. There was an insatiable taste for "bloaters," as they were called. Probably an insatiable thirst after eating them, too. In any event, alewives were eagerly sought after by Maine natives. In the June 12, 1879 issue of the Belfast, Maine, *Republican Journal,* there is a story about the alewife fishery at Damariscotta Mills and Warren. These towns reserved the right to sell the fish for town income. The yield that year at Warren was an estimated one million fish, and the selling price was 40¢ a hundred. To assuage the feelings and resistance of local inhabitants, who previously had had free harvesting access to the Georges River, the Warren town law specified that "every male citizen shall be entitled to two hundred alewives, at a certain rate, and every widow the same number free."

As time passed, more and more towns claimed alewife rights. Some were sold to speculators and some were retained. Eventually the state made it perfectly clear, as only bureaucrats can, that those fish swimming up and down the rivers and stream belonged to "the people," and regulation of the resource was appropriated by Augusta. Such is the case today. Communities that border alewife streams are granted exclusive privileges upon application to the proper authorities. But if a municipality does not exercise this right, then the state will assign these rights to individuals. A few large fish processors bid rather outrageous prices for river rights in the mid-1970s when they had strong overseas markets for this fish. Failing to get them, the processors then offered to purchase all the fish from the towns. Some accepted. Some did not. The lobstermen were gravely concerned about this "sellout" as they termed it, and the larger community-owned alewife operations seemed to be sensitive to the lobstermen's needs, although most harvesting operations are inland, away from fishing communities. A compromise was struck giving lobstermen first shot at the fish, with the companies getting the surplus.

Lobstermen in pickups drive long distances to get alewives, and there is no assurance that they will come home from the alewife trap with bait. Sometimes it takes a week of driving before "the fish ran last night."

Alewives are salted like herring but are also used fresh and strung on whole. When cut up, kyacks are stuffed in bait bags a la herring cuttings. The lobster jury verdict on alewives is unanimous—finestkind. Price per bushel to lobstermen in the spring of 1982 was an average of $5, from the traps.

Racks. Although brim usually denotes redfish, other fish racks are used. Flatfish, or flounder, is *the* bait of Massachusetts fishermen, and they are used in Maine although there are not as many groundfish processing plants in Maine as in the Bay State. Racks of cod, haddock, pollack, and hake are fine bait. They stay on good, say the fishermen. Skiff fishermen are associated more with heads. They pick them up at neighborhood fish markets having a store owner–filleter who cuts his own fish.

Sculpin. This is the ultimate trash fish. Not only is it ugly, real ugly, it's all head with very little meat on its bones. It has sharp, infectious spines all over its ugly head. The sculpin is despised by all but the lobsterman, for the sculpin is the best bait going. Fishermen get them in their traps, which the fish enter to steal bait. The sculpin is speared in the head, a couple of slashes are made down its flanks, and it is strung on the bait string. For sure, the next haul will produce lobsters in that trap. As a bottom-scrounging species, it undoubtedly is a fish very familiar to the lobster, and he has acquired a taste for it. Sculpins do not put down well and turn soft and slimy, like mackerel, when kept in bait barrels. And to handle any amount of them a lobsterman would need iron mittens.

Crabs. There is a controversy about using crabs for lobster bait. Some places they do it, some they don't. Examinations of lobster stomach contents have provided evidence that crabs are the single largest component of a lobster's outside-the-trap diet, and many lobstermen were well aware of this crab preference long before any research had been done on the subject. Casco Bay fishermen have used crabs for a long time. There are pockets of crab users farther downeast, but by no means is the practice widespread. In the last 20 years, lobstermen have been saving the larger crabs they take from their traps and selling them to crab pickers. In this sense, big crabs are too valuable to be utilized as bait. Penobscot Bay has more crabs than any other place on the coast, yet fishermen there resent crab baiting. It's another income resource that they see threatened by indiscriminate use. Rock crabs, *Cancer irroratus*, were valued at between 15¢ and 20¢ a pound to fishermen in 1982, so they were well worth keeping off the bait line.

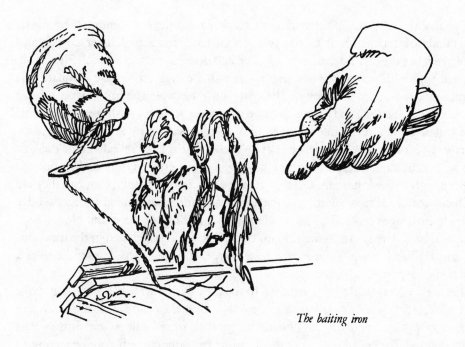

The baiting iron

Smaller crabs, however, are sometimes run through with the baiting iron and strung on in tandem with bait bags containing fish. But rarely, unless he runs out of other bait, does a lobsterman use crabs alone. Dead crabs sour very quickly in a trap, in about two days, and fishermen have an aversion for sour bait. This may be the main deterrent to crabs.

Artificial bait. Fake bait, it's called, and it comes off the wall at times. There are more weird fake baits than places in Maine you can't get to from here. The most serious of the fake baits is a meal, or paste, manufactured from fish waste. It is essentially a fish meal. To this are added ingredients that practically eliminate odor and stabilizers that give the bait an almost unlimited shelf life. The paste does not freeze in the winter nor rot in the summer. The advantages are many. None of the bait-fetching rituals are needed—no trips to the sardine factory or salting and storing headaches. The meal comes in convenient 5-gallon plastic tubs that can be easily stored aboard a lobsterboat.

Because it is a mealy paste, the method of using it involves some kind of a container other than bait bags. These are half-pint round plastic cups with screw-on covers. Molded into the bottom of the bait cup is a small tab with a hole in it, so that the cup can be strung on a bait string. The cup lids come perforated with several holes to allow the release of bait scent. The frugal fisherman, never one to buy new when an adaptation will do, borrows the family ice-cream scoop, which is the ideal tool for filling bait cups. The consistency of the paste is remarkably on the order of chocolate whorl.

But alas, the supposedly better mousetrap cheese has never caught on. Thousands of pounds of this artificial bait have been offered gratis to lobster co-ops and fishermen, but the takers have been few. The bait does have its drawbacks. First of all, the bait cups with perforated lids aren't perforated enough to release adequate bait scent. So extra 3/32-inch holes have to be bored into the cups. The bait obviously can't be placed in bait bags, handy around the boat, because it would wash away in an hour. The bait also has a real tendency to congeal in cold water. It doesn't dissolve well. Instances of lost traps recovered weeks or even months later revealed that the bait was still in the cups, settled into cementlike globs. Fishermen claim the bait doesn't have enough of the important oils that are the attraction of natural bait, and they are probably correct. Traps baited with redfish or herring, when hauled after a two-day set, will show signs of small oil slicks where they come out of the water. Not so with fish-meal bait. Perhaps the same amount of oil per ration is included in the meal, but the natural bait has a much slower release factor, allowing it to deteriorate over a much longer period of time.

There may be a social stigma attached to the use of artificial bait. Something about going lobstering with a 5-gallon pail of mush, a bushel of sundae cups, and an ice-cream scoop. One hundred tubs of complimentary artificial bait sat gathering weeks of mildew and backward glances at the Vinalhaven cooperative before retreating to the mainland aboard the ferryboat with its perplexed manufacturer.

Still, a few lobstermen use the stuff. They are mostly skiff fishermen, part-timers. The 5-gallon tub gives 150 baitings, and the cost is in the neighborhood of $30.

The plastic bait cup has enjoyed more success than the fish-meal bait it was designed to hold. Filled with herring cuttings and fished alone or with bait bags, these are in widespread use today. Bait in mesh bags is preyed upon by unwelcome guests, while the bait cups, with only small holes for predator entry, preserve bait much longer. Consequently, the trap fishes longer. The cups are about 50¢ each in quantity lots, while the lobsterman can knit a bait bag for 15¢ if he doesn't count his time, which he doesn't. His rationale is that he's here on earth anyway and has to fill up that time doing something.

Trying to find the ultimate bait at the end of the rainbow has been an elusive but interesting search. A Dr. Harry Lee of Stonington supposedly used Freon gas mixed with fish oil. This mix was packaged in a container that released the gas slowly. The premise was that the gas would absorb the oil and dissolve in seawater, liberating the globules of odor. Well, after a compensated trial run in the Deer Island Thorofare, the verdict announced was that "the bait was good but not as good as what we have." This was a euphemism for "t'want worth a shit."

Lights were thought to attract lobsters. Lights of every conceivable shape and content were tried. Bottles filled with radium salts (the old watch-dial trick) and glass bottles coated on the inside with herring scale lacquer. There was the small bottle filled with a dose of mercury; when hung in the trap it would gently rock to and fro in the tide, reflecting surface light rays. Of course, somebody should have told these guys that light is pretty well absorbed below 80 feet.

It was thought that simplicity was the light-lure answer, and an electric light was tried. This was a tiny bulb connected to flashlight batteries. Then there were the Christmas tree bulbs, the white coffee mugs, and the infamous kerosene-soaked brick. All had their shot at creating a better lobster menu. The tactics employed by the artificial-bait inventors were at times intense. The lowly hair-brained lobster was elevated in intelligence and stature to an international jewel thief. All the lobster really desired was a generous hunk of dead fish to munch on.

If lobster bait is a science, then salting it is an art. The best definition of a finestkind lobster bait is, "It'll draw a crow but drive a skunk." The betweens is the catch. There are lobstermen who use salt sparingly, and they and their families are preceded by their custom wherever they wander. Lobster bait permeates like penetrating oil. A fisherman who has filled bait bags for 50 years has veins of half blood and half fish gurry. The gurry ratio increases in direct proportion to the amount of salt he uses to put down his bait.

Fred Dodge, an old-timer who fished from Penobscot Bay's Islesboro, used to put his bait down with very little salt and lots of seal oil. On a hot, summer day Fred could be detected downwind the day before he left his house. Fred shot seals that fooled around his fish weir, this being in the days when seals were legal game. Fred would string up a seal carcass over his hogshead barrel full of herring and let the mammal oil drip, drip, drip in the hot, heady days of August. It was blowfly heaven, but eventually the thick layer of oil would cap the bait tub tighter than paraffin on strawberry preserves. Only when Fred broke the crust did the odor escape. It is said and recorded that nothing, absolutely nothing, stank more on the face of the earth than Fred Dodge's seal bait. A skin transplant would not cure anyone coming in contact with it.

There are Fred Dodge followers today who salt bait by the sparing handfuls, but seal oil is a missing ingredient as there is a head price of $10,000 for shooting one.

Bait used within three to four days can usually be treated lightly, but anything stored longer than that needs some sodium-chloride attention. The best bait put-downers salt liberally (say, 80 pounds to five bushel), and after a few days, when the bait turns to pickle (leakproof containers must be used), the bait is re-salted. This procedure produces a sweet lobster bait that will last for years.

Lobstermen who don't salt heavily claim that lobsters like fresh rather than salty bait. Others claim the opposite. A majority will admit that crabs like fresh bait better, a plus for those keeping and selling crabs and a minus for lobstermen who find crabs a pest. It is also claimed that lobsters will not so readily enter a trap full of scampering crabs.

All sorts of schemes have been tried to preserve bait by other than the ages-old methods of salting and freezing. Drying is fraught with problems. American custom once tolerated acres of open chicken-wire flakes full of drying fish, but no more. Air-quality laws would zap the sun-bait machine in a second.

One of the most famous bait-keeping episodes involved an experiment by some intrepid agricultural engineers at the University of Maine. They developed an ultraviolet apparatus that emitted a low-level humming noise and a spooky bluish light. Theoretically, the emissions would zap the considerable bacteria in the fish offal and conquer the spoilage of guts and heads. The device was installed at Willard Kelley's lobster pound in Steuben. In his bait shed. It was inserted into a half-filled, 55-gallon drum of unsalted herring cuttings. Being electric, it was plugged into a 110-volt wall outlet.

This scientific hum, drum, and light show continued for several days. When the engineers came to inspect their apparatus, they noticed that the lobstermen were giving it a very wide berth. They wouldn't go anywhere near it. The engineers began questioning them.

"Ain't good for ya," said one.

"Wouldn't touch that bait with a 10-foot gaff," said another.

These replies intrigued the learned college boys, who by interview, deduction, and intuition pieced the story together. It seems that when the machine was first left in the bait shed and the engineers departed, the lobstermen all came forth to inspect the gadget. It was humming. It was giving off an intense, eerie, blue-greenish light. It was plugged into an electrical source. It was spooky. A fisherman remarked after a few minutes that he doubted that the thing "would be too kind to one's balls." The verdict was in.

The engineers tried their damndest to shoot down the sterility stigma, but when the bait went untouched for weeks (although the spoilage-retardation theory was upheld), they gave up. Never, never would such a device be used on the coast of Maine, whether it worked or not. No lobsterman was about to lose his manhood over a barrel of fish heads.

Bait problems do not cease when a trap is baited and submerged into cold Atlantic waters. Baits have predators other than the expected lobster. Among the more prevalent are sea fleas. These ravenous little ($\frac{1}{16}$-inch) microplankters descend upon freshly baited traps like locusts on a cornfield. Quite alone, they can strip a bait bag in 30 minutes. The only defense against these fleas is the plastic bait cup, although they do penetrate the openings, which are just a dite larger than the flea.

Starfish love a free lunch, and the asteriid sea star is the most common bait molester in Maine. These five-armed critters crawl along surprisingly fast on their tube-footed suction cups. One marine scientist with nothing better to do spent a summer among the stars. In November, he wrote a rather terse paper calculating that a starfish could travel a mile a week—if he wanted to. And there are other species of stars that gobble up the lobster-bait ambrosia. There are blood stars, mud stars, margined stars, spiny sunstars, and purple sunstars. They are beautifully colored in hues and tints of red and orange and yellow. Lobstermen have absolutely no use for starfish, believing them a true appendix of nature serving not a single function in the scheme of things. Fishermen's wives are more broadminded and request that their husbands bring home a pail or two of stars on occasion. The sea warrior reluctantly does, and wives spread the stars in the sun, sprinkle them with salt (to prevent spoilage and shrinkage), and let them dry for a week. The stars are then placed in a cardboard box and stored in the attic. Come Christmas they are used along with shells from the shore to trim the tree.

The green sea urchin in Maine is widely known as a "whore's egg." The exact correlation is lost in coastal lore, but it is reasonable to assume that if whores could lay eggs, like woodchucks could chuck wood, they would resemble sea urchins. This fullaspines fellow will eat anything, including, some fishermen suggest, rocks. They cover considerable distances on hundreds of tubular feet. In some areas they infest the bottom, and a trap can come up containing two bushels of urchins. It takes awhile to clear those traps. The urchin also figures quite prominently in another aspect of fishing. Lobsters, being shy creatures, like to hide in kelp. The main diet of sea urchins is kelp and seaweeds. When urchins become quite numerous they invade kelp beds and strip them naked. Lobsters move off to other hiding grounds. It's a known cyclic ritual between the urchin and kelp and is reflected in the lobster landings. In years of good kelp cover, lobstering is better. In the times of urchin abundance, lobstering is poor. The marine scientists have been slow to accept this theory although it is one of the more universal lobsterman beliefs.

Snails find their way into lobster traps. Primarily, they are the larger species such as whelks and winkles. They are called "snorts" by fishermen, and it needs scant explanation once one has seen a snail sans shell. These shelled gastropods sneak about on rubbery mantle feet and chow down on anything within reach. They particularly like soured bait. There is a small fishery for whelks in Maine. Regular lobster traps are used, although the top-opening crab pot works just as well. A Jonesport fish company, Three Rivers, once had a thriving business with whelks and winkles. It purchased the snails in 5-gallon pails from fishermen, steamed them, and removed the meat, which was marinated in spices and super-secret sauces. The product hit the big time in the ethnic market. Then the company ran out of whelks. One reason was that patches of snails were quickly depleted. Another was that those catching snails were quickly called "snort fishermen," and this handle was a little hard to take with some of the boys, who refused to winkle anymore. Unfortunately, the Italian people have to get their whelks outside Maine to cook up a batch of scrumptious *scungili*.

Little fishes show up regularly at the lobster-trap feeding trough. Cunners, juvenile flounders, cod, hake, pollack, sculpins, sea ravens, sticklebacks, whiting, tommycod—a bibliography of fishes. Big fish enter also, and large bottom feeders such as cod are frequently caught in traps.

Estuarine shrimp enter the traps, especially in the fall months. These nonmigrating species—*Pandalus montagui, Crangon vulgaris,* and *Dichelo pandalus*—are small, about 3 inches at maturity, with insatiable appetites. As an important part of the estuarine food chain, these little fellows get fat by feeding on just everything smaller than they are. In turn, they are food for every fish that swims in the bay.

There is another voracious bait thief. The krill. These half-inch, translucent flea-like critters are the mainstay of baleen whales. The estuarine variety are predominantly horned krill and are found during the day on muddy bottom, rising into the water column at night. For some reason, there are occasional upwellings of krill, and windrows of the dead wash ashore and are greedily eaten by foraging seagulls. The habits of estuarine mysid and euphausiid shrimp are not well documented by the scientific community, but lobstermen will attest to their attraction to lobster bait.

It's doubtful that seals or porpoises bother lobster traps either for the lobsters or the bait. The main reason they don't is that they can't get into a trap. The entrance rings are rarely larger than 6 inches in diameter, since lobsters over 5 inches long (carapace) are illegal. This is about a four-pound lobster. There is no incentive to make the mousetrap door larger than the mouse.

The question of whether seals would actually go into a lobster trap after bait if they could negotiate the opening was conclusively answered in the summer of 1979.

In the spring of that year a field agent in the Maine Department of Marine Resources started a project to determine whether West Coast fish pots could be used in nearshore areas along the Maine coast. There were several objectives. To obtain fish for fresh food sales. To catch lobster bait. To see if large, oversize (illegal) lobsters were living in shallow habitats. The agent had constructed typical West Coast sablefish pots, 8 feet long and 34 inches square, with two tunnels, or heads, made exactly like lobster pot heads only larger. The head openings were 20 inches across.

The traps were set in 80 feet of water in June 1979, off Seal Island in upper Penobscot Bay. They were baited with oversize bait bags containing about five pounds of salted herring cuttings. The bags were hung in the second "parlor" of the fish trap, and they were left on a three-day set-over. In the second parlor of the first trap hauled was a dead, mature seal. The seal had obviously negotiated two 20-inch heads to get at the bait. The seal had drowned, but there were no visible signs that it had struggled to escape. None of the meshes of the webbing that covered the trap were broken, although seals can tear through twine with relative ease. There were no marks on the hide of the seal. There were no cuts on its mouth where it might have tried to chew through the trap frame. It was a very sad mystery. The other trap hauled that day contained only a few crabs and a codfish.

There was a seal haul-out about a half mile from where the traps had been set, so the fish traps were moved across the bay into shoaler water and at least five miles from the nearest seal haul-out. About two weeks passed during which the traps caught only fish, crabs, and lobsters. Then, one August morning, one of the traps yielded two drowned seals. A large one and a small one. Probably mother and offspring. Again, the trap was not damaged, nor were there bruises or abrasions on the seals to show that they might have struggled to get out.

Because of the tragic catching consequences of the fish pots, they were removed from the water the rest of that year. When next they were used, the heads were bisected with heading twine to form a cross at the entrance, quartering the available open space. This probably had some effect on the oversize lobster results, but no more seals were taken with West Coast fish pots.

A 400-trap fisherman is providing a lot of daily free lunches for the little denizens of the deep. He is spending between $2,500 and $6,000 a year for bait, depending on where he lives. Actual figures for bait expense are hard to come by. Only the IRS has a ballpark figure, and those agents don't return calls. However, fish heads and offal are as essential as boats to the multimillion-dollar lobster industry. To paraphrase an old proverb, "For want of a fish head, the whole damn battle was lost."

A lobsterman "ain't particular" about his wearing apparel. A wool shirt bought is a wool shirt worn through thick to thin. He will wear what is nearest when he rises in the morning. He cares not a whit about style, only that a piece of clothing is held together in some semblance of order and that specific garb for a selected site is usually worn there. A hat, for example, is usually worn on the head. Lobstermen are not eccentric in dress, they just don't give a damn.

The custom of wearing 100 percent wool one-piece "union suits" seems to be fading with the newer generation. The old-timers, the one-color fishermen, wore thick, ungodly itchy, vintage, trap-door, all-wool long johns year-round. The only concession to summer heat was the rolling up of sleeves to the elbow. Even a bear sheds most of his insulation in the summer months. Dogs shed. Seals lose a couple of inches of fat in August. But not those fishermen of olden days. Two sets of union suits would last a long time. Too long, some would say.

Maine fishermen have an affinity for wool hats. For year-round wearing. They used to be all-wool, lined and with pull-out ear flaps. These red-and-black and green-and-black checkered caps were pretty much the head uniform of the day for years. They got very oily around the band, and the oil and salt water would mix into a greasy white concoction that, by osmosis, would take over the entire cap in about two years. The size didn't matter much. If it was too large, newspapers would be stuffed under the ear flaps. If too small, the fisherman would simply slice the headband halfway through and stretch the whole to head size. The old wool caps are fading from the scene, probably because they don't make them anymore or the wool became adulterated with cheapo cloth and the fisherman said the hell with it if he couldn't get two years' wear.

The knit wool hats are the replacement. Navy watch cap style. Some of them are freebees and that makes them popular. If a lobsterman buys a $10,000 Caterpillar diesel engine for his boat the company will usually give him a 70 percent wool watch cap with a "CAT" label machine-stitched on the front. One size fits all. The way to a lobsterman's heart is through his head. The color of the hat doesn't matter if it's free, but if the lobsterman has to buy one it's usually a gaudy blaze orange so that he can wear the same hat deer hunting. (Maine law demands one item of a hunter's outer clothing be fluorescent.) These flamboyant lids are usually made in Formosa. Not many orange sheep in Maine.

There are a couple of other styles. One is the long, long-visored cap that is L.L. Bean's concept of what a real lobsterman wears upstairs. The bill of the cap is so long a *real* fisherman would have to turn it backward to drive his pickup. None of the Bean caps have been seen on bona fide lobstermen since Dana Andrews and Cesar Romero made the movie *Deep Waters* on Vinalhaven in the 1950s. Lobstermen got paid $5 a day for wearing Bean caps and Brewster mackinaws.

The "Greek" style fishing cap had a splurge in popularity. They hit LaRochelle's Clothing Store on Commercial Street in Portland in the early 1970s, and they couldn't keep them in stock. There was a run on the bank. First thing an offshore fisherman did upon getting ashore from a trip was to buy a Greek cover. This style hat is still popular with Maine humorists who play guitars, sing off-key sea chanteys, and get discounts at L.L. Bean.

Fishermen's wives knit apparel for their spouses, and fisherman rib-style sweaters and hats seem to last for generations. More than one lobsterman departing this world has entered the next wearing his best homemade fisherman sweater.

Lobstermen rarely wore anything on their hands until recent years. Inshore summer fishing wasn't particularly cold work, and mittens and gloves were cumbersome. Also, either a man had "fisherman's hands" or he did not. If a man's hands got cold in the summer working around the water, he might just as well go into milking cows for a living. For years the traditional cold-weather hand covering was the fisherman mitten. These were home-knit using raw wool, real raw, with all the oils and even burdock bits and pieces. They were knit thick and oversize and prewashed in hot water to shrink them. The mittens were knit long for a purpose. They were obviously wet all the time (fishermen wet them before putting them on, in fact), and the water accumulated in the tip of the mitten. The fishermen then simply slapped the tip of the mitten on the boat rail or some other hard surface, and the water was knocked from the end. The wet wool would stay warm from the friction of the hand inside. Fishermen still wear them, but most all are home-knit by relatives.

Insulated gloves and mittens came onto the marine gear market about 10 years ago, and winter lobstermen, scallopers, and draggermen purchase them by the hundreds of gross. The insulating qualities are quite good, and they are waterproof. The problems are that the gloves are hard to put on, the cotton wrists are always wet and cold, and when the gloves and mittens do get wet inside, as they always do, they take forever to dry out and are freezing cold until they do.

Wristers are woolen, tubular-knit "sleeves" that a fisherman pulls on to cover the arm from wrist to elbow. This prevents chafing of oilskin jacket cuffs, and it covers that area of the arm normally exposed when working traps. Wristers prevent "chilblains and pinboils" on the arms. They are also used by Maine woodsmen but are rather difficult to find except in specialty stores such as a ship chandler. They, like the mittens, are made of raw wool and preshrunk. The repeated wet-dry cycle shrinks the stitches over a period of time, and they become molded perfectly to the individual user's arm. The very first knitting project for a daughter was once a pair of wristers for Dad's Christmas stocking.

The newer breed of lobstermen wear cotton gloves summer and winter. A box of "dunkers," which are blue cotton with an elastic gathering band across the back, will usually last a fisherman a season. Twelve pair, a pair every couple of weeks. More gloves are lost overboard than wear out.

Jackets, sweaters, and shirts are cotton flannel and wool. The lobsterman dresses in layers. The mornings are cool, and as the day progresses, a layer is shed according to the whims of weather. Dark green wool pants, like the old Johnson brand, are favorites. All lightweight cotton pants are called khakis, no matter what color they are. They are never called chinos. Matching cotton shirts are favored. Khaki pants and shirts in green are the most popular. There are macho lobstermen, quite naturally. From spring to fall, they never waver from beltless Levi's, which hang at perpetual half-mast revealing a never-setting moon cleavage. This seascape is topped by a sweatshirt with sleeves ripped off at the shoulder seams and a polyester, adjustable-band baseball-style cap touting one beer or another. The macho allegiance is to hops, not diesels.

The lobsterman's dress sock is white and cotton. If the country ever awakened to its senses and elected a lobsterman president, he would be inaugurated in black tie, tails, and white socks. A lobsterman can be singled out in any crowd, no matter his upper sartorial splendor, by his white socks. A Rockland haberdasher who sold white socks to island lobstermen for decades said the reason related to him was that colored socks "poisoned the feet." In any case, fishermen wear white socks even under wool socks in the cold months. Raw wool homemade socks are the best, and with white liners, they last for years.

Fishermen's boots have come a long way. They were once all-leather and kept half waterproof and half flexible with lard, turpentine, linseed oil, and chicken fat "tried out" on the back of the kitchen wood stove. The legendary stories of lost feet from wet and frozen leather hi-cuts are frightful. Vulcanized rubber came to the rescue of suffering feet quite recently. In 1929, only nine percent of boots *and shoes* were made of rubber, but today, rubber boots are the first piece of clothing a fisherman purchases. Wet feet, unlike wet hands, are not tolerated.

There are several styles of rubber boots, and they repeat themselves like the cyclic nature of the sea. The first popular boots were knee length. This style faded in favor of three-quarter length or "over-the-knee" boots. Nowadays, the knee style is back. The three-quarter boot is favored by fishermen who hate to wear oilskin pants, since the added length gives some protection against wet thighs and legs. The shorter boots are lighter. In the three-quarter boot, there is a cinch strap at the top that is cut off immediately after purchase. No upstanding fisherman would be caught dead with boots sporting functioning cinch straps. After removal, sometimes a marline loop is tied into the ex-cinch hole to hang the boots. Then there is another style of boot. The biologist boot. These are made in Taiwan, and the left and right feet are interchangeable. All Taiwan-made biologist boots come in size 8. They come in one color, olive drab, which is the only color the Oriental manufacturers know (from watching World War II movies), and they are hip length with straps that wrap around the wearer's belt to hold them up. Every marine biologist and scientist has a pair. They are standard government fishcrat issue.

The rubber boots don't necessarily come off when the lobsterman comes ashore. He wears his boots to the beer store, co-op meetings, movies, and to town when he needs to go to town. He paddles around his house in stocking feet much like the Japanese fisherman. The dress shoe, when the wife absolutely, positively puts her foot down against wearing rubber boots to weddings and funerals, is the Romeo slipper. This is an elf-like half-slipper type of footwear with no laces, stretchy side pieces, leather sole, and rubber heel. It's the perfect shoe that is not a shoe. When a lobsterman is forced into conventional shoes because he doesn't want to spring for a new pair of Romeo's, he will reluctantly wear a pair of his discarded wicked-lace shoes. However, once the laces are tied, usually in a square knot, the fisherman never unties them. He just wiggles in over a crunched-down heel until there is no resistance left in the leather, and out of shape and out maneuvered, the shoe surrenders to the inevitable power of the white-socked foot.

Oilskins were once just that. "Raingear" is a new sissy kid in the cove. The oilskins of seafaring stories were made of cloth, usually cotton, and treated with oils to make them waterproof. They froze stiff in the winter and mildewed in the summer, and to keep them anywhere near impervious to water, they had to be rubbed down with warm oils every month. Oilskins required maintenance just like boats and nets and engines. Taking care of oilskins was one of the first lessons learned by sons of fishermen. In the book *Saturday Cove* a fisherman remembers himself and his father sitting on a herring fish weir on a cold November morning watching for fish flashes, like match scratches, down deep in the cold blue-black waters of the weir pound:

> The boy fisherman would have his hands inside his worn rubber boots as they were cold from the chill of the wind born as a cross child of land and sea. The hand-knit collar sweater would be cinched high with a big blue moon button found and claimed from an abandoned attic sewing basket. And over all, Christmas present oilskins now mottled yellow with rutted work lines creased like country roads across a giant field of wheat.

Technology and plastics hung the oilskins on an attic peg with hoop skirts, and the emerging raingear must be considered a welcome improvement. Raingear or "foul weather gear" is a misnomer, because a fisherman uses his raingear as working gear. Sunday supplement pictures of lobstermen in full battle dress on sunny days are accurate . . . . Well, the sou'wester is a bit much. A lobsterman wears rain pants, or sometimes just an apron, to stay dry from the water coming up, not down. Aprons are worn in the summer because they are cooler and provide the same amount of protection. And there are those lobstermen who just *hate* pants.

Canadian and Scandinavian raingear is the most popular, and expensive. Sixty bucks a set for the good stuff. The large American companies didn't follow their excellent rubber boot products with modern-day oilskins, and the foreign gear jumped into the void. For years and years, *the* foul weather gear was Canadian Black Diamond. (It's still around.) If a boy fisherman received a present of Black Diamond jacket or pants, he would wear them more proudly than a titled English laddy his Eton blazer. Today's pants are constructed identically front and back so they can be reversed for added wear. But today's jackets are fastened with grommets that often pull out and never seem to get replaced. There was always that attic blue moon button around to remedy open spaces in the old oilskins. The time and place of wearing determines the names applied to raingear, especially the jacket. When this is worn to the store on an unrainy evening, or to the dock just for the hell of it, or to get an armful of wood from the barn, the jacket is called a slicker.

"Where's your pa, Junior, land sakes, he was here just a minute ago."

"Gone down t'the co-op I guess, Ma, his slicker's gone."

The rain hat is always called a sou'wester, like a pint a pound the world around. The sou'wester has become quite stylish. L.L. Bean sells them to assorted away states where customers like to dress up in the garb of native Mainers. But Maine lobstermen rarely wear sou'westers. They are under cover of a pilothouse roof all day long and need warmth on their head, not waterproofing. The design of the sou'wester, however, is so perfect that the style hasn't changed in 300 years. A soft crown with short, turned-up front rim and long back ending below the jacket collar line. The hat acts as a perfect rain gutter. Somewhere on a lobsterboat one can find a sou'wester, but for head protection the fisherman likes his kindly wool hat and an occasional jacket hood. The hoods are not worn much because it's hard to hear 360 degrees with a hood covering up the ears.

The Maine lobsterman doesn't rush out and buy survival gear or safety equipment other than that required by the Coast Guard. The lobsterman runs afoul of the law if he doesn't have a life preserver for each person aboard, ring buoy, day and night flares, fire extinguishers, bell, night running lights, and an upfront, very visible plaque warning himself that pumping oil overboard can bring down a fine of 10,000 clams. But the other stuff such as life rafts, survival suits, and even an anchor, for heaven's sake, are not mandated by law, and the fisherman on the smallish lobsterboat operated nearshore rarely has such equipment aboard.

There are several reasons. One is the old story that a lobsterman can't swim and if he fell overboard he'd drown anyway. True, most of the old-timers could not swim. Taking dips in year-round 40-degree water was not a pastime of lobstermen. Even the sometimes Saturday night bath in tepid water was a chore. But the majority of contemporary fishermen can swim. They are not accomplished Buster Crabbes but can keep their heads above water for respectable lengths of time doing the Friendship crawl or the Beals Island dog paddle. Fishermen have an uncanny ability to hang onto things, which relieves them of learning to swim. Lobstermen under the influence of sinful spirits have been falling off wharves and docks for hundreds of years. Although positively incapable of fundamental decisions on land, once in the water some rational and spiritual sixth sense kicks into gear and they grasp and cling to anything solid or floating. Lobster lore is pregnant with tales of fishermen clinging to wharf spiling for days, unable to speak but hugging those slippery poles through tide and time. Fishermen falling overboard are often found floating accompanied by the smallest chip of wood. Lobstermen have divine faith that when they do go overboard, something will be there to grasp. It's simply a calculated risk with the odds on their side. So why learn to swim? The new breed swims because of outside social contacts with the schools and "Y" and not because they believe mastering a few arm strokes will save their skins. Of course, lobstermen are born fatalists, and learning to swim only serves up a devil's advocate to their doctrine and who needs another quandary?

The temperature of the medium in which a lobsterman works probably influences his attitudes. Long before government created whole divisions of experts to study hypothermia, the lobstermen were fully aware of the condition. They called it freezing your ass off. Today, everybody from the Coast Guard to Sea Grant has jumped on the hypothermia grant wagon and traverses the fishing ports of the country giving lectures on freezing your ass off.

The lobsterman learned from his father, and his father before him, that once in 40-degree water, a person has precious few minutes to disassociate himself from it. In the winter, falling overboard can even shock a fisherman to death. Water is a wonderful conductor of body heat and there is little use in trying to prolong the inevitable, the lobsterman's logic goes.

There are tragic stories of lost and drowned fishermen. If a lobsterboat is found with engine running but nobody aboard, fellow fishermen search the immediate area very quickly. The finding of the living is paramount. But, as time passes, there is the inevitable hauling back of the fisherman's string of traps to look for a body fouled in twisted pot warp. A life taken by the sea reinforces the fatalism of those who trespass upon it.

There is no question that safety equipment would save lives, fisherman logic aside. The documented evidence cannot be refuted that chances of living through an overboard ordeal are much higher wearing survival suits and life preservers. But the arguments for lifesaving gear must take into account working modes of fishermen. It is next to impossible, for instance, to tend traps wearing an approved life preserver. By law, they must provide certain levels of buoyancy, and this is accomplished by bulk. Slender inflatables are not approved. The Mae West's worn by John Wayne while flying Marine Corsairs all over the South Pacific in World War II were romantic but unacceptable in the table of regulations surrounding the Pepsi generation. And although life preservers must legally be aboard a boat, they are thrown forward to the fo'c's'le, which is the very worst place they could be stored. An engine fire cuts off access, and water coming aboard a boat heads almost always like a torrent into the forward below-deck areas.

Pit Ginnis was a lobsterman who fished around Penobscot Bay in the 1940s. One day his motor up and quit. The old Chevy had seen better days. The points had carbon warts on them bigger than a bullfrog. You could throw a fixed tomcat through the gap in the spark plugs. Pit was never one for preventative maintenance.

Anyway, on this day Pit swore and yelled and fumed and ground his battery nearly to death. The Chevy wouldn't even cough. Pit eased a little gas into the carburetor. A little more. A sputter. More gas, and more . . . .

Then the whole boat exploded into a mass of wood splinters, engine block, wholesome lobster bait—and Pit. Luckily, it was summertime, the water was tolerable, and several other lobstermen were in the vicinity of the disaster. Easing through the debris, another fisherman saw Pit about midmess hanging onto his half-submerged bait barrel.

"Christ a'mighty, Pit!" yelled the rescuer, "what the hell happened to your boat?"

"Sonofabitch blew up. Backfired, the bastard," sputtered Pit.

He was hauled aboard, bait barrel and all, because Pit wasn't about to let go of anything solid unless he could swap it for land.

"Pit," said the savior, "if'n you hadn't found that barrel, you'd drowned f'sure. Ain't you got any life jackets aboard?"

"Naw," Pit said, sitting high on his bait barrel and dumping seawater out of his high-top sneakers, "them things are useless as tits on a clam."

One can only surmise what Pit Ginnis would have thought of survival suits. These flotation exposure suits came to U.S. fishermen via Europe and Canada in the late 1960s, but they received scant notice by fishermen until about 1975. Exposure suits must meet certain criteria of the Coast Guard and Underwriter's Laboratory to be approved. Brand-name manufacturers will argue their individual merits, but the exposure suits are all basically the same. Tests for approval include ease of donning (they come in sizes), 22 pounds of sustained buoyancy (average person weighs 15 pounds in salt water), orange color, air-release valves, mobility, ability to provide hypothermia protection for a minimum of six hours in 32-degree (Fahrenheit) water, and ability to bring wearer to upright position in 10 seconds. The suit must be constructed of closed-cell flexible foam. It is the material of the suit that gives the buoyancy, not the air inside. Some brands have collars, whistles, strobe lights, and chemical light sticks in external pockets. Waterproof flares can be attached.

They are expensive—$250 to $300. That's a lot of cash on the bait barrel for a lobsterman. He looks at this gear as an offshore expense, and he doesn't fish offshore. And then there is that burdensome life-jacket argument. It takes time to fetch a survival suit (away up in the fo'c's'le with the life preservers), put it on, and abandon ship. The lobsterman will take what time he has with a sinking boat to try to save that boat, not his fanny. His last seconds before sinking will be on the radio yelling for help from nearby fishermen. He is alone. He cannot save himself and his vessel at the same time.

But there certainly are a growing number of lobstermen who carry exposure suits. And there are happy-ending stories. And sad, tragic, heart-breaking endings. Several years ago a lobsterboat caught fire late in the afternoon in the western waters of the state. The flames were seen from shore as darkness approached. Two young, healthy, vigorous lobstermen had been aboard. The search for the men was continued all night by the Coast Guard and friends of the missing lobstermen. In the dark, grey, early morning light, a CG helicopter found the lobstermen floating face down. They were unconscious in their exposure suits when taken aboard the aircraft and rushed to a hospital, where a medical team had been alerted to the men's condition. Because of the nature of hypothermia, it was not known if the men were dead or alive. The prolonged cold cools the body to incredibly low temperatures. To the 80s, 70s, and even lower. Then, only the core functions of a human being contain life. The heart. The brain.

Hypothermia procedures were commenced—the gradual warming of the body. But the men were dead. A Coast Guard inquiry could only make educated guesses as to why the men perished in that cold water wearing approved "survival" suits. One man was not fully wearing his suit. Water was inside both garments. One lobsterman had a deep cut and contusion on his head. The inquest suggested that the boat had exploded from diesel or hydraulic-fuel fumes. A break in a hydraulic hose spraying onto a hot engine can easily cause an explosion. The investigation theorized that following the explosion, one of the men was unconscious and the other put an exposure suit on his unconscious partner. This was an incredible task, which he completed, but he may have physically exhausted himself doing it.

Because these "survival" suits had been advertised in glowing terms, fishermen took the deaths of the two lobstermen twice as hard. The word passed quickly on the coast, and so-called survival suits still have a hard time passing muster in Maine.

But there are happier endings, and several cases of fishermen wearing suits in life-threatening situations dramatically document that they are, indeed, life savers.

It's an unusual Maine lobsterboat that has an inflatable life raft aboard. They cost into the thousands of dollars and when-friends-are-near-fishing, who needs one? Some boats do carry a punt or skiff atop the pilothouse, but these are in the minority. A lobsterman usually owns one punt at a time. He rows this from wharf to boat mooring, and that's it. Wear it out, build another.

There is a piece of survival gear that a few inshore fishermen carry, probably the same ones that would have exposure suits and inflatable rafts, and this is the EPIRB—Emergency Position Indicating Radio Beacon. There are several models.

The larger ones hang on brackets in the pilothouse, upside down, and when a sinking is imminent, the EPIRB is thrown overboard or attached to the life raft. The positioned weight flips the radio, activating the battery, which starts the radio transmitting on an emergency frequency. The smaller models can be inserted into the external pocket of an exposure suit and secured with a cord. They are hand-activated with an off-on switch. The small ones are a bit larger than a pack of cigarettes. They have a range of 150 miles and their operating life is about 70 hours in 50-degree water and 24 hours in 28 degrees, which is about the surface temperature on a cold, blustery Gulf of Maine winter day.

These fairly inexpensive radios ($75) have a bonus factor along the Maine coast. They have simultaneous and continuous dual transmission on international civilian and military frequencies when activated. The omnidirectional antenna sends a signal to an altitude of 40,000 feet, where it can intercept commercial aircraft. Hundreds of European in-coming flights pass over Maine waters every day. These aircraft monitor the emergency frequency, and a distress signal, usually accompanied by loran bearings, is passed to the Coast Guard. Fixed-wing aircraft and helicopters from Cape Cod can be on-site off the Maine coast in 45 minutes, often sooner. The aircraft can home in on the distress frequency with surprising closeness.

Nevertheless, exposure suits, inflatable life rafts, and portable rescue beacons remain pretty much supercargo to lobstermen hauling their traps off the ledges and granite outcroppings and among the spruce-covered islands of what the poets love to call the rockbound coast of Maine. The lifesavers are nice gadgets to read about and maybe some day . . . well, when the lobsters run good. The farther a lobsterman fishes from his familiar landmarks, the more serious he becomes about gadgets. Offshore lobstermen with gear 20 to 30 miles to sea have this survival gear aboard as surely as they do cases of beer and girlie magazines.

Fishing gear to the lobsterman is in the eye of the beholder. One man's exposure suit may be another man's union suit. One fisherman may not leave his mooring without a life raft, another wouldn't accept one as a gift. There are staples in gear— the bread, the butter, salt and flour of the trade—and there are frills. That is part and parcel of lobstering as the individual, fascinating, independent, mysterious business it is.

After Pit Ginnis was hauled from the bits and pieces of floating wood that were once his lobsterboat, he was asked if he was going to hang up his oilskins. After all, everybody advised Pit, he'd had a long, rewarding life on the water. But he was getting on.

Pit replied, "Hell no, I'll quit when I wear out my baitin' iron n'not one goddamn shag terd sooner."

He didn't, either.

THREE

The Boat

Shorty Gage, the eccentric lobsterman friend of Cap'n Perc Sane of Saturday Cove and *National Fisherman* magazine fame, claims to own the perfect Maine lobsterboat. Fictional Shorty (or is he?) repossessed the 50-year-old craft from a mud bank where the previous owner had left her to die. In peace. Shorty was never one to pass up a bargain, or opportunity, and dug the 30-footer out of the tidal flats in several pieces. The house and deck came fairly easily, but Shorty was about 20 tides freeing the hull from its grave of clam shells, blood worms, and black goo patted down by a few thousand tides. Shorty would shovel mud like hell on low tides and drink beer on the floods, a perfect existence for Shorty.

Once the boat was free, he winched the mess to a high bank and for a year patched the whole back together with the precision and innovation of a brain surgeon. Today, Shorty's lobsterboat floats at a Saturday Cove mooring, more or less, and outside of the irritable Coast Guard, which have Shorty listed as a permanent hazard to navigation, the boat and Shorty live a unique, troublefree lobstering existence on Penobscot Bay. Troublefree also means maintenance-free.

The boat is mostly an auto junkyard that floats. Power comes from a scrapped 6-cylinder Chevrolet engine that turns a 2½-blade propeller. Shorty puts an old peach can over the exposed carburetor, since flames usually belch forth when the stuck float valve causes a rich, rich feed. One time, a boat moored 100 yards downwind had its gas fume detector go off, Shorty's boat was such a floating ball of gases. For some strange reason, the boat and Shorty haven't exploded. Shorty steers with a 1956 Buick steering wheel linked to a sheet-of-tin rudder via a clothesline-and-pulley mechanism that can't turn the boat fully because of the many knots in the linkage. Shorty used to haul traps by hand, but a few years back he rigged up a hauler. His power takeoff via frayed V-belt to assorted shafts and gears and universals runs a cast-cement winch head. There are no reduction or kick-out gears, so the winch runs as long as the engine does and at the same speed as the V-belt. Even idling, Shorty can haul 200 feet of pot warp in four seconds. The traps surface about 75 feet away and head toward his boat like torpedoes. Shorty throws the warp off the winch head just before the trap scuttles him.

Shorty is hardly ever afloat after dark, but just in case, his running lights are candles in olive-bottle lenses painted green and red. He keeps a couple of Roman candles wrapped in Cosmoline for flare emergencies. His boat has a perpetual leak, more an ooze like magma pushing up from the earth's bowels and ready to erupt. But only a few times has Shorty thrown a plank. For just such a waterborne catastrophe, Shorty keeps a bushel of sawdust aboard, which he heaves overboard near the leak. The water rushing into the hull draws the sawdust with it in obedience to an obscure self-caulking law of physics. If a butt joint goes, or the rupture eats sawdust like pigs swilling slop, then Shorty has a couple of surplus U.S. Army blankets that he heaves over the side. They usually do the trick until he reaches the cove and grounds out. A few fistfuls of oakum and white lead later, and Shorty floats off on the tide for another routine day of lobstering. His boat, which, by the way, is named *Oatmeal*, defies the law of gravity, and if the Smithsonian ever wants an original floating machine to display, then Shorty Gage's *Oatmeal* should be the obvious candidate.

The original Maine lobsterboat was not built for lobstering; it was simply a boat that floated and could be rowed upon the waters with confidence that it would not sink. It was a water vehicle for transport and for fishing. The specialization came sometime later. The first boats used by fishermen tending their lobster traps were small rowing boats—skiffs, dories, punts, and peapods. The drudgery of "ash sails" gave way to the sailing boats—the Casco Bay Hampton boats and the Friendship sloops. The earlier models were centerboarders. The Friendship sloop keel boats became very popular with lobstermen about 1890. They had greater depth in proportion to beam and length and, of course, carried greater loads. The Friendships became larger and even carried gaff topsails. The huge single headsail gave way to the double headsail rig. These sail changes allowed the lobstermen much more control of their sloops in varying winds. Lobstermen "beat" down a string of traps and "hove-to" while hauling. This demanded much more maneuverability than the large mainsail alone could offer.

The first powerboats came along at the beginning of the 20th century. The engines, two-cycle and ponderous, presented a problem for the double-ended peapods and Hampton boats with their fine lines and pointed ends. These bulky engines had to be installed right in the middle of the double-enders, that being the only place with enough bearing to support the weight. Obviously, the engine was right in the way and interfered with the lobsterman's work.

Friendship sloop

About 1915, Maine boatbuilders solved this problem by widening the standard double-ender toward the stern. This shape, called the "pumpkin-seed" shape, although still double-ended, was widest at the point one-third the boat's length forward of the sternpost. This shifted the point of greatest bearing aft, allowing the engine to be mounted farther aft and giving the fisherman more working room amidships. Later, builders began building covers and engine boxes, enabling the lobsterman to stack lobster traps on the stern. These pumpkin-seed models came to be the standard lobsterboat around Jonesport and Mt. Desert. Powered by Knox and other two-cycles, the 22- to 28-foot boats served Maine lobstermen right up through World War I.

Downeast boatbuilders were, and are, an innovative bunch, and various other lobsterboat designs were tried. Ephemeral stern configurations such as steamboat sterns, torpedo sterns, and tugboat sterns came and went on the flood and ebb of fashion. And there was a flurry of other designs, including the Jonesporter of the 1940s with its cut-off tumblehome stern. But it would be difficult to talk of present-

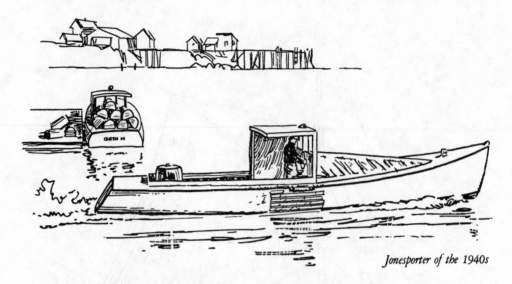

Jonesporter of the 1940s

day Maine lobsterboat design and not mention Will Frost and his kin. Will may not have been the dean of lobsterboat builders, but few surpassed him for design. He had boatyards along the coast in Portland, Jonesport, and Beals Island, and he built not only lobsterboats but trawlers and rumrunners. The Depression wiped out the family yards. Son Bert migrated to yacht building yards in Boston, Cape Cod, and Rhode Island, working in Herreshoff's Bristol yard, for Baltzer Boats, and for Chester Crosby. In the mid-1960s, Bert owned the Frost Shipyard in Jonesport.

Will Frost's grandson was Royal Lowell, who died in November 1983. Royal Lowell designed more than 200 boats, including the first fiberglass lobsterboat models. He learned well under "Grampy" Frost, who showed him how to make half-models, take the lifts off, and loft the lines. "Grampy" thought his grandson should have some formal training, so he paid for Royal to study at the Westlawn School of Yacht Design in Connecticut. Royal left in a month because he knew more than the instructors.

The Will Frost heritage is rich and alive in Maine today. Doug Dodge, a present-day boatbuilder on Beals Island, is another of Will Frost's grandsons. Dodge possesses an added gene of boatbuilding brilliance. His uncle was Harold Gower, a pioneer in the building of the Beals-Jonesport lobsterboat. Gower was perhaps one of the first to build a lobsterboat with significant deadrise aft. And Will Frost was the first to make popular the square-sterned lobsterboat that came out about 1927.

Boatbuilders have made changes over the years in the Beals-Jonesport model, such as greater length and width, more sheer, more rocker and more tumblehome. But as lobstermen began setting more gear and running farther to sea, the basic design— with underwater flat sections providing bearing to support deck loads and countering a tendency of the propeller to haul down the stern when used with engines of great horsepower—has remained the same to the present day.

Maine lobsterboats were traditionally built of oak frames and timbers and planked with cedar. Wood, wood, wood. And then in the early 1960s an upstart, a new kid on the block, came to town, and the repercussions are still vibrating throughout the length and breadth of coastal Maine.

One of the first fiberglass boats came from Cy Cousins's Webber's Cove Boat Yard in South Blue Hill. The yard had built a few of the 40-footers for the U.S. Navy for use as personnel carrier boats. Cy decided that Maine lobstermen could use a few.

He took a bare hull to an Ellsworth shopping center and set the hull on a cradle for display. In due time, the lobstermen passing by would stop, take a turn around the hull, and get back in their pickups and drive off. One day, a contingent of lobstermen arrived in a beat-up old Buick. Four creaky doors opened and out stepped six rubber-booted fishermen, each holding a warm pint of Ballantine Ale. It was obviously a planned from-afar inspection party with all the credentials needed to tell the folks back home just what the hell this plastic boat thing was all about.

For at least 10 minutes the fishermen patted, climbed, stroked, kicked, and eyed Cy Cousins's alien from outer space. They huddled amidships. Then the first and only words were spoken. Pointing to the scribed waterline, the inspection team leader said, "Well, boys, that's where they put that sonofabitch together and that's where the fucker will come apart." They en-Buicked and sped away toward parts downeast.

There was another theory quite popular with lobstermen about the time "plastic" boats came on the scene. It didn't originate with fishermen, but they embraced the hypothesis with open, calloused hands. It seems that someone with exclusive divine rights to a higher, loftier plane of physics came up with the story that molecules of plastic, fiberglass included of course, are held together by magnetic powers home-ported on a star in the universe unbeknownst to man. All well and good. However, the time will come, the time will surely come, when the universal alignment will get out of kilter and the magnetic force will be neutered. Without this mysterious space-age glue, all things constructed of plastic will fall apart. Suppose, said the lobstermen disciples of this antimatter theory, you are out hauling traps one day and all of a sudden your boat disintegrates into a billion, billion molecules of oil. Only your cotton shirt will be left to swim home in. If this supposableness could not be proven, neither could it be disproven, and there are lobstermen working today in their oak and cedar boats who wryly smile when passing a fiberglass-enclosed colleague, knowing full well that someday he will be treading water in a large slick of plastic beads.

Despite the universe a-kilter theory, fiberglass lobsterboats have become the norm on the Maine coast in the last few years. The wood-fiberglass argument can be heard today in about every harbor and fish house. The once thriving wooden-boat shops on Beals Island are still there, turning out magnificent craft made of wood, shaped and formed by experienced boatbuilders who learned their trade from fathers and grandfathers. But they are fewer. And fiberglass-boat shops are sprouting like lawn mushrooms after a week's rain. There are myriad schools of thought on why lobstermen turned to fiberglass. The main reason seems to be maintenance. And it's a fair and strong argument. If a fiberglass boat's bottom is properly prepared with a quality bottom paint, there is no reason why that boat cannot stay in the water for a year or even more. A boat out of water is a liability. Wooden boats have more of a tendency to attract the algae and mussel spat that foul bottoms. And, of course, a wooden boat will become heavier and heavier the longer she stays in the water. The fiberglass hull will not absorb water, and launching weight is just about hauling weight.

Glass-boat owners claim that well-maintained boats are an investment in that the boat will actually appreciate in value over the years—up to a certain point, of course. Others claim this is not true, that any boat depreciates. Distilling a few hundred classified ads for used fiberglass lobsterboats shows no hard and fast argument either way. It depends on the individual boat and the tender loving care she has had over the years. (Maine lobstermen take extremely fine care of their boats.) But the starting, asking price for a four-year-old lobsterboat in standard glass-hull design, rigged for hauling, is about $50,000. That is generally $10,000 to $25,000 less than that vessel would cost new.

Wooden-boat owners make the same claim as to appreciation, but things happen to a wooden boat. The glass hull is constructed in one piece, but wooden hulls are constructed of hundreds and hundreds of pieces joined together by skilled craft. The laws of nature being what they are, forces are perpetually trying to separate these pieces, and the odds seem greater that an object built in one piece will outlast one built in many.

The wooden-boat fisherman has some compelling aesthetic arguments. Wood has been around millions of years, and man has an intimate knowledge of its function, strengths, and weaknesses. Fiberglass is a mere sprout and hasn't been around long enough for builders to know just how it fits into the longevity scale of things. Indeed, some of the earlier small boats made for the Navy developed serious structural cracks when used in the cold waters of the Arctic and Antarctica. Some fishermen claim that standing and working all day on a fiberglass deck is the same as standing on cement—with the same leg muscle fatigue. Others say that the fo'c's'le and other enclosed areas in fiberglass boats "sweat," causing constant dampness. And then there is the "feel" of a wooden boat, an indefinable sense of responsiveness and character and compatibility that fiberglass has yet to possess. The glass builders will counterpoint vigorously, showing their trophies from "The World's Fastest Lobsterboat" races and other competitions. And they do, indeed, win the lion's share of contests between the two types of boats.

Lobsterboats are occasionally built in steel and aluminum, but the biggest deterrent to metal boats is maintenance. Lobstermen can fix broken wood. They can even learn to mend plastic. But working with cutting torches, welders, sand blasters, and chipping tools is not the thing that lobstermen are made of. And yards that do metal maintenance are few and far between.

Lobstermen don't like steel for another reason—"They are just plain goddamn ugly." Fair comment. Steel does not lend itself to the moldability and flexible shapes that can be gained in either wood or fiberglass. One lobsterman said steel boats reminded him of "two washtubs and a hen coop floating down the bay."

Aluminum boats do not have the form and weight drawbacks inherent in steel, but there are very few yards building in aluminum. Many years ago, Alcoa Aluminum tried to interest several Maine boatyards to build in that material. It was just after World War II and surplus aluminum was a problem. A few boats were built in Maine, mostly small sailboats, but the experiment was not successful. The earlier boats— both in aluminum and steel—had electrolysis problems, and at that time that metal-eating gremlin was as foreign to Maine fishermen as electronics and hydraulics. Aluminum and steel are currently gaining favor, however, and will be more common in the future.

Whatever the design of a lobsterboat, the gearing out of the craft has progressed pretty much to a standard list of mechanics and electronics.

Nothing since the internal combustion engine has altered lobsterfishing as much as the hauler—first, the mechanical, and then, hydraulic. Hand hauling of traps is still a common occurrence in Maine, especially with skiff and part-time fishermen, but when strings of gear reach the hundreds, other means of lifting are required. Power takeoffs are used. In early versions, pulleys rigged to the engine shaft and then to V-belts driving other pulleys or gear linkages powered a winch known as a niggerhead. Two or three turns of pot warp were taken on the turning head, and the leverage ratio multiplied many fold, greatly easing the aching backs of lobstermen. These early niggerheads usually did not have throw-out clutches and ran constantly when the engine was turning. This caused some nasty accidents. Loose clothing got wound on the heads, pulling fishermen into the whirling dervish like moths to a flame. The most common malady, the "riding turn," reached epidemic proportions when niggerheads first came into the fishery. A fisherman's hand would be caught between the winch head and the warp, drawing the arm into wrenching distortions and usually breaking a few bones before the engine stalled or the turns slipped. The riding turn was especially prevalent during the winter, when fishermen wore gloves or mittens. Many old-timers have fingers and hands permanently formed like the Coriolis effect. Another problem was the exposed linkage of the hauler, with shafts and pulleys and gears strung along under the rail of the boat. One lobsterman likes to tell of the time one of his pant legs got caught in the hauler shaft and ripped his pants, shirt, and jacket right off his body. "I was left ballicky bare-assed," he says, "and that's a sight."

Amazingly, there are still lobsterboats with pants-stealing and riding-turn niggerheads operating on the coast. But in the 1950s, the hydraulic sheave hauler was born. This device literally revolutionized lobsterfishing. It is quite simple. The boat's engine shaft drives a small hydraulic motor. Flexible hoses connected to the motor, with a small oil-expansion tank and speed-control valve, drive a hauler. This hauler is essentially two disks bolted together with a small V-space between them. The pot warp is placed between the two disks, which the fishermen call "shivs," and as the hauler starts spinning, via the position of the hand control, the warp is drawn tight between the two disks. The action retrieves the line at any speed desired by the operator. Hydraulic fluid is compressed oil, and it offers amazing power for the space it occupies. One of the very first hydraulic haulers in Maine was the Hydro-Slave, and thousands have been sold. The haulers are relatively simple to install and maintain, with lobstermen doing both.

Even the outboard-skiff fishermen are into hydraulic haulers. The setup principle is like that in the large-boat installations, except the power to operate the hydraulic pump comes from the top of the outboard flywheel. The only outward change is altering the outboard fiberglass cover to accommodate the height of the flywheel addition. Some of the skiff and small-boat lobstermen use electric haulers. These get their power from an auxiliary battery.

The lobsterboat engine can be one of nearly a hundred makes or models. The early boats were powered with 6-cylinder Chevy engines. The 4-cylinder Jeep engine was popular right after World War II. But like the boy with a toy, fishermen began trading and installing bigger and bigger "mills." Buick and Oldsmobile engines became the rage in the 1960s. The 325 h.p. Buick gas engine with 2:1 Warner "Velvet" drive was considered the golden dream of a boy fisherman. He had to someday race his buddy Billy, who wanted a 403 Oldsmobile. Big gas engines were definitely "in" for many years. But the fishermen who didn't care to race began

Today's lobsterboat

buying diesels, and today probably three-quarters of the lobsterboats are diesel powered.

Diesel engines are much more expensive than gas engines at original purchase, but diesel has some decided advantages. One is its design, which eliminates the gas-electrical system, and if there is one place that a finicky plugs-points-distributor system is not needed, it is around the salt water. Because of the ruggedness of the diesel block and compression system, the diesel usually lasts longer than gas. The nautical miles per gallon is better. And a decided plus is safety. Gasoline fumes are deadly explosive, while the flash point of diesel fuel is much higher. Although some tragic fatal boat accidents have been properly attributed to ruptured hoses that sprayed diesel fuel on hot engines, explosions are a rather uncommon occurrence in diesel-powered boats. The resale value of diesel engines is also much higher than for gas. The two main disadvantages are cost, as mentioned, and maintenance. Although fishermen are quite familiar with gas engines and take them down to their bare blocks for valve jobs and other overhauls, fishermen are not that versed in diesel mechanics. A fuel injector is not a spark plug. A fuel injection pump is not a simple carburetor. And diesel service, usually from "the city," is very expensive. A lesser problem is that diesel fuel is not readily available in some ports, although that scarcity is changing very rapidly with the popularity of the diesel.

Some lobsterboats are equipped with cages around their propellers. In places where "you can walk on the traps" a cage is nearly a necessity. Otherwise, a fisherman running through trap gear all day would have a ball of warp on his propeller shaft that evening resembling a basketball. It also would make for very strained relationships with fellow fishermen. Cape Porpoise Harbor, where the buoys look like solid confetti on the water, is an example of lobstering ground where prop cages are used. The argument against them is that they do cut a boat's speed somewhat and they are expensive, being constructed, usually, of stainless steel. They sometimes do not last long, whatever the construction material, if the boat has an electrolysis problem (which the fisherman probably first discovers either when his cage drops off or when he hauls in the fall and finds the cage looking like a ball of reinforcing rods).

A lobsterman fishes his ground by familiarity. He knows the ledges and rock piles and bottom configurations as he knows the path home. But few boats are without electronics in some measure. Depth sounders are in common use. The lobsterman will use his sounder most frequently when fishing in shoal water during the shedding season and when "setting off" in the deeper water during the fall, when lobsters begin to move out of the bays and inshore depths. The fisherman will set strings in different depth contours to determine just where the lobsters are traveling. At these times, his sounder is extremely helpful.

Occasionally, sounders will be used for navigation in the fog. Compass courses are followed, but with an eye on the recorder for good luck. Sounders also have preset minimum depth alarms so that eyes don't have to be glued to the dial or paper. With

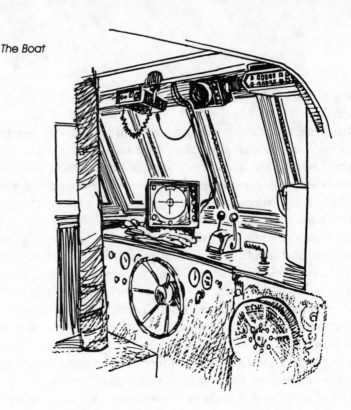

The pilothouse

paper-recording sounders, lobstermen can read a bottom. They can tell by the width of the returning echo whether the ground is mud or hard. Rock piles and ledges, favorite lobster habitat, leap from the machine like firecrackers. Instinctively, a fisherman not familiar with an area and sounding it for the first time will take "marks" on a particular hard bottom or rock pile by eyeballing prominent landmarks—sort of a redundant backup, or maybe he really doesn't trust the electronic world as yet.

Radar (derived from the words radio detecting and ranging) was once thought of as "sissy stuff" by lobstermen. Probably it was because the sets were so expensive that hardly anybody could afford them. The argument, however, was that if a fisherman didn't know his way around without radar he shouldn't be out there in the first place. And so for a long time, price and vanity kept the radar confined to the larger fishing vessels. Eventually a few showed up on small boats, and these fishermen were going out on days when others stayed home and cursed the fog. Lobstermen soon discovered that radar was not a sissy fellow after all.

Radar works by radio energy in the form of pulse signals transmitted from an antenna located atop the boat. The signals strike objects, called targets, and are reflected back to the antenna, which receives the signals and displays them electronically on a cathode ray tube or scope. Position can be determined from one target, since both bearing and range are available from the scope. Radar echoes are received from all kinds of things—buoys, land, buildings, other boats. In addition to finding desired targets, the radar will display signals returned from waves, referred to as "sea clutter." However, sensitivity control knobs can reduce this effect.

Once a lobsterman begins using his radar he acquires a great flair for running to his traps in fog so thick the bow of the boat may not be visible. With ranges and bearings from known landmarks or buoys, he can find his gear in just about any weather. And, of course, there is the safety factor of awareness of what is around the boat. Some lobstermen work in bays—Penobscot Bay, for instance—where large and numerous oceangoing vessels steam at 18 to 20 knots right through lobstering areas. These large vessels cannot maneuver in confined areas and cannot quickly alter speed. A lobsterman fishing in the middle of the bay between Rockland and Vinalhaven in pea soup fog had better have radar if he expects to claim longevity as a virtue.

The newest electronic device sending the lobsterman to the bank loan window is loran. And loran has come a long way, baby. Loran A has been superseded by loran C (loran meaning long range navigation at sea), which was developed by the military because the signals could be received slightly beneath the sea surface and could be used by submarines. Loran is a hyperbolic navigation system. The sending and receiving in precise time delays of pulse transmissions from a "chain" of stations, usually designated as master and slaves, can be computerized in a very small, simple-looking box taking up no more room than a couple of loaves of bread in the pilothouse. This electronic marvel is amazingly accurate, nearly troublefree, gives latitude and longitude, computes way stations, stores memories of wrecks and fishing grounds, gives speed over ground and estimated time of arrival to the second, and rings out a signal when you get within 20 feet of your destination, also flashing an A-R-R-I-V-A-L sign. Lobster fishermen tell their wives they just cannot live without a loran.

Lobstermen use two kinds of radios, the ever-faithful and chatty citizens band and the Coast Guard–monitored VHF "marine service" radio. The FCC regulates both, but in the case of CB, the government has pretty much thrown in the towel.

With inexpensive radio communications, the lobsterman (and his wife) embrace the means of breaking the day's monotony. And, well, the radios just might be handy in case of emergency, shore or waterside. The FCC found out early in the big-brother monitoring business that provincial language patterns were not about to be altered no matter the damn rules. But for a while, mobile FCC vans zeroed in on racy highway CBers and closed them down via license revocation. That is, if the operator had a license. It was a little harder to nail boats on the water. Today, the CBers and the FCC are adversaries only in the sense that the FCC pays very little attention to CB activity. A constant XXX-rated station will probably get a call-warning from the FCC, but little else. The Coast Guard adamantly refuses to monitor the so-called CB emergency standby station, Channel 9, and what regulations come in the box are discarded with the wrapping paper. CB is the old phone party line, the backyard tattler, the smoke signal, the two-cans-on-a-string method of water communication along the coast of Maine. Lobstermen do not use call letters. They are "Dirty Water

Harry" and "The Preacher" and "Dockside Dink" and "Snot Sleeve" and "Wherefuckarewe." Each fishing community will have a different standby channel, and wives will leave their sets tuned to that station all day long. Their lobstermen husbands are a lot more chatty than their stoic, reticent Maine reputations lead one to believe. "Putting on" is a CB game lobstermen play.

"You on, Rock Rider?"

"Yo, come back, Dink."

"Well, I dunno, hauled four pairs down by the fart hole. Only got five pounds a trap. Ain't worth it hardly, is it, Rock?"

"Naw, same here, Dink. Six pounds a trap. I dunno, every goddamn year things get Christly worse. I dunno, may put this slab on the bank come fall n'let mother plant peas in her. I dunno, things are pretty sour."

"Know whatcha mean. Well, got a pair coming up. Out."

Rock and Dink were not talking to one another. They were playing to the CB audience. Other acts take other tacks like:

"Roosterfish, I just hauled 22 pair n'got a horny slime eel, two one-legged crabs n' a half-bushel of whore's eggs. How's going me f'a six-pack 'til I get on my feet?"

The weather act is good listening:

"You on, Cement Ass?"

"Finestkind, you got me, Puker."

"Jaysus, some goddamn sea out here, ain't it? I been takin' water right over that box of choc'late donuts in the fo'c's'le f'an hour now. I think my lights is coming unhooked inside me or sumpin. Ain't seen my bow stem since 'round nine this morning. Maybe it ain't on there."

"Finestkind, Puker."

"Jaysus, left a streak of bottom paint on that last sea longer than a pig's pecker. Water runnin' through me like a rain gutter. Oh, I'll haul right through, though, Cement Ass, 'cepting maybe if'n I come apart you gonna be around?"

"Finestkind around, Puker. Out."

The fog plays to a large CB audience theater.

"You on, Clam Hole?"

"Yo, Sweet Jesus, ain't it some thick?"

"Thick, you say! Hauled one warp a minute ago n'came up with Silas Green's heifer which was tethered out behind his barn. Christly, Clam Hole, Silas hailed me, picked up his heifer which I'd throwed in my lobster tank, n'told me that I'd been hauling down in his lower pasture f'half the morning. Thanked Silas f'pointin' me back t'the harbor."

"Yo, Blackback, gotcha. Yep, I got turned 'round a couple times this morning, too. Threw an anchor over t'have a cup of coffee n'piece of apple pie n'damned if'n the Greyhound bus didn't pull up and stop. People got out n'walked all 'round me. I sold two crates of lobsters f'tourist prices 'fore the bus took off."

"Shit, Clam Hole, some people have all the luck."

"Way she goes, Blackback, well gotta sign off, there's another bus slowing down."

It's no secret that thousands of CB radios are purchased in Maine by people who will never push the talk button. It's pure, unforgettable downeast entertainment. The only cancellations of the long-running show are from CB rain, otherwise known as "skip." This is a radio frequency phenomenon: When atmospheric conditions are just right, transmissions bounce around canceling local talk like a downpour on a picnic. And for the last few years (it runs in cycles) skip in the daytime has wiped out the lobsterman soaps to an annoying degree. Early morning is the best listening, however, before the sun and skip rises, and just for those times only, the best buy in Maine entertainment is a $40, 40-channel, free-for-all peephole into Maine wit and humor.

The antithesis of the CB is the VHF-FM marine telephone. After all, the government had to take a communications stand someplace. This was it. When the old AM marine bands became very cluttered with the advent of more marine radiotelephones, the government turned to VHF in the 1960s. Although the signal was not as strong, it opened up far more channels for the boat operator. There are 89 marine VHF-FM channels. And they have different functions and assignments. There are international, safety, commercial, noncommercial, port, Coast Guard, public, state, and NOAA weather channels.

Channel 16 is the standby calling, receiving, and distress-calling channel, and all vessels including most lobstermen do monitor this station. Range varies considerably, but generally over water, VHF can be received an average 25 miles. And so lobstermen fishing from a port are within static-free communications with one another. Also, many co-ops, lobster buyers, chandlers, and boatyards have shore VHF bases, which are usually manned during fishing hours. Private marine operators, such as the Camden marine operator, relay messages between land and water stations via telephone connections. Bay pilots have shore VHF stations. Both the FCC and Coast Guard oversee operating regulations. And they are strict. Fishermen do not object, for they rely on VHF as the saving factor when emergency assistance is required. The Coast Guard response time for bona fide Maydays coming in over Channel 16 is bureaucratically immediate.

The inshore lobsterboats have few other electronics. They rarely have RDFs (radio direction finders), although a few old sets still clutter up pilothouses. Fume detectors and sniffers are usually the human kind, and any lobsterboat with an autopilot would be shelled and sunk. Power hailers can't compete with downeast lung power when needed. The compass, hardly an electronic, is a staple, but their sizes and prices range from the ridiculous to precious. Lots of fishermen claim their compass as their only true friend—their wife, mistress, and salvation. And they tender commensurate loving care.

Lobstermen have no use whatever for a chart. "Useless as tits on a bull," old Pit

Ginnis would say. Charts are for boatmen who don't know where they are going, a condition not compatible with lobsterfishing. If a lobsterman doesn't need a chart, why would he need such things as parallel rules, plotters, protractors, and dividers? He doesn't. Now, a good leadline is another basket of fish.

The lobsterman will equip his boat with the required lights, horns, bells, life jackets, and life ring. He may even throw in, on his very own, an adequate anchor (fisherman's style preferred) with at least 50 fathoms of anchor rode. He will instrument his boat with only what is necessary, add a respectful automatic bilge pump, maybe a small searchlight, some plastic washdown pails, and brushes—and then get to hell fishing.

The boat and gear will probably be American. It is unlawful to operate in U.S. waters a foreign-built commercial boat over 5 net tons. What foreign boats there are in Maine are Canadian Maritime–built—the Novi's—and generally under 35 feet in length. Since U.S.-documented boats must be over 5 net tons, and boats that fish commercially in the territorial waters (outside the three-mile state limit) must be licensed and documented, non-U.S.-built commercial-fishing boats are effectively eliminated from offshore fishing. Most lobsterboats in Maine, however, fish in state waters and are state-licensed rather than federally documented. The main reason is the hassle of getting the boat documented. There is only one CG documentation office, Boston, in all of New England.

Maine lobstermen have an individualistic custom in naming their boats. More often than not they are named for sons, even though the fishermen follow the normal sea tradition of calling boats a "her" or "she." A lobsterman might refer to his boat as "she's a good old girl" when the name on the bow is *Donny M.* The Donnies and Bobbies and Billies outnumber the Susies and Betties and Barbaras. There are compromises such as *Donny-Sue* and even acronyms concocted from the first names of the family—the Billy, Elizabeth, Sam, and Steve becomes the *BESS.* Lobstermen also take considered pains in having the boat-name paint job a first-class application. Usually there is a sign painter or talented artist in a community who does the names on all boats. Block letters, shaded letters, Old English, and other styles surrounded in filigree make for handsome hailing ports.

The Maine lobsterboat is the fisherman's working world, and he will maintain that structure oftentimes with more diligence than he devotes to his domicile. After all, his house has a co-captain, and his boat does not tolerate that shared responsibility. The model development of the lobsterboat came through compatibility with the seas upon which the lobsterman works. But design had to accommodate the whims and idiosyncrasies of that independent fisherman. The lobsterman mixes mores and structured ideologies like no other artisan. And so perhaps the evolution of the Maine lobsterboat came about through a handful of pragmatism, a pinch of eccentricity, a dose of science, a bit of wit, and a headful of respect for the sea, which is after all the final reviewing stand.

Whatever, the Maine lobsterboat is an elegant lady.

FOUR

The Lobster

In small pockets along the Maine coast lobsters are traditionally called "spiders." And that they are, more or less.

Animals without a backbone and having external skeletons are classified as arthropods—"arthro" meaning jointed and "pod" meaning leg. Included among the arthropods are crustaceans, insects, and arachnids, which are the spiders. Each of these is further subdivided by taxonomists, whose passion it is to break broad groupings down into narrow ones. Crustaceans include decapods, or 10-legged critters, which are lobsters, crayfish, crabs, and shrimp. (There are others that don't taste very good and won't be mentioned.) The scientists who have zeroed in on the American lobster have labeled the genus *Homarus* and the species *americanus*. These same gentlemen and ladies claim the "Maine" lobster is the only true lobster, and those who have taste-tested southern spiny lobster and Maine lobster side by side surely would have to agree.

The "Maine" lobster ranges along the Atlantic seaboard from Labrador to North Carolina and is found in waters a foot deep nearshore to over 1,000 feet deep off the edge of the continental shelf. The offshore lobster fishery in the canyons of southern Georges Bank, Stellwagon Bank, and Tillies Bank operates at great depths for the same lobster that might be found under the seaweed at low tide on Vinalhaven.

The lobster has 21 segments, 14 of them in the head and chest area (cephalothorax) and seven around the stomach or abdomen. The top and sides of the upper body are covered by the carapace, and this is what is used for the measurement of the lobster for legal and scientific purposes. The sharp, bony spur jutting forward from between the eyes is a rostrum. Shrimp have a similar appendage. The eyes are stalked, movable, and compound. The lobster has two sets of antennae, short and long, which are used as sensory organs. The mouth is a mess to look at but very efficient. One would assume that a lobster grabs a hunk of food in a manner reminiscent of King Henry VIII and stuffs it in his mouth with his big fat fist. Nope, the lobster eats daintily with mandibles and things called maxillae, which pass food to the jaws for crushing.

The lobster has claws, of course. Those two big ones out front are called chelipeds. Behind those are four pairs of walking legs; the first two pairs are hinged. The abdomen, we mentioned, has seven segments, and each has paired appendages. From the first pair, the sex of the lobster can be determined. It is the only visual way to label the lobster a boy or girl. These appendages on the male are hard and bonelike, while they are light and feathery on the female. It should have gone without saying. Anyway, the next four are called swimmerets and help in forward swimming. The last pair are flattened and with the telson make the tail fan. The fan is used for swimming backward. The lobster has a four-speed transmission stuck right under its belly.

It's only fair that if we eat a lobster, we should also understand how they eat. The digestive system is made up of the mouth, a short esophagus, stomach, digestive gland, and intestine. Food is ripped apart by all that front-end hardware, enters the mouth, and passes through a short esophagus into the stomach. The cows could learn

a few things from lobsters, who have been around a lot longer. The lobster has three stomachs. The first stomach is sort of a how-do waiting room from which the food passes to number two, which is a gastric mill where the food is ground very fine and then passed to the third, or posterior stomach. Here, the juices from the digestive gland (tomalley, and now nobody will eat tomalley) start digestion, and the food in solution is distributed throughout the body. Waste material is extracted from the blood by the "green gland" and excreted through openings at the base of each second antenna. Other waste continues through the digestive tract and is excreted through the anus, which is in the tail.

The circulatory system of the lobster is an open one. That is, the blood mills around a lot, rather than traveling narrowly defined routes through closed veins and arteries. The blood cavities, called sinuses, surround the important organs. In these spaces the blood sloshes like the wash water in a Bendix, bathing and feeding the organs. The heart has one chamber and is located forward of the thorax. The blood of mammals and lobsters differs. Oxygenated mammal blood is bright red and the nonoxygenated is dull red. But in the lobster, the oxygenated blood is bluish and the non-oxygenated blood is colorless. Sawing a lobster in half will not create a gory red mess all over the floor. The lobster does not have red corpuscles. The oxygen-carrying pigment, hemocyanin, is a copper compound and is in solution, while that of mammals is an iron compound, hemoglobin, and is in the red corpuscles. The lobster does have white corpuscles.

Pit Ginnis was giving a group of tourists a biology lesson on lobsters and was asked if lobsters had blood.

"Not a goddamn drop," Pit stammered. "They pump salt water through a flapper valve."

"Amazing, just amazing," said a tourist.

"Tell ya another goddamn thing," Pit said, waving his hands around like he was knitting bait bags. "They ain't got tongues, Adam's apples, or ears, but they do have scales."

When another tourist told Pit that he had never seen scales, Pit said, "Hell no, you never saw 'em 'cause you ain't no lobsterman."

Getting back to some more scientific stuff. On each side of the body, enclosed by the curved lower edges of the carapace, are the gills. There are 20 on each side, each with numerous filaments deployed around the central axis in an arrangement resembling a bottle brush. There are two openings into the gill chamber. Water enters in back and leaves from the front. It is fanned out of the chamber by the second maxillae, which are also called gill bailers. Once every few minutes the gill bailers reverse their beat for a few strokes to wash silt or sand that has settled on the gills back out the gill chamber entrance. Since respiration occurs as blood passes through the gills, the lobster would smother if the gill bailers should stop beating.

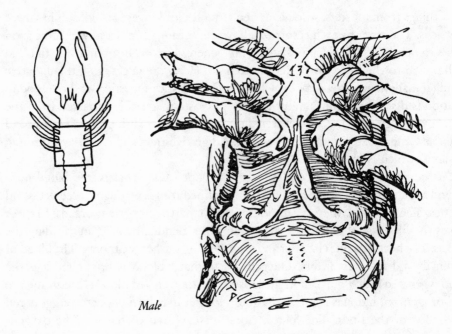

Male

Carbon dioxide diffuses from the blood through the thin walls of the gill filaments, and oxygen is removed from the air dissolved in the water.

The reproductive systems are quite adequate. The female sex organs, ovaries if you will (or coral, that orangy stuff found in the body cavity with the tomalley of a cooked lobster), consist of a couple of cylindrical rods connected by a short crossbar resembling the letter H. They may cover two-thirds of the body, from the stomach to the fifth segment of the abdomen. The openings from the ovaries to the outside are found at the base of the third walking legs. The seminal receptacle, an opening on the undersurface near the junction of the thorax and abdomen, is the third part of the female reproductive system. The male testes also form the letter H and are in the same position as the female's ovaries, only much smaller. The opening from the testes to the outside is on the back side of the basal segment of the last pair of walking legs.

Scientific literature states that reproduction in the lobster is of the sexual type. Pit Ginnis would have loved that. Lobster sex means that the male lobster mates with the female, usually when she is in a soft condition after shedding. He does this by rolling the female on her back and inserting his sperm into her seminal receptacle using his modified first pair of swimmerets.

The mating behavior of lobsters has been studied at some length. Biologists suggest that the most successful matings occur less than three hours after the female sheds her old shell. As she sheds, she releases a hormonal substance that attracts the male. And apparently this hormone attraction decreases quite rapidly with time. If a male is transferred to a tank with a female that has molted within the last 12 hours, mating will usually occur. But mating seldom takes place if more than two days have elapsed since the female's molt.

A male that has successfully mated with one female is capable of mating with another a few hours later, suggesting that multiple paternity is not unusual. A female will mate with males both larger and smaller than herself, but the chances of success are greatest when the male is slightly larger. Comparable size may be necessary for successful sperm transfer, for a female mated to a smaller male will often attempt to mate a second time if a larger male becomes available. Opportunities for multiple paternity, therefore, are limited by both size and time. A much larger male could easily displace a smaller male for possession of a female but males that are too large for a given female show little interest in her, and in any case females reject the huge studs, which are said by many lobstermen to be the salvation of the lobster industry. And it should be recognized that a male that is too small is unable to turn the female over for mating even if the female desires to do so. Some scientists have stated that there is an intermolt mating of previously inseminated females. Not so, say colleagues on the other side of the question, because the gelatinous sperm mass hardens in the seminal receptacle of a mated female and after about 10 hours is sufficiently hard to prevent penetration by another male.

After mating, according to conventional wisdom, the sperm cells are held in the seminal sac until they are needed. This could mean 9 to 12 months later, when the female extrudes (lays) her eggs. She lies on her back, and the eggs pass through the opening at the base of the second pair of walking legs and over the sac, where fertilization takes place. If the female did not mate, and the eggs therefore cannot be fertilized, she may nevertheless extrude her eggs but may drop them after a few weeks rather than carrying them "full term."

Just before mother lobster lays her eggs, she grooms her swimmerets very carefully of all dirt and sand. Then, as the eggs emerge, they are covered with a gluey substance. After fertilization, they are guided along her stomach area by her swimmerets, the glue causing them to stick to one another and to the swimmerets. The eggs are greenish-black, and their number depends upon the size of the lobster. A female lobster with a carapace length of 3¼ inches lays an average of 10,000 eggs; a 4½-inch lobster produces, on average, 38,000.

This conventional wisdom is questioned in one respect by some lobster biologists. These dissenters point out that the seminal receptacle contains a sperm plug, which forms an apparently impenetrable barrier between the spermatozoa and the outside surfaces. This plug is little changed after egg-laying and fertilization. How then, does the sperm get outside to reach the eggs? The conscientious objectors claim that the sperm never does reach the outside, that fertilization takes place inside the lobster. This is accomplished by two new internal ducts formed for the specific purpose of passing the sperm from the seminal receptacle to the oviducts. If that is correct, then

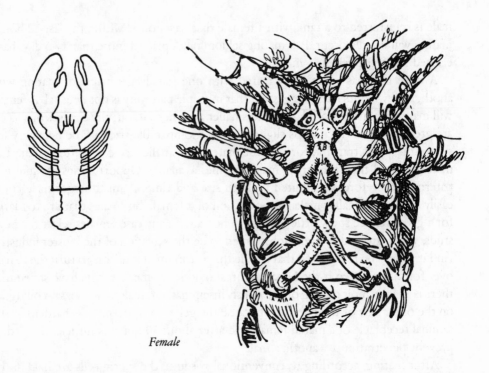

Female

lobsters are fertilized in a manner similar to crabs—and that is news any way you count the eggs.

There is evidence, also, of multiple egg laying. That is, a female can lay fertilized eggs twice in succession after only one mating. The theory goes that a female receives enough sperm to lay two batches without an intervening molt.

Anyway, mother lobster carries her eggs around on her belly about as long as mothers ashore—10 months. Come birthing time, she arches her tail upward and vigorously agitates her swimmerets. Off come the eggs, which now have become transparent, revealing the eyes of the embryos within. The eggs hatch from the female over a one- to two-day period. The newly hatched lobster does not resemble its mother. It is about a third of an inch long with very large eyes, and its double walking legs have hairlike projections that allow the larval lobsters to swim near the surface. During the free-swimming period, which lasts 15 to 25 days, the larvae shed their shells three times, changing their appearance somewhat each time. Each between-molt period is called a stage. At the fifth stage, the lobster settles to the bottom. The young lobsters are extremely defenseless and vulnerable until they sink to the bottom and find home in a sand or mud burrow or under a rock. More than 99 percent of them die during the free-swimming phase.

Because larval lobsters are at or near the surface for as long as a month or more, a major oil spill during this period in the summer could literally wipe out the total lobster year class for that area. And because small lobsters feed exclusively on plankton, which also would be killed by the metric ton, the oil spill scenerio is a scary one.

"You ain't got the brains God gave a lobster," is an old chestnut heard along the shore. The lobster ain't too brainy. What's there is a small whitish mass at the base of the rostrum, between the eyes. Two nerves run down either side of the lobster from the brain to the tail, with branches in every tail segment.

The sense organs are the eyes and sensory bristles. The eyes are compound, like those of the housefly, but probably aren't much use because the lobster is active mostly at times (night) or in places (great ocean depths) where there is little if any light. Lobsters cannot see in the dark, although some lobstermen can. It is the bristles that are most important. There are two types, chemical and sensory (touch). The chemical bristles that detect taste are located around the mouth. Those that pick odor from the water are on the antennae. Remove these and the lobster has to stumble over breakfast before he finds it.

The sensory bristles are distributed all over the body. One amazing group of these functions as a balancing organ. Seems that at the base of the first antennae there is a tiny pore opening into a water-filled sac called a statocyst. On the floor of this sac is a ridge of sensory bristles, and interspersed among them are extremely fine grains of sand. Any movement of the lobster causes the bristles to sway and the grains of sand to roll over them, which stimulates the nervous system to make the proper balancing response. Humans got their idea for ears from the lobster.

While on the subject of amazing lobster stunts, how about a neat trick called autotomy, or reflex amputation? If a lobster is caught by an appendage—or perhaps merely shocked by rapid changes in temperature or by rough handling—it can "throw" that appendage, which could be a claw, walking leg, or antenna. Tricky enough—indeed, brave—cutting off your own hand, but the real act starts at the next molt when the lobster begins replacing that which was lost. With each succeeding molt the appendage will grow larger, until it "catches up" with the rest of the critter.

The lobster reaches full growth by increments, and from its hatching size of $\frac{3}{16}$ inch (length of carapace, also called gauge measure) the lobster must shed 25 old shells and grow 25 new ones to reach a legal length. All this house refurbishing takes place within a time span of 5 to 7 years. Lobsters have to molt because they get too big for their britches. Those lobsters just below and within the legal size range increase about 14 percent in length and about 40 percent in weight with each molt. That means that a lobster right at the legal minimum gauge length of $3\frac{3}{16}$ inches, weighing about one pound, will increase to $3\frac{5}{8}$ inches and approximately $1\frac{3}{8}$ pounds. Given enough time (and no one really knows how much time is enough) he can grow to between 30 and 40 pounds. Lobster lifespan is the stuff of myth, and supposedly responsible people have said a lobster can live a hundred years or more. But lobsters lie about their age.

Scientists have devoted a lot of time to this molting business, enough time to add a few twists to the straightforward too-big-for-their-britches explanation of the process. It seems that before the lobster casts its shell, most of the calcium salts in the shell are absorbed into the bloodstream and deposited in a pair of sacs called gastroliths, which are located in the walls of the stomach. As the calcium salt transfer is going on, the fleshy parts of the lobster are absorbing large amounts of water. This is the reason that the body size of the lobster increases during the molting period.

Lobster biologists claim that the molting process is under the chemical control of two small glands, the sinus glands, located at the base of each eyestalk of the lobster. If, for instance, the eyestalks or sinus glands are removed, the lobster will molt sooner and more frequently than an unmolested lobster. Regrafting reverses the molt and retards shedding. This would suggest that it might be possible to manipulate the sinus gland hormone and prevent shedding when lobsters are in great demand. This would be a tremendous marketing breakthrough, but hold the enthusiasm for a commercial molt inhibitor, say the scientists. The lobster is not that easily conquered, and it has other biological functions that are backups to the sinus gland's hormonal triggering mechanism.

The amount of calcium in lobster blood has been shown to be a definite sign of shedding. Normal (non-molting) lobsters average 65 milligrams of calcium in every 100 cubic centimeters of blood, whereas the molting lobster has about 77 milligrams of calcium per 100 cc of blood. Drugs that are known to increase calcium levels in human blood have an opposite effect on the lobster, depressing calcium levels in shedders. So much for interspecific pharmacodynamics.

Lobster biologists are still seeking methods to alter the lobster shedding process despite the knowledge that growth is constant with life. Experiments have shown, for instance, that a lobster bound tightly with copper wire will die in attempting to cast its shell. Molt prevention escapes the scientists at this time, but their pursuit of "why" clashes most vividly with the lobsterman's "big britches" modest concerns about the life and times of the lobster. Researchers claim they will one day understand the secret of the lobster's unorthodox way of growing only in that short interval between the discarding of the old shell and the donning of the new.

There are some general and accepted ideas on where lobsters live. The preferred environment is a rocky bottom, though lobsters do move around throughout the seasons, crossing large areas of mud bottom in the process. But for every concept there is a disclaimer. Lobsters do sometimes live on sandy and muddy sediments, especially in deep water. They dig burrows when no rock formations are available and live quite comfortably.

In 1982 some scuba divers made a night dive onto a bed of mahogany quahogs in the Penobscot Bay area. The site had been investigated a couple years before, and photos had been taken. The surface of the bed, about 60 feet in depth, was shown by the photos to be hard-packed sand with numerous old shells and many "pit" marks. The small depressions were a mystery until the night dive, when hundreds of lobsters were observed apparently digging for the quahogs, which were only an inch or so beneath the sand. The lobsters had come out of a nearby area that was riddled with burrows.

There have been many attempts to locate artificial reefs for lobster habitat in Maine waters. Most proposals have fallen by the wayside for a couple of reasons. First, most of the coast except the western, sandy area has abundant ledges and rocky bottom. And second, the artificial reefs were to be constructed of old tires, and lobstermen were not very receptive to having their waters filled with what they called "garbage." There was indeed cause for concern, because artificial tire reefs have been shown to leach oils and chemicals into the water for considerable periods of time.

A suitable habitat must include a source of food, of course, which brings us to the question of a lobster's diet. Outside the trap, that is. In two separate research investigations, the stomach contents of lobsters taken from the wild by scuba divers were examined. In Newfoundland, rock crabs and spider crabs were found to make up half the stomach contents. Starfish comprised 10 percent of the diet with sea urchins next at 7 percent and then jellyfish, clams, mussels, periwinkles, and worms, in that order. Fish was a mere 3 percent of the diet.

A study in Connecticut also identified crabs as 50 percent of the diet, followed by snails, worms, mussels, fish, eel grass, sea squirts, and sea urchins.

Some biologists believe that lobsters supplement their animal diet with microscopic plants collected on the gills. They also speculate that lobsters eat various species of seaweeds.

Maine lobsters have more to worry about than several thousand guys with fast boats, tricky traps, and enticing bait. There are diseases, parasites, natural predators, and pollutants.

One prevalent disease, caused by a bacterium, is gaffkaemia, which scientists and fishermen alike refer to as "red tail." It was once thought that infected lobsters had red abdomens, and although this proved not to be so, the name stuck. Red tail exists in the wild but is rarely, if ever, a problem. It is when lobsters are pounded in large holding areas under adverse conditions that red tail can be devastating. Hundreds of thousands of lobsters were lost during an epidemic in the mid-1940s. Another serious outbreak in the 1970s prompted lobster pound operators to use scuba observers weekly during the summer to detect the disease. The disease seems to accelerate with increased water temperatures in the summer and early fall and is further abetted by lowered salinities. Lobsters with terminal-stage red tail are actually suffocating. The bacteria multiply in the blood, destroying the hemocyanin, the oxygen-carrying agent in the plasma, and the result is asphyxiation and death. The infected lobsters are extremely weak, and they collect at the edges of the lobster pounds in the shoal water, trying to get more oxygen.

Unfortunately, the cannabalistic nature of the lobster serves him in ill fashion where red tail is concerned. As the diseased lobsters die, they are torn apart by other lobsters and eaten. This releases still more bacteria into the confined pounds. Pound owners sitting on a quarter million dollars of live lobsters are extremely keen observers of their stock in trade. If there is a sharp increase in the number of dead and weak lobsters, especially if the water temperature has reached 45 degrees Fahrenheit, the pound may be in real trouble. Although the disease is not harmful to humans, the dead lobsters cannot be reclaimed, and some losses are tremendous.

At the University of Maine, biologists have been attempting to control gaffkaemia. In the mid-1970s, a graduate student in UMO's Department of Animal and Veterinary Sciences developed an injectable vaccine against the disease. The success was varied and it was certainly labor intensive, for each lobster had to be individually injected. However, the university sought and received a patent on the vaccine. More recently, UMO professor Robert Bayer and a group of graduate students used a pellet mill to prepare a food of flour, fish meal, and an antibiotic called Terramycin, a very common medicine used in treating a variety of animal diseases. Although the medicated pellets have enjoyed some success, obstacles remain. Bayer's research has shown that the medication is a feeding deterrent (although hungry lobsters will eat just about anything). He is quick to say also that the medication does not provide immunity; it is a short-term prevention. Lobsters treated (fed the pellets) in the early stages of red tail, and treated long enough, probably can be cured. The already weakened lobster will probably die.

Several pound owners and operators are not that enthused with the university's work, citing the cost factor. To date, the medicated lobster food has been prepared and distributed on an experimental basis by the university to a few selected lobster pounds. The cost on a commercial scale has not been addressed, at least not publicly.

The dissident pound operators may have a point. In 1983 the cost of commercial trout chow used by aquaculturists was about 30¢ a pound. This FDA-approved feed contains fish meal, soy bean flour, and several antibiotics and medications. Traditionally, lobster pound owners rely on fresh, fresh-salted, or frozen fish to feed their impounded lobsters from fall to winter and possibly into the spring if they are not sold earlier. The average price for these fish is 5¢ a pound.

One lobsterman who was told about what was going on "up t' the university" said, "Holy Christ, now they've done it, we're gonna have FDA-approved lobsters."

To which his buddy added, "I'm hangin' it up."

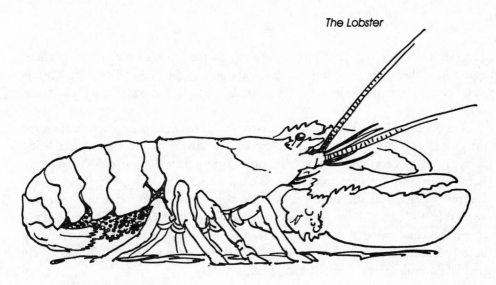

Egg-bearing female

Another problem facing our friend *Homarus americanus* is a shell disease. It was first noted at Yarmouth, Nova Scotia, in 1936, and became known in Maine in 1948 when a shipment of lobsters from Canada showed shell lesions. The lobster shell has three layers. The outer is composed of chitin (the stuff of fingernails); inside this is a layer of lime, which gives the shell strength, and a living layer that secretes the other two. The shell disease eats away the chitin, much as the enamel of a tooth is eaten away, exposing the layer of calcium carbonate beneath. As this in turn gradually dissolves, it leaves the living layer vulnerable. The lobsters may look bad but survive, unless the disease eats away the shell surrounding the gills and fatally impairs gill function.

Water temperatures and salinities have great importance in lobster habitat. When lobsters are taken from the wild, where they seek optimum conditions, and are thrown into holding pounds, lobster cars, and airport terminal show-off tanks, they are faced with tremendous biological problems. Salinity, for instance. Lobster tissue and blood are about the same concentration as surrounding seawater. When a lobster is taken from 3.5% salt water and dumped into a tank with a salinity of, say, 2.5%, the lobster's kidney is not able to maintain its internal balance. In an effort to equalize salt concentrations inside and outside its tissues, the lobster takes up more and more water. The cells become distended and burst. With the internal functions destroyed, the lobster dies.

The higher the water temperature, the lower its oxygen-carrying ability. Add the overcrowding factor to warm water and the result is lobster mortality. Lobsters do have a remarkable ability to exist in water temperatures as high as 70 degrees Fahrenheit—if they are not crowded. Lobster pound owners utilizing pumped recirculating water systems were faced with a puzzling mortality problem in the early 1950s. Red tail, low dissolved oxygen, and high temperature were ruled out, but still lobsters were dying like flies after a Maine fall day. The problem was a gas disease.

Too much nitrogen was dissolved in the water by the action of the pump impellers, especially if there was a seal leak on the intake side of the pump. The poor lobsters were getting the equivalent of the "bends," which can kill or cripple scuba divers.

Friend lobster living beneath the seemingly safe cold deep waters does not escape man-made pollution either. Lobsters are close relatives to the insect pests being sprayed with chlorinated hydrocarbons, organic phosphates, and arsenic compounds. Lobsters are extremely sensitive to these commercial insecticides, which eventually, via freshwater runoff and atmospheric fallout, find their way into the inshore ocean waters. In 1972, Bob Dow of the Maine Department of Sea and Shore Fisheries found that chlorinated hydrocarbons in trace dilutions of 1 part per 5 billion resulted in 100 percent kill of larval lobsters within 24 hours. Lethal toxic levels for lobsters in the wild are unknown. Pretty heady stuff.

Detergents and other cleansing agents carried into seawater from households and commercial laundry facilities are also toxic. But lobsters are so forgiving at times. A Belfast lobster dealer was cleaning several of his recirculating tanks and instructed his young helper to complete the job while he was away for the day. The young man, probably attuned to television advertising and without specific instructions, buzzed on up to the store and purchased a half dozen boxes of household detergent. He scrubbed and scrubbed, and later in the spic-and-span day he transferred several hundred pounds of lobsters back into the clean tanks and turned the water on. The owner returned to the biggest bubble bath the city had ever seen. The detergent-laden water hitting a 5,000 rpm pump made bubbles prodigiously. The water was immediately shut off to these tanks, and all anyone could see was hundreds of lobster antennae sticking up above the soap bubbles like submarine periscopes. They were probably sending out Maydays. Anyway, the lobsters were moved to fresh tanks and the mess was cleaned up. Surprisingly, no lobsters died from the experience.

Metals are also toxic to lobsters. Copper causes the highest rate of mortality. Copper pipes, fittings, and other components are not used around lobster tanks. Zinc is the second most toxic. Zinc mines where the metallic residues could be carried into tidewater are a concern for lobster pound owners. Lead and aluminum have some effect on lobsters, also.

And if the lobster escapes all this, would you believe that he may suffocate to death because mussel spat (small seed mussels) have collected on his gills?

With the range of lobster enemies so huge, why doesn't the human predator do something about returning lobsters from whence they come? The artificial rearing of lobsters is a story within itself. And surrounded with controversy.

People have attempted to hatch and rear lobsters since 1885 in the United States. The first attempts were limited to hatching the eggs in jars and immediately releasing the fry. Between 1885 and 1903, a total of 880 million fry were returned to East

First-stage larva

Coast waters. At the beginning of the 20th century, however, fishery biologists realized that this method was ineffective. Most of the fry were destroyed because they were so vulnerable so soon after birth. Like throwing a baby out on the street.

The advantages of raising lobsters through the early stages before release were recognized from work done in 1897, and the first such rearing station was put into operation at Wickford, Rhode Island.

By an Act of Congress on February 4, 1901, a lobster hatchery was established in Maine. It was on a nine-acre site on McKown's Point in West Boothbay Harbor, the location of the present-day facilities of the Maine Department of Marine Resources. The program began with the release of first-stage lobsters, but a few fourth-stage were reared experimentally. In 1937, the Maine legislature approved construction of a lobster-rearing station at Boothbay adjacent to the federal hatchery, and a cooperative lobster-rearing program was started. Maine purchased egg-bearing lobsters and held them in the federal tidal pound at Pemaquid. In the early spring they were taken to the hatching tanks in the federal building, where natural hatching of the eggs took place. The first-stage lobsters were then collected and transferred to rearing tanks in the state building, which had heated salt water. The larvae were allowed to molt three times into the fourth stage before they were released into coastal waters. It was assumed from previous research that lobsters at this size, about ¼ inch, had a far greater chance out there in the cruel sea than lobsters at the just-hatched stage.

The cost of the propagation was not examined that closely because from a biological point of view, the resource was the important thing. But the cost, in the end, was too high. In 1939, 1,395,000 fry were delivered to the rearing station and an estimated 160,000 fourth-stage lobsters were released. In 1948 there were 66,730 fourth-stagers from 1,446,000 fry. And these were eyeball estimates. To make matters worse, there was growing evidence that the fourth-stage lobster, the age being released, was still in a planktonic state of mind and had not at this age taken up bottom residence, which would afford much greater protection. With this in mind, the hatchery biologists estimated that less than 10 percent of the released fourth-stage lobsters would survive to reach the minimum legal size, and further, that even under ideal environmental conditions the hatchery program could make only a 1.5 percent contribution to the annual catch.

It took about 15 days to raise the lobsters from first to fourth stage at a temperature of 65° Fahrenheit, with a survival rate of 34.6 percent. When the rearing tank temperature was reduced to 58°F, it took 25 days to reach the fourth stage, and the survival rate was 16.9 percent. Modest though they are, these figures were challenged as being too optimistic. All scientists agreed that the seawater used at Boothbay Harbor would have to be heated if there were going to be any successful rearing results.

The true cost of that heating was not assessed for some time. The records ignored it even when changes in the heating equipment were recommended. The rearing capacity of the station was 294 tanks, and with a flow of 2½ gallons per minute per rearing tank, the volume of water used every 24 hours was between 850,000 and 1,000,000 gallons. Since a gallon of seawater weighs about 8.7 pounds, some 80,000,000 Btus were required each 24 hours to raise the temperature of the seawater about 10°F. (The seawater at Boothbay Harbor averages approximately 45°F.) And this was in the days of pennies per gallon for oil. Today, the cost would be mind boggling.

In 1950, the state-run propagation of lobsters was given a death blow. A report stated that the success of lobster rearing in Maine had been so poor and the procedures so expensive that the practice could only be characterized as a useless expenditure of time and money and ought to be abandoned. It was.

The federal-state failure in Maine didn't cut any ice in Massachusetts, where the Department of Natural Resources has a lobster hatchery at Oak Bluffs, Martha's Vineyard, operated by John Hughes. The Bay State officials involved with the lobster hatchery program believe it is essential "toward the reinvigoration of the lobster industry." The Oak Bluffs facility raises lobsters to fourth stage and then releases them in the wild, as did the Maine program.

The raising of lobsters from larvae to legal market size is being attempted in several parts of the world. Private and federal monies (the Sea Grant program has invested more than $2 million in the artificial rearing of lobsters) continue to support lobster culture programs that show very little future pay-back. They are encouraged by statements from such sources as the National Marine Fisheries Service, which has estimated that in 1980 the world demand for the American lobster exceeded supply by 40 million pounds annually. Lobsters, however, don't like cloning. Because they are cannabalistic, they must be housed in individual compartments, which makes for interesting (and expensive) petit-condo fabrication. Then there is the diet situation. Lobsters are picky eaters. In captivity, they often insist on exotic foods such as brine shrimp at $10 a pound. And because lobsters feed continuously, brine shrimp in the raw cannot be thrown into the tanks a couple of times a day. The lobster food must be able to retain nutrients in the water. This feeding quirk has spawned the development of a lobster food pellet made of brine shrimp and soy lecithin. But lobsters are not exactly craving soy beans for supper. The researchers admit that a commercially viable pellet is well down the road. In the meantime, the shrimp diet of "domestic" American lobsters can escalate the cost of a one-pounder to about $150.

Transplanting adult lobsters from the East to the West Coast has also met with disaster. Puget Sound and the Columbia River in Washington received some Maine-caught lobsters in the early 1900s. The 30,000 lobsters were never seen again. Although a few lobsters were recaptured from a batch liberated near Prince Rupert, British Columbia, in 1954, such programs were terminated as being fruitless. It should also be noted that marine biologists liberated several lobsters in Great Salt Lake, Utah, for which they should be indicted on cruel and abusive treatment charges.

When the state-federal hatchery program was dumped in the early 1950s, another controversial scheme took its place. It continues today and is called the "seeder program." The idea, which came strictly from the industry, was that the state would purchase egg-bearing lobsters from pound keepers and release them along the coast. Lobstermen in general thought the plan would be the salvation of the industry by maintaining an adequate spawning stock. The pound owners were in complete agreement (some said they fathered the plan) because egged lobsters were illegal and would have to be liberated anyway. Under this program the pound owners received full market value for a product they legally should return, free, to the sea. It became apparent over the years, however, that the state was running out of berried females to buy, as the lobster biologists had claimed all along. There were few females producing seed because most (about 80 percent) were being caught before they were mature and capable of reproduction. Nevertheless, a Lobster Fund was created by statute whereby $5 of every $10 license fee would go to the fund for the seeder program. This was updated to $10 when the license fee went to $33 (and $5 for every $13 under-17-years-of-age license) in the mid-1970s.

With the scarcity of seeders, the state changed its purchase program to include females that were not berried. The lobsters released in this program are V-notched in the tail (the same mark Maine lobstermen give to berried females before throwing them back), which makes them illegal to possess even if they are not carrying eggs. Many fishermen who were in favor of the seeder program for berried lobsters balked

Fourth-stage larva

at the "all female" rule change. However, the DMR had a tiger by the tail. The Lobster Fund did not lapse and the monies could not be used for anything else. With 8,500 licenses contributing $10 apiece to the fund, $85,000 a year was enriching the DMR coffers, with no place legally to spend the money. In the fall of 1982 the DMR distributed 29,724 pounds of V-notched lobsters, valued at $85,082.25 (state-bought at an average of $2.86 per pound), at 40 locations along the Maine coast from Biddeford Pool to Machiasport. They were released in lots from 200 to 1,000 pounds, between October 21 and November 15. This fall program was supplemented by a spring distribution of an undetermined number of pounds.

The lobster biologists are not very enthused with the seeder program. Instead, they support an increase in the minimum size of a legal lobster, a measure they say would dramatically increase the percentage of female lobsters that spawn at least once before capture. The seeder program, they say, will do little to change the spawning population. This argument is murky, however, since biologists have also said that the lobster population will sustain itself if an average of just two young per mature female survive to maturity. Given the incredible number of eggs one female can produce during her reproductive lifetime, the critical factor, these scientists say, is not the number of spawning females but rather the subsequent survival of their young.

Sometimes the method of releasing lobsters comes under fire. The task falls to the wardens, so two targets are rolled into one.

"Well, Junior, I see they put some more punched lobsters out the other day," said a fisherman sitting on a wharf cap timber and squinting down the bay at nothing in particular.

"Where'd they set 'em this time, Fiddy?" responded his wharf mate.

"Same's always."

"Dumped 'em right off the wharf again, I guess, huh?"

"Same's always, Junior, drowneded 'em right off the wharf like a grain bag of kittens."

The wardens do have a problem in some cases. Supposedly, they distribute by boat over a fairly large section of the designated waters, but they have crates of live animals that do not appreciate broken-down motors and churning seas. Since they can't take them home for overnight holding in refrigerators, they may resort to dumping the animals off the wharves in one resounding clump, usually when all the Juniors and Fiddies are around to witness the deed.

So, with all the controversial lobster programs weaving in and out of the industry, how is the Maine lobster holding up under all the fishing effort, bureaucratic shuffling, and management schemes that change with every new political power? Pretty well, thank you.

In the last 40-odd years there certainly have been many changes in the lobster industry. Lobster landings in 1940, for instance, were 7,644,735 pounds, taken from an estimated 222,000 traps. At the conclusion of World War II many fishermen returned to their profession, and traps in the water jumped to 378,000, with 19,132,785 pounds landed from Maine's inshore waters. In all but two years between 1949 and 1982 the landings have fluctuated between 17.5 and 22.6 million pounds. The lowest figure was 16.4 million pounds in 1974. But there has been a dramatic increase in the number of traps in the water. The scientists call this fishing effort. In 1982 there were an estimated 1,846,000 lobster traps being fished along the Maine coast. It's not certain how the state and federal lobster scientists estimate numbers of traps, however, except by personal observation and interview. The state lobster license application did not request this information until 1980, and although the lobsterman is now asked to provide it on a section of the application that will be torn off for confidentiality, lobstermen distrust the system and routinely underreport their actual trap numbers. A survey of commercial lobster trap builders revealed that none had ever been asked the number of traps they build during a year. And a very high percentage of wooden traps are built by the lobstermen themselves. Yet any management approach must incorporate an estimate of fishing effort, rough as it is.

Annual trap loss depends on the severity of the weather. Some years a lobsterman might lose 40 percent of his gear through heavy storms, which move the traps along the bottom until they end up broken on the shore or far offshore where they "drown" in water deeper than their pot warp length and are lost forever. A lobsterman with even a moderate trap loss of 15 percent from his total of 400 will be building or buying 60 traps to replace his gear. But many overbuild, anticipating a further loss the coming year. More traps enter the water via this philosophy. And then there are the new fishermen coming into the business. In 1962, there were 5,658 lobster licenses issued. That year, 22 million pounds of lobsters were landed. In 1982, there were 8,500 licensed lobstermen and just about the same poundage caught. Using these and other statistics, the lobster fishery managers scream about the "overcapitalization of the fishery." They define this as a condition whereby the input of vessels, fishermen, and technology is greater than that necessary to harvest the maximum sustainable yield—the surplus yield or maximum yield per lobster recruit.

This theory has been around for quite some time, and considerable pressure has been exerted by the state and federal agencies and even private enterprise to limit entry into lobstering. Sometimes the pressure backfires. In the mid-1970s, the State of Maine began to make noises that lobster licenses would be frozen in the near future. Applications increased by 4,000, and all were issued licenses. Parents were purchasing licenses for their preschoolers. The abnormal number of licenses for that year was plugged into the statistics and models and other bioeconomic apparati used by scientists and other fishery managers with no footnote on the cause. And obviously, catch by effort and related statistics were shot to hell. Incidentally, a one-day-old baby can still get a lobster license in Maine. The enabling law merely states: "Eligibility. A lobster and crab fishing license shall only be issued to an individual and shall be a resident license."

A word about lobster landings. The landings in Maine are actually compiled by the feds—the National Marine Fisheries Service. The source of these very important statistics, important because they are the basis (along with estimates of fishing effort) for most all lobster management plans, is the established lobster dealers along the coast. Each month, NMFS personnel, aided by Maine DMR personnel who are cooperators in the program, visit each of these dealers and obtain the number of pounds landed or purchased by that dealer in the preceding 30 days. The figures are confidential and are coded so that individual dealers are not identified outside the primary collecting offices. But like the fishing effort estimates, these figures are imperfect. There is the tendency of all government functions to ride with the status quo, so new dealers and sources are very frequently overlooked in the landings picture. It is obvious to anyone who has witnessed the mom-and-pop lobster marketing operations on the Maine coast that a helluva lot of lobsters are not going through the "established" dealers. The smaller lobstermen, for instance, sell almost exclusively into the retail summer tourist trade. There they can get close to retail, off-the-shelf prices, whereas selling to a dealer would net them more than a dollar a pound less. If one of these lobstermen is bringing ashore 500 pounds per week, that's $500 more in his pocket. And the lobster license authorizes the lobsterman to sell his own catch, so no other reporting device such as a wholesaler's license exists as a record of these landings or sales.

The feds do not claim to document every pound of lobsters that comes ashore. They admit to about 10 percent error. But what if 20 percent (1,700) of the state's 8,500 lobstermen were selling outside of the reporting dealers, at, say, 350 pounds a week for 26 weeks? That would amount to 15,470,000 pounds a year of unreported lobsters—68 percent of the 1982 Maine reported landings! Pretty far-fetched, claim the feds. It could be, claim some close-mouthed dealers.

Maine still leads the United States in lobster landings. The ferocious-looking creature seems to be holding his own despite many doomsayers. In 1978, the director of research at the Maine Department of Marine Resources, Vaughan Anthony, who has since returned to his National Marine Fisheries Service position at Woods Hole, Massachusetts, said the lobster industry was about to collapse. He gave a litany of factors from decreasing offshore stocks to colder water over the next 25 years as signs of the impending death of the lobster industry. Anthony's remarks drew the ire of Commissioner Apollonio for creating a near panic among many fishermen.

Anthony wasn't the first. In 1903, Herman Bumpus of the United States Fish Commission predicted that without help or relief many local lobster populations would soon be exterminated. In 1956, Harold W. Look of Rockland, writing in the local newspaper, called for strict and quick protection for the offshore lobsters, which were then being discovered by the RV *Delaware* in experimental tows at the edge of the Continental Shelf. He stated that the offshore lobsters were the same species as the inshore stocks, and because the *Delaware* had caught only large lobsters and no juveniles, the offshore population must be "seeding" the Maine coast. He cited the counterclockwise Gulf of Maine currents as the mechanism for this seeding, saying, "It is well known that one flood tide on the southwestern shore of Nova Scotia equals two ebb tides. That surplus water must go somewhere. It does. There is a westerly current along the coast of Cape Breton, Nova Scotia, Maine, and Massachusetts, sweeping out to sea by Cape Cod. Beyond the shoals is the Gulf Stream heading north and east. To illustrate: A Rockland, Maine, boy was lost overboard 100 miles southeast of Nantucket and was found by Leslie Dyer at Seal Island, not too many miles from the boy's home. A sealed bottle cast overboard off Cape Cod was found by Birger Magnuson of Vinalhaven on the shore of Brimstone Island, not far from Seal Island. And in the days of the Boston boat, less revolutions were logged on the trip from Rockland to Boston than on the eastbound trip." Using drift bottles and current meters, oceanographers have further documented this counterclockwise drift. The argument that offshore lobsters seed the coast is a plausible one and has never been refuted.

Today, however, there is a thriving offshore lobster fishery and yet the inshore annual landings in Maine seem to be holding near or over 20 million pounds.

In 1964, Ed Myers of Saltwater Farm in Damariscotta was so alarmed at the prospects for a future lobster industry that he refused to ship lobsters out of state during the months of August and September, when lobster shedding and mating are at their height.

Myers said, "Fishing pressure on the lobster stocks has increased geometrically and most heavily at the time when reproduction and recovery from the ordeal of shedding are at their peaks. The number of traps has doubled in the past twenty years, and there have been improvements in gear and electronics and the seakeeping quality of lobsterboats."

He advocated legislative action to ban lobstering statewide in August and September, a suggestion, he admitted, that would not make him King Neptune at the Maine Lobster Festival. He said that the lobster, like the green turtle of the tropics, would become almost as extinct as the dodo bird the way things were going. Nearly two decades later, lobster landings in Maine had increased 3½ million pounds.

Clearly the American lobster has a mind of his own, and just as clearly the people who know the lobster are no mind readers.

FIVE

The Buyers

The lobsterman in this century has never had a problem selling his catch. The old tales of using lobsters for fertilizer under hills of corn and five-pounders going for a nickel are exaggerated without question. After all, lobsters are a tasty food with an easily shucked exoskeleton, and what housewife wouldn't prefer a simply made lobster stew or salad to the tedious task of preparing those other bony things that come from the sea?

Our warped retrospect of lobster fertilizer and such arises partly because we forget that prices were commensurate with the times. We should remember, but rarely do, that these were the "good old days." The City Fish Market in Belfast, Maine, catered to a fish-loving populace and did a thriving business. E.F. Bramhall, proprietor, was an ardent advertiser in the city's weekly newspaper, *The Republican Journal*. In 1907, the prices for seafood were "quite reasonable except for salmon," according to the historians of that day. The advertisements read: "flounder, 15¢ a dozen; halibut, 22¢ lb.; clams (shucked) 10¢ pint; cod, 9¢ lb.; scallops, 15¢ pint; haddock, 10¢ lb.; fresh Atlantic salmon, 52¢ lb." And those locally caught Penobscot Bay lobsters were selling for 22¢ a pound no matter the size, but the preferred were two-pounders. Mr. Bramhall's account ledger indicates that lobster sales were equal to sales of other seafood, although prices were almost double that of fish. Of course, lobster could never compete with flounder at 15¢ a dozen. And flounder, incidentally, is still one of the best-selling fish in the world, but the draggerman is receiving about 85¢ a pound for his efforts while Mr. Bramhall's modern-day counterpart displays "sole" fillets between rows of lemon halves for $3.50 per pound. And if one wants to get shocked into fish-price perspectives, those 20¢-per-pint retail scallops of Mr. Bramhall were bringing an ex-vessel price to scallop boats in October 1983 of $7.65 per pound in New Bedford, Massachusetts. The retail ticket was outasight.

The Maine lobsterman doesn't have much truck with fish prices except when he wants to build a fish chowder and checks out the price of whole haddock, which he reluctantly buys with a few choice remarks about just who in the fishing industry is getting rich. Lobstermen prefer to exclude the middleman wherever possible, selling direct to the retail customer. This is for obvious reasons. The wholesaler's profit, or a part of it, goes into his pocket. Most fishermen selling direct will "take off" a few nickels from their price, so that persons buying direct from the lobstermen claim they are getting a helluva deal. Actually the price is about the same. The lobsterman didn't get off the turnip boat yesterday. The part-timer and small lobsterman is usually the one selling direct to consumers, however; it's a matter of logistics. The little guys can store their smaller catches in floating sunken cars, using their home as a place of business. After all, mom or the kids are always around to answer the phone.

Selling direct has other advantages besides price. These are "casual sales" in the reasoning of the lobsterman, requiring a cash transaction only and the IRS can go fish. The small and part-time lobsterman usually builds a summer clientele over the years or inherits one from his father, and those summer folk can eat a lot of lobsters, especially when they are bought from the local lobsterman and are flipping fresh from the cold, salty waters of the Maine coast. The purchase transaction is a continuing source of summer talk among the folks from away.

"Well, everybody, we are having lobsters tonight. Hope you can eat a few selects I buy from Harold over in the cove. I get them wholesale, of course, have been for years, pay just what it costs Harold to catch 'em. Harold always saves me the few selects he gets each hauling. You have never tasted anything like them, right, Martha? Say, why don't we all go down to the wharf and watch Harold bring them in from his car. Wouldn't that be the old school tie?"

Following a phone call, all meet Harold at the wharf and watch as he rows, backwards, out to his buoy in the cove and hauls a brown scummy bunch of boxy slats into his punt. Filling a plastic 5-gallon pail, Harold rows back, backwards, to the dock, where he is immediately surrounded by mid-cocktail hour giggles and gaffs from the folks from away.

"Jesus Christ, Harold, these are beauties," says the host.

"Oh, just average, Albert," says the old salt shyly, hitching up his beltless green wool pants.

The ladies giggle and then chorus an "oooohh" as the host replies, "Average, my ass, Harold, you saved them special for me, didn't you?"

"Now that could be, Albert," says Harold, putting the host into the inextricable position of paying top dollar or facing humiliation at the lobster dinner boil.

"Tell you what," says the host, "how about I pay you a bonus, Harold, on top of the regular price?" Albert folds three crisp twenty-dollar bills into Harold's salty, scummy hands.

100

The lobster car

"Aw, Albert, now you didn't have t'go do that," says the lobster catcher as he transfers the bills to his shirt pocket bank, the one with the button padlock.

Happy as clams on a coming tide, the folks from away return to their interrupted cocktail hour to hear the host once again expound on the what-a-goddamn deal he gets from Harold over in the cove on the price of lobsters.

Meanwhile, back home, Harold throws another alder stick in the kitchen Clarion stove and smiles at the finestkind of prices the summer folks are paying this year.

The home-seller lobsterman is faced with a problem, however, when fall comes and the summer folk have shuttered all their shingle cottages and returned to city ways. This takes place, unfortunately, just when the lobstering is the best—the fall months. Now the entrepreneur is faced with a surplus of perishable goods. He must take sou'wester in hand and visit the wholesaler and accept middleman prices. Some lobster dealers are outright belligerent with these guys and refuse to buy their lobsters. But most could care less and purchase whatever from whomever on their terms. A lobster is a lobster is a lobster.

By far, most Maine lobster poundage traffics through the lobster dealer, and he comes in all sizes. The dealer is the one who buys direct from lobstermen, or from other "buyers," and then sells to various levels of the trade from the retail restaurant to another wholesaler. Some dealers offer bait, supplies, and even cash up front to their fishermen to keep traditional and dependable sources of product. Other dealers will have nothing to do with bait, believing that lobsters alone are headache enough to handle. Obviously, only the shore-based dealers can supply full services at their own docks and wharves. Many dealers operate from inland or at another middleman level requiring little more than a truck. It should be evident that "middlemen" in the lobster business have an indefinable geographic and economic location, and they seek their own individual levels according to market supply and demand.

It is, claim most of the lobster dealers, supply and demand that sets the lobster price at the fisherman and dealer levels. This fails to wash with lobstermen, who believe that the price is set by dealers, perhaps in collusion, as "low as they dare." It is a fact that there is nowhere the lobstermen can turn for authoritative price guidelines. It is the dealers who determine the price of lobsters.

That price is set on a number of factors, one of which is the ageless supply-and-demand equation. Through the winter and spring months lobsters are scarce because there are few offshore lobstermen, and the price goes up. The bay or nearcoast lobstering nearly ceases during the period from December to April. There is another hiatus during the July-through-August period when a majority of the Maine lobsters are burrowed beneath rocks acquiring new shells. When "new shells" start moving into traps, the price gradually falls to the lowest point in the year, during September to November, when the large catches occur. This is the supply-and-demand argument used by most all dealers.

The Canadian lobster industry is tied very closely with the U.S. industry. In fact, dealers claim to a man that the Canadian lobsters "enhance" the price paid to U.S. fishermen. The Yankees have a hard time swallowing that wisdom, but it is a fact that without Canadian lobsters at certain times of the year, many dealers would be out of business. Imports of live Canadian lobster in 1982 accounted for about 30 percent of the U.S. market. Although Canadian buying by Maine dealers varies considerably, those that do admit the 30 percent figure is quite accurate. The bulk of this foreign buying is in the winter months, when the American lobstermen couldn't begin to supply the market. During the Christmas season, for instance, there is a heavy demand for lobsters, right at the precise time that Maine has few to sell. The Maritime Provinces of Nova Scotia and New Brunswick know their way around the lobster business and play a key opportunist's role in the U.S. lobster market at this time. In the fall months, when the U.S. harvest is the greatest, the Canadians close their seasons.

At one time, about 10 years ago, there was an influx of Newfoundland lobsters to U.S. markets. The volume was considerable and it depressed prices quite a bit. The lobsters were small, however, and there was considerable loss through mortality. Newfoundland lobsters are smaller than Maine's, and the Newfie lobstermen have small tides and considerable freshwater runoff and use "rather old" bait, all of which conspires to produce what one Maine dealer called that "Newfie garbage."

The Maine lobster does not immediately crawl from lobster trap to table. The logistics of handling a fluctuating supply of perishable live product were solved

The lobster pound

nearly a hundred years ago with tidal lobster pounds. These are enclosures within small coves and other protected shore indentations, all with some natural impoundment characteristics but with help from manmade additions. They are, in effect, dams with slatted gate openings allowing the ingress and egress of the changing tides. The pounds, however, are deep enough so that lobsters are not exposed at low tide. With each flood, new salt water and accompanying nutrients are brought into the pound, and on each ebb the wastes are flushed to sea.

There are approximately 56 tidal lobster pounds in Maine with a combined capacity of about 4,225,000 pounds of live lobster. The pounds come and go and change ownership, but Maine has a nearly constant capacity to store 4 million pounds of lobster in any year. The figure is actually considerably higher, because there are many live-lobster pounds with considerable capacity that are nontidal; they must pump seawater through their systems because their locations will not allow them to use the free tidal energy.

When the market price is at the season perigee, owners begin filling their pounds with "cheap lobsters." The larger pounds start first—some can store 200,000 pounds of lobster—and the smaller ones begin in November. The length of time the lobsters are held is the name of the lobster game. Fortunes have been made and lost on lobster speculation. Having a pound full of live lobsters in the winter is like driving a truck full of old, unstable dynamite down Pikes Peak without brakes.

The risk is quite easy to comprehend. Assume that pound owner Salty Dog began filling his 100,000-pound-capacity facility in September and by hook or crook (lobstermen presume the latter) he paid an average price of $2.10 per pound. One might innocently assume that Salty could unload these on the Christmas market for $3.25 per pound and make himself a neat little profit of $115,000. Disregarding such things as shrinkage for a moment, probably Salty is a true lobster entrepreneur and plays his hunch, gamble, or whatever *Homarus* speculators play. Salty waits. The price goes to $3.50. Next week it goes up again. For every 25¢ the lobster price goes up, Salty makes another 25 grand. It's not hard to see Salty's gambling blood beginning to boil. At around $4 per pound, Salty decides to wait just one more day to unload and then spend the rest of the winter in West Palm Beach. Well, overnight, some Canadians and Newfoundlanders plus a half dozen countrymen decide to unload, too. The price drops $1 and Salty Dog has just watched $100,000 go down a clam hole. His one big shot of the year fizzled like a wet firecracker from Formosa.

That was the simple scenario. Salty obviously had a few more problems and expenses. He and most of his colleagues need ready cash to play the lobster game, for lobstermen don't play with wooden matches. So, bank loans at 14% enter the profit-and-loss ledger. Salty must feed his lobsters while they are confined, at the standard formula of one bushel of bait (fish cuttings, racks, brim, etc.) per 1,000 pounds of lobsters per week. Bait can run $5 per bushel. Then, there is the weather. Extremely cold temperatures can freeze the surface of lobster pounds, which are located next to the shore where freshwater runoff can reduce salinities, thus raising the freezing point of the water. Most lobster pounds operate in the same manner when removing the lobsters. They haul drags over the bottom to catch them. Cutting and removing the ice first is fairly cost intensive.

Theft (pounds are usually in isolated, remote areas of downeast Maine and subject to guerrilla tactics by unsavories) cannot be disregarded, and the ever-present red tail can literally wipe out a lobster pound in a couple of days. Dead lobsters, incidentally, are not a total loss, and they are not taken to the dump. Dead lobsters, whether in summer or winter, in small or large lobster pounds, are cooked and picked for the meat. However, the wholesale price of lobster meat is about $8 per pound, and the same lobsters live would sell for three times that. It takes about five live chicken lobsters (one to 1¼ pounds) to produce a pound of clear meat. (Lobster lovers purchase millions of gallons of water a year.) And so, dead lobsters are not a profitable item, as Salty Dog will find out if he continues to play the lobster game much beyond Christmas.

Some dealers play the overseas game, especially around Christmas when there is a tremendous demand for American lobsters. Although the Canadians supply the bulk of lobsters to Europe, several Maine dealers are involved in air shipment of lobsters to Britain and France, the latter country importing nearly 4 million pounds a year from the U.S. and Canada. Although Europe has a small lobster population, it is scarce and getting thinner each year. In the Scilly Isles off the Cornish coast of England, a 150-pot lobsterman might haul a day's catch of three or four lobsters from his beehive withie pots, hardly a contribution to the European people who have long enjoyed the taste of succulent shellfish.

The U.S. commercial airlines jumped into the air freighting of lobsters about 15 years ago, and today, lobsters are not only shipped via jet overseas, but are also shipped to domestic markets through the Midwest, West Coast, and southern states. Surprisingly, there are no large commercial air shipments of lobsters from Maine. The air freight lobster terminal of the United States is Boston, for Maine airports do not handle the huge, wide-bodied jets that accommodate very large containers, called LD-3s, in their bottom cargo holds. These jumbo shipping crates hold 2,500 pounds of lobsters in fifty 50-pound subcontainers.

All the cargo airlines have special tariffs called seafood commodity rates, which include lobsters. The regular freight rate for a 2,500-pound package like the LD-3 from Boston to Los Angeles would be about $1,200. The tab for a lobster shipment of that same weight is only $500. It would be impossible to ship the same distance by truck for that amount. Overseas air freight also has a special commodity rate for lobster shippers, although the expense is considerably higher. Lobsters shipped to Switzerland, for instance, cost $1.05 per pound rather than the average $2 per pound for general freight cargo. The obvious original reason for air freighting was the speed of delivery of a perishable live product, but the low shipping expense, because of considerable deregulated competition, is a bonus that developed in the late 1970s.

Shipping lobsters via air is nothing new. During World War II there were several air bases in Maine, and sitting around the fire with a bunch of the old pilots, one can still hear the "lobster run" stories. "Training missions" by the hundreds, originating in every quadrant of the country, flew into Brunswick, Portland, Bangor, Belfast, Bar Harbor, and even Aroostook County. Olive-drab duffle bags swiftly climbed back into the wild blue yonder, and that evening the officer's mess, wherever, featured live Maine lobster. Command staff officers found reason to schedule air maneuvers with fuel stopovers in Maine.

Late one July afternoon in 1944, a bunch of kids were cooling off at the Belfast City Pool (on the shores of Penobscot Bay) when they were startled by a formation of aircraft coming up the bay about a good wave height off the water. George Kelly, who was the airplane nut of the sophomore class and a regular spotter in the Belfast observation tower (that is, the tallest building in town), yelled, "They're Curtiss P-36 Hawks!" Maxine Bacheldor and Barbara Ramsdell and Polly Banks inquired if they were friendly hawks, but most of the still-wet kids had already jumped on their bikes and headed for the airport. The planes, two abreast, made their approach and landed about the same time the bicycle brigade arrived on the tarmac taxi strip. The engines coughed and stopped (George said they were 1,200 h.p.) and the propellers jerked to a quivering halt. Canopies slid back and six Smiling Jacks replete with flowing silk scarves, leather helmets, and shiny leather jackets with furry collars stepped onto the olive-drab wings of their star-emblazoned Hawk aircraft, and then to the soil of Maine.

The squadron leader beckoned and half the sophomore class advanced in unison, rather expecting John Wayne or Errol Flynn to offer a welcome handshake.

"Hey, kids, where is this place, anyway?" asked the dashing aviator.

"You're in Belfast, Maine, sir. Welcome," answered George.

The pilot asked for a map. He said they were on a training flight from some place in upstate New York; they had run into some rather bad weather and lost their bearings.

George said he would get a map right away from Hammons Texaco Station downtown if the pilots would wait.

"Sure, kid," said Smiling Jack, as the girls came closer and George jumped aboard his Silver Flyer and peddled madly down the dirt access road.

"Hear you have lobsters up this way?" said the leader. And immediately the training mission and the lost squadron and the emergency landing congealed into the real mission of the flight of Curtiss Hawks. Of course, half the sophomore class were not to realize the real reason for decades.

Lobsters and area fishermen were discussed among the assembled and diverse generations, and when George returned with the free Texaco map of the New England states, another sophomore contingent had already left to round up lobsters. Father lobstermen returned in about an hour with boxes and bags of dripping live lobsters, and the pilots pooled their pokes and came up with a fair cash price for the lot. The containers were crammed under seats and behind instrument panels, and one pilot stowed his parachute behind some unscrewable plate and sat on his box of lobsters.

Laden with the finest of officers' mess fare imaginable, the pilots climbed aboard, while one, obviously the junior officer, went from plane to plane inserting a starting shell. Those old, chunky Curtiss Hawks were thoroughbreds in their day. The first were delivered to the United States Army Air Force in 1935, and the single seater was the first monoplane to incorporate a retractable undercarriage and enclosed cockpit. However, they needed some help to get started. A device resembling a huge shotgun shell was inserted into a mechanism and fired from the cockpit to turn the 1,200 h.p. engines over.

On signal from the squadron leader, the pilots fired their engines and the metal props melted from an object to a blur and the pilots with a wave taxied down the runway and took off two by two and headed down the bay from whence they had come. Half the sophomore class scrambled for the ejected starting shell cases, all but George Kelly, who wondered, mostly to himself, why they had forgotten his Texaco map, which was laying beside a clump of unmowed jimsonweed.

Shortly after World War II, old pilots were buying up old airplanes and wondering what the hell they could do with them to make a buck. One enterprising pilot was Jack Dodge of Owls Head, Maine. Jack became a legend, having taught thousands of people how to steer an airplane through the skies. He was a bush pilot extraordinaire with what is called the natural talent and "feel" of an airplane. Following the war years, Jack returned to the Rockland area and dabbled in most anything for a buck, but fishing and flying were his two loves. He spotted herring schools for purse seiners—one of the very first in the country to do so.

Jack somehow managed to buy a surplus C-47, the military version of the legendary DC-3. This incredible aircraft of the 1930s was the most widely used airplane in the history of the U.S. Air Force and still is in service around the world. Jack knew a good cargo plane when he flew one. The interior was stripped for astounding loads in the 10,000-pound range, and its twin 1200 h.p. engines, 200+ m.p.h. speed, 23,000-foot service ceiling, and 2,000-mile range made it an ideal flying lobster car.

Jack's objective was to load the "Gooney Bird" at Rockland and fly lobsters into either Boston or New York. The lobsters would be packed in wooden barrels in wet sawdust. The barrels were topped with a small cake of ice and a couple of handfuls of rockweed and covered with burlap. The initial flights were a great success. Air time to Boston was less than an hour, compared to seven or eight hours by truck, resulting in far less mortality and "ocean fresh" lobsters that Jack promoted with considerable zest.

The old, olive-drab C-47 with its painted-out military insignia and its single pilot, Jack, could be seen taking off and landing at the Rockland strip at frequent but odd hours any day of the week.

As time passed, the sawdust-barrel air highballing of lobsters faced competition from improved truck routes, better highways, and sturdier shipping containers. And Jack's old C-47 was getting senile. Continued dripping of salt water throughout the airframe acted like acid on the steel and aluminum skeleton. The starting mechanism of its piston engines failed faithfully, and Jack resorted to winding a rope around the prop spinner, tying the other end to a jeep, and, in four-wheel drive, taking off down the taxi strip to turn over the big engines. And Jack had an enforced habit of buying only enough fuel to last from one point to another in the shortest straight line. It's said that Jack Dodge had more dead-stick landings in a DC-3 than any other pilot alive or dead. Local gas stations thought nothing of seeing Jack drive his old Chevy pickup into their place with a flat "Gooney Bird" tire in back. With the coming of the 1950s, Jack's Flying Lobster Airline drifted into the things that tall tales are made of, and the venerable DC-3 was sold for parts that are probably still in the air someplace in the world despite a coating of Maine salt water.

Commercial airlines, specifically Northeast Airlines, started carrying lobsters on scheduled runs, and that practice continues today with jet service to Maine by such airplanes as the 727, which carry the smaller, expendable cardboard containers supplied by the lobster dealers.

Lobster dealers supply a variety of markets within and without Maine. These vary from other wholesalers to retail restaurants to supermarkets. In recent years, there has been a trend to holding and displaying live lobsters in see-through, self-contained tanks. The original setups were nothing more than an ordinary tank with artificial salt water and a recirculating water pump. The restaurants used them primarily for promotional purposes. To select one's lobster dinner was the ultimate in cuisine. There were many problems, and lobster mortalities were considerable. The reason was generally the fault of the nonfiltering system. The lobsters gave off excrements and these accumulated until the water became murky and foul. If the water wasn't changed on a rather frequent basis, the lobsters became weak and died. Also, it was difficult to regulate "shelf life." That is, the first lobsters in the tank were not necessarily the first to leave, and new ones were dumped on top of old ones until the old-timers either threw in the towel or tasted like one when cooked.

Improvement in live lobster tanks came quite rapidly after retailers got a taste of the possible shrinkage involved. Nevertheless, modern tanks are not without maintenance problems. The water should be changed at least on a six-month basis, and more frequently if the tank has a high-volume use. And there is the price. The going rate for a 300-pound-capacity self-contained unit (biofilter, pump, and additional carbon filter, with ½-inch acrylic siding and wood base) is about $4,500.

The alternative to water-fed tanks and the assorted paraphernalia is dry refrigeration. Lobsters live a surprisingly long time out of water, and many middlemen lobster dealers have most of their lobsters presold and require only a short holding time between purchase and sale. A large reefer unit does quite well. A thousand pounds of lobsters in crates make a compact unit of merchandise. Still, the clear-sided lobster display tanks are about the only answer for retail establishments utilizing the same sight-selling technique that has proven so effective for the wire racks of goodies surrounding supermarket checkout counters.

And speaking of supermarkets, many such chains use lobsters as a leader, complete with high-intensity advertising. These promotions usually happen around the lobster glut time in the fall or when a dealer suddenly finds a market or a sale gone sour. The supermarket will buy in quantity, say 4,000 pounds, and turn a refrigeration case into a two-day seafood act. The lobsters are sold at "fisherman's prices," and the promotions are usually very successful, especially if the supermarket is subtly pushing another product such as turkeys in an adjoining display case. But large stores are not the usual purveyors of lobsters. One reason is the fluctuating price. Another is the supplier. A dealer doesn't want to fiddle around with a chain buyer on price and inconsistent purchases. And large market chains seem to have an aversion to seafood in general for some reason. They usually leave the merchandising of seafood to the specialty seafood stores and markets, preferring to handle meat products. When seafood products are carried in inventory, they are usually frozen and processed—battered fish sticks, battered fillets, battered, battered, battered.

The Maine lobster has endured more sales pitches than a carnival girlie show. There were a slew of pails-by-mail companies in the 1950s. For years the back cover of *Down East Magazine* carried a full-color list of various size "clambakes" one could order through the mails. And a shipment was guaranteed to arrive alive anywhere east of the Mississippi. For about 25 bucks the suffering lobster addict could order (phone or write) a half dozen lobsters, a peck of clams, and a clump of authentic

Maine seaweed, all nestled nicely in a 3-gallon tin can. Upon receipt, the purchaser had merely to take an ice pick or some other pointy object, drive a few holes in the top of the can, and set it on the stove for about 20 minutes. An instant Maine clambake. There are a few of these lobster-order houses around today, but most gave way to other, more voluminous ways to sell lobsters. Today, a half dozen chicken lobsters and a couple of pounds of peanut-size steamers delivered by a friendly UPS driver will shame a C-note. Gourmet feasting, it's called.

There are companies in Maine, and other states as well, that "put on" Maine clambakes. Some have permanent sites and daily schedules. Others cater clambakes bringing everything, including the seaweed, to the site of the convention, picnic, class reunion, or whatever. A few include a boat trip to an island in the lobster-clambake deal. Cooking, in all, is outdoors in the traditional seaweed blanket. The customer gets a couple of lobsters, a plate of steamer clams, an ear of corn, a potato, and later a cup of boiled coffee and a slab of blueberry cobbler. The lobsters usually come from a lobsterman, but the large caterers work through dealers, where they may pay more per pound but have a reliable supply.

Restaurants in Maine do not sell the quantity of lobsters one would think, although during the tourist season lobsters are a must item on Maine menus. Handling live lobsters presents problems. Unless the restaurant has one of those expensive display tanks, the lobsters must be refrigerated, and therefore buying cannot be in any volume. Restaurants close to dealers can run over and pick up a few pounds when that party of 12 arrives and all order baked stuffed you-know-what, but very few live lobsters are kept on the premises. Another concern of the restaurateur is the price fluctuation, and just about every eating place will leave the lobster price

on the menu a blank space. The markup on a lobster dinner, even in Maine, is considerable. A 1½-pound lobster cost the Maine native or visitor an average of $13 in 1983. Restaurants usually purchase lobsters from their regular seafood distributors, which are high in the middleman ranks, and they therefore pay more than, say, a primary wholesaler. Lobster meat is another matter. This product can be frozen quite well and has a considerable shelf life. Restaurants can also get "deals" on lobster meat, and the meat is a familiar product that meshes comfortably into the portioned logistics of such menu items as stews, rolls, and salads. The live lobster is the only live product handled by restaurants and is therefore an "outsider." But restaurant sales of *Homarus* account for hundreds of thousands of pounds a year.

The Yankee roadside peddler is another purveyor of lobsters. Although diminishing in numbers, the peddler was once a very common tradesman, especially on the backroads of rural Maine where housewives did not "get t'town very often" but craved the taste of the sea. The "fish man" traveled his accustomed route with strict regularity and would always carry a few clams and lobsters along with his more mundane stock of cod, haddock, corned hake, and flounders. Special orders for special occasions, such as lobsters for birthdays, would arrive the week following the order as sure as the dog barked at the farmhouse gate. It's not hard to imagine the genuine treat of a farm family member opening his eyes to a steaming, rounded kettle of red lobsters on a table thoroughly accustomed to a menu of field and meadow vegetables and farm animals. And it's not surprising that boys and girls raised on the farm grow up to be compulsive lobster eaters. They usually got that way because of the exciting weekly visits of the "fish man."

Yankee peddlers today travel fast and distant with their salty wares. The fish men of Maine in panel-body pickup trucks leave their homes in the early evening, and morning finds them on weekend sites in shopping center parking lots and busy street corners as far south as Washington, D.C. Fresh-caught Maine fish is their thing, but thousands of pounds of lobsters ride in these out-of-state marine caravans. One peddler from Rockland sells an astonishing amount of lobsters from the back of his pickup truck parked in the YMCA lot in Reading, Pennsylvania. During Christmastime, he makes three trips a week with only lobsters. Many are orders taken from a previous week's visit, and some are simply sales generated by probably the best advertising medium in the world—word of mouth.

Pickup trucks with seafood signs scatter to the four directions from Maine throughout the year. Seafood gypsies, maybe, but they are a significant distributor of Maine lobsters, and one source that rarely gets plugged into the industry facts and figures. One state economist was asked his estimate of the amount of lobsters sold by these Yankee peddlers.

"Oh, I don't know, but it's hardly worth worrying about."

Maybe the pickup brigade wants it that way.

Another consumer of the Maine lobster is the visiting yachtsman—as distinguished from the visiting carsman. There is no seaward tollgate to tally the boats that visit the Maine coast each year, but there is hardly a harbor, port, cove, or gunkhole that doesn't play frequent host to a hulled visitor. And many of those captains and crews will seek out a "mess of lobsters," usually from the harbor fisherman. Some even intercept lobstermen when they are hauling. The purchases of visiting boatmen run to the tons and tons of lobsters served on everything from teak tables to hatch covers.

The lobster was once the most highly touted product in the state. Every level in the industry promoted the "Maine" lobster. Lobstermen's associations, dealers, wholesalers, retailers, and state agencies conceived every imaginable advertising tool from tie clasps to stuffed lobster pillows to a never-ending stream of recipe and how-to-eat-a-lobster pamphlets. For every lobster served, there was a Maine lobster bib and a place mat with the dismembering process outlined by the numbers. Every visiting dignitary was presented a lobster gauge as his keys to the city. Complimentary lobsters paid for by state tax money and funneled through every imaginable state agency were shipped to the White House and to foreign embassies. Hedda Hopper, the late Hollywood gossip columnist, wrote once that the stars "dined on fresh Maine lobsters, compliments of the chamber of commerce."

Somewhere along the way, however, some bright bureaucrat began to question the amount of money plowed into maintaining the star status of *Homarus americanus*. His thinking was on track, for the Maine lobster, like the Hershey chocolate bar, needed no advertising. It self-sold. Today, the Maine lobster is generic; there is no "good" or "bad" brand. State agencies and chambers of commerce print and supply a few recipes and the venerable lobster bib, but public-agency lobster hype is definitely low key. The commercialization of the lobster has been transferred to the private sector—the dealers who fight for the market—and if one controlled the lobster logo he would be deeper into riches than the combined oil sheiks. The lobster buyer, whether in those moored sailboats in secluded coves or the seated guest around the fancy restaurant table, certainly needs little urging to dine.

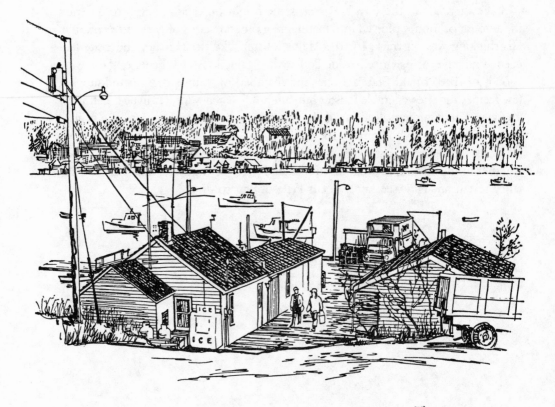

The co-op

SIX

The Scientists

The role of the lobster biologist in this fiercely independent industry is undoubtedly an antagonistic one. Lobstermen refer to these scientists as "bug chasers" or "pointy heads," or as one fisherman characterized a group of biologists who had concocted a unique management proposal—"those dark side of the mooners." And sometimes the name calling gets downright dirty.

At a regional meeting held to examine the issues surrounding a veiled limited-entry idea, about 20 lobstermen listened for an hour to state biologists, who presented graphs, tables, and 50 miles of technical language supporting their point of view. As often is the case at these hearings, the attendees showed no visible sign of persuasion one way or the other; they just sat expressionless while the professional data rolled on, and on, and on.

As the biologists rested their case and leather briefcases snapped shut in unison, the chairman inquired if any of the lobstermen cared to speak. Heads twisted ever so slowly. Feet shuffled. Thumbs twiddled. The group was about to send out a scout to challenge the invaders, but the chairman was unfamiliar with the pause tactic used by fishermen for centuries. At face value, the pause denoted acceptance, concession to evidence, or utter defeat.

"Well, since there doesn't appear to be anyone speaking against this proposal, I will adjourn the meeting," said the chairman.

As the head table started to rise, the scout rose also from the back row of folding grange hall chairs. "MR. CHAIRMAN." The two words froze the head table like an ice pick.

"Mr. Chairman, I got a few words t'get off my chest 'bout all this coming down hard on business."

The head-table oarsmen dropped into their seats. "Well, certainly, Mr. Errrrr, please go right ahead with your comments. That's why we are here, you know," said the chairman.

"Okay, I appreciate it. First off, these shitheads don't know one ..."

"Whooooa there, mister," said the chairman, half rising from his folding platform, "we can't have any of that. This hearing will be conducted with decorum. If you wish to speak, please contain your remarks to the issues and not personalities. There will be order."

"Sure. What I meant was—what's decorum—was that any asshole could see it won't work out because ..."

"That's enough, that's enough right now," half-yelled the chairman, now fully standing and thumping his fist against his leather briefcase.

The scientists moved their chairs closer together, circled their wagons, while the fishermen sat with their same stoic expressions, leaving the skirmish strictly to their appointed scout.

"Sure," said the scout, "what I was saying 'fore being interrupted was, balls, there ain't no way ..."

"This meeting is over, gentlemen," said the chairman, rising with his flock.

The fishermen had presented exactly the view they wanted. None. But the presentation of scientific "evidence" was neutered by a couple of chosen words that were intended to divert the biologists from their cohesive proposal (which the fishermen really didn't understand) to a defense of their personal fannies. The fishermen had no animosity toward any of the panelists; they just executed their ageless battle plan—when confronted by a superior opponent, then pause, divert, and conquer.

Scientists get a bum rap from fishermen. There is no doubt about that. And inwardly and personally, many if not most lobstermen do have considerable respect for the marine biologist. They cannot, for social reasons, wear their feelings on their oilskins.

The adversary relationship is more the result of the system than personalities. Biologists work in an exact science, and fishermen rely on experience and intuition. Never do the twain seem to meet. The scientist rarely operates in a total or "holistic" sense with his science. His realm is a carefully circumscribed sphere, and his investigations, the results of which are not made public until they have passed the test of his profession, are similarly closely defined. The very worst thing that can happen to a scientist is to have his methods and conclusions considered suspect by his peers. Partial or fragmented information with possibly far-reaching implications is rarely available from biologists. Even in such a small state as Maine, where marine biologists are surprisingly few given the tremendous range of coastal environments and the financial importance of the fishing industry, a biologist exists professionally as an individual stone in a rockpile.

The fisherman, on the other hand, is enveloped in the cyclical nature of the sea from birth, and he understands the interrelationships of marine life without necessarily comprehending scientific disciplines. His instincts and observations—like those of all worldly animals—are keen, because through these he must survive. The scientist can postulate theory for decades or experiment within a cozy laboratory over a lifetime and survive quite well in a cruel world. The fisherman going to sea each day as a hunter has no such luxury.

An example of the two philosophies involves the urchin-kelp-lobster abundance relationship referred to in an earlier chapter. There are biologists who spend lives studying the Echinoids—the sea urchins and sand dollars. Others carry on a specialized study of ocean plants. Others, of course, study lobsters. It is common for scientists related to all three to be under one marine administration, or even one roof, and not really know what their colleagues are doing. And maybe not care. The lobsterman, however, is hauling a hundred or more traps each day. He sees the biological changes of the saltwater life. His eyes, not theories, tell him when the sea urchins eat the kelp that hide the lobsters. He understands the balances of nature although he cannot explain them. When the balance wheel tips, as it always does, the kelp beds will be stripped clean by an overpopulation of spiny green urchins. Molting and juvenile lobsters will lose their shelter and hiding places, and predators will become fat and successful. Then, the satiated urchins will have eaten themselves out of house and fodder, and they will die as nature intended. Slowly, the kelp beds return. Ever so slowly the lobster refuge again comes to life.

Through observation, lobstermen can predict abundance and scarcity, often with more accuracy than lobster scientists, who view the same terrain through far different parameters. This, obviously, leads to suspicion and confrontation. There are far right and far left examples of the inability of the two factions to unite. But the middle ground is where most of both groups take up residence.

Communication seems to be a key to much of the alienation. The two languages, for instance, couldn't be farther apart. Terms such as "catch-effort trends," "fecundity," "ovigerous females," and "logarithmic models" have no dominion in the common fisherman dictionary of "pot warp, a sleeve full of snot, and he's a pisser." Growing up on opposite sides of the creek tends to separate linguistics.

It is the responsibility of fishery managers, administrators, or fishcrats, if you will, to coordinate, assimilate, and disperse scientific information through broad enough channels so that even the common wharf rat will understand the meanings. Unfortunately, most top fisheries administrators come from a political soil fertilized primarily by cuttings from the science side of the fence. It is a rare day that the sun shines on a fishcrat who has risen from oilskins to pinstripe suit, from a beat-up old Ford pickup truck to the status suburban Volvo, from a haunting vessel mortgage to a stock portfolio.

If there has been a villain in the fisherman-scientist long war on words and ideas, it has to be the administrators of bureaus, departments, and councils of fisheries trade and commerce. The scientist himself would rather be left alone in his research sphere, explaining on his own terms and time through technical publications his funded work.

One of the best research projects ever done on the American lobster is a continuing one in Maine by Jim Thomas (who retired in 1984) and Jay Krouse of the Maine Department of Marine Resources.

In most lobster-catching states, the reported monthly and annual landings (in pounds) of commercially harvested lobster are the basis for management decisions. Though these simple landings figures are a far cry from detailed catch-and-effort data, they are easy to obtain and work with. Historically they were used in Maine as well, but long before the Magnuson Fisheries Conservation Management Act of 1976, which ultimately would require the collection of accurate catch data for all species, biologists Thomas and Krouse instigated the DMR Lobster Research Project. This involved the establishing of 153 sampling sites from Kittery to Cutler. Ten of these sites are sampled each month. The sampling points are actually dealers or cooperatives that buy lobsters directly from fishermen.

While at one of these sites, the survey crew interviews any lobsterman who delivers his catch to that dealer that day. The interviewer logs information such as the number of hours spent hauling traps, the number of fishermen on each boat, the number of traps hauled, and the number of days these traps were "set over." (Lobstermen do not usually haul the same trap every day. It is allowed to "fish" for two to five days, and this is called a set-over in scientific jargon, which is very close to the fisherman's term—a "soak.")

Back to the sampling methodology. While the interview is going on, the rest of the sampling crew counts the entire catch aboard the boat and records total poundage. Ten lobsters are selected at random and are individually measured, weighed, and sexed; condition of shell (hard or soft) is noted, as well as the number of culls. There is surprisingly little resentment of this scientific diversion among the lobstermen. The confidentiality of the data collection protects the fisherman, and it stood the test of the 1974-75 blanket audit of the Maine lobster industry by the Internal Revenue Service. The IRS did not request the DMR data, although the question begs as to what would have happened if they had.

When the sampling crew returns to its West Boothbay Harbor base, the information is analyzed with particular emphasis on the measured lengths of the sampled lobsters. "Length frequency" analyses (a term scientists bandy about at all fishery meetings) allow the biologists ultimately to estimate the number of legal-sized lobsters that are caught each year. This is a marked refinement of the less revealing landings figures, which are reported as poundage rather than numbers of lobsters. They can also estimate the number that die from natural causes. They call these two components "fishing mortality" and "natural mortality," and over the years the biologists have estimated that removal by fishing ranges from 85 to 90 percent, and death from natural causes runs 5 to 15 percent.

The surveys have shown that 90 to 92 percent of the yearly catch is between 3 5/16 and 3¾ inches of carapace length—a size range of half an inch. The entire Maine lobster industry is trading and depending on this narrow range. Above 3¾ inches there is a startling drop-off in the number of lobsters caught, and lobsters measuring 4½ to 5 inches, the maximum legal length, make up less than three-fourths of one percent of the catch. The scientists say their estimate that 90 to 95 percent of the legal lobsters are caught or die naturally each year proves that most lobsters do not have a chance to remain in the wild population and grow to a larger size. They claim that their length frequencies from sampling support this conclusion. Further, the sampling crews ride aboard commercial lobsterboats and compare the number of legal and sublegal lobsters caught. They have found an exceptional number of "shorts" caught in traps, but a dramatic drop in numbers of lobsters over 3 5/16 inches, the minimum legal size.

From laboratory studies, biologists know that a just-legal lobster of 3 5/16 inches, after shedding its old shell, will increase half an inch in length and add about a third of a pound in weight. Weighing this factor against the measured rates of natural mortality, they conclude that if more lobsters were allowed to age and grow for a longer period of time before being caught, the loss of lobsters to natural causes would be more than offset by the increased size of those remaining, up to a point. At a certain size and age of lobster, as growth slows and natural mortality increases, the balance tips the other way. They say this balance occurs at 3½ inches, and this is the size that would give the greatest catch in pounds.

It is apparent where the scientists are heading with their publicized research—increasing the minimum legal size to 3½ inches. Realizing that such a move in one year would eliminate the Maine lobster industry, the biologists would like a phased-in five-year plan, with incremental increases of 1/16 inch per year. They claim that this would result in some loss to fishermen during the period but that after the five-year plan is completed there would be an 18 percent increase in the catch by weight, or an added bonus of $3 million (1980 prices) to the Maine coast lobstermen.

The scientists throw still another strike at the complacent lobster hitter. Most of the lobsters entering the fishery legally (3 5/16 inches) each year are not yet mature and capable of spawning. This, coupled with the data showing that nearly all of the available legal population is being caught each year, is a somber indictment of those who traditionally block any legislative attempts to increase the legal minimum size.

The lobstermen, almost to a man, claim the increase will put them out of business. They cite as evidence the scientists' conclusion that 90 percent of all legal lobsters caught lie within that half-inch size range.

A bunch of lobstermen sitting around the wharf at Winter Harbor were discussing the increase in length.

"Cripes, they keep pushing us up in measure n'who in hell will buy 'em?" asked one.

"The filthy rich, the filthy rich, same as always, Sam," answered another, throwing his whittling to the tide.

The fishermen realize what the wholesalers do, that a legal 3½-inch minimum would drive the per-pound price up almost a dollar. The "chicken" lobster of today, the size most served in restaurants, would be illegal under the increased minimum proposal. The minimum then would be a "select" in the 1¼- to 1½-pound size. Given present-day restaurant prices, a typical lobster dinner would increase by at least $5; the "live" retail cost would have a hefty rise all along the coast where those boiled-lobster tourist stands greet the migrating summer folk.

The fishermen say the scientists have a point, biologically, in their arguments to raise the minimum length, but either do not consider the important socioeconomic factor or misread it. Also, the fishermen don't believe they would recoup their losses in anything close to the five years the biologists say it would take. In either case, the increase may be a moot point with the adoption in 1983 of the American Lobster Fishery Management Plan. This plan was authored by the New England Fishery Management Council following public hearings along the northeast coastal states. Such a plan was mandatory under the 200-mile-limit bill. In the plan, all states must conform to the minimum 3³⁄₁₆ inches in federal waters. After much debate the states have unanimously agreed, which will also make the federal law applicable in the territorial sea or state waters from shoreline seaward three miles. Obviously, any attempt to increase the minimum size would now have to be ratified by all member states, and that would start a lengthy and protracted lobster war. Theoretically, any state could arbitrarily change any of its state lobster laws, but in practice, the feds and other lobster-catching states probably wouldn't allow that to happen.

If the scientists are climbing the walls over the opposition to an increase in the minimum size, they are absolutely livid and suicidal concerning Maine's maximum-size law, which forbids the taking of lobsters with a carapace length over five inches. The biologists have been bonkers over this law for about 40 years.

Maine is the only lobster-producing area in the world with a maximum legal size. (There are more than 35 states, provinces, and countries where one or more of the three species of true lobster, Norwegian *(Nephrops norvegicus)*, American *(Homarus americanus)*, and European *(Homarus vulgaris)*, are landed.) The first maximum-size limit, 4¾ inches, was established in 1933. Two years later it was raised to five inches. This limit has been in effect since then except for a two-year increase to 5³⁄₁₆ inches, after the minimum size was raised to 3³⁄₁₆ inches from 3⅛ inches in 1958.

The biological excuse for the Maine law was taken from the late, great lobster guru, Francis H. Herrick, whose monograph *The American Lobster* was the definitive study of lobsters when it was published as a United States fisheries bulletin in 1895. In this work, Herrick revealed the anatomy and physiology of the American lobster in naked detail. For one thing, he observed that the number of eggs produced did in fact increase geometrically with increased overall length of the lobster. And—or so the reasoning went—the more eggs there are, the more lobsters there will be.

Robert L. Dow, former commissioner and research director for the Maine Department of Marine Resources, and a lobster guru in his own right, thought Herrick's conclusions were all wet. Dow said that if Herrick's assumption was true, the Gulf of Maine would soon be filled from surface to bottom with not only lobsters but fish and all other marine species as well. Survival of the young, not numbers of eggs, Dow believes, determines future population levels.

The real reason for the maximum size limit was not biological. It came right at the height of the Great Depression, when there wasn't any demand for large lobsters because of high prices. Most observers, however, point to the World War II era and the Rockland lobster dealers as the factors that probably closed the minds of Maine lobstermen to any suggestion that the maximum size limit be abolished. The dealers—A.C. McLoon was the most prominent—found themselves paying higher prices to fishermen. At the same time, the retail and restaurant demand narrowed down to a very specific size lobster—one from 1¼ to 1½ pounds. This was a "serving size" for restaurants and a "convenient" or one-per-person retail weight. At that time there was a very limited market for picked lobster meat. If fishermen presented dealers with large lobsters, even the 3½-to 4½-pounders that were below the legal maximum, they were a dealer liability. The dealers had to pay price per pound for what they viewed as a very slow-moving and perishable product. Their problems would only be compounded if the maximum law were eliminated and fishermen began landing six-, eight-, ten-, and fifteen-pounders.

McLoon and his colleagues in Rockland began a prolonged campaign to sell the idea that the big, oversize males were the "great studs" patrolling the bottom byways and sleeping with every female they encountered. And the oversize females were the "big mamas" who could spill out millions of babies at a sitting. The combination of these two oversexed crustaceans was what kept the bread on lobstermen's tables, claimed the dealers. The biological hypothesis was highly suspect, but the propaganda was beautiful. The fishermen fell hook, line, and bait barrel. The legislators wouldn't even listen to the biologists who tried to explain the sex life of lobsters at public hearings. In vain the biologists pointed out that large males cannot mate with smaller females (and the scanty observations of oversize lobsters that have been made indicate that most are males). To no avail they argued that large lobsters shed infrequently, so that oversize females, if they do exist, would not mate regularly. The political heat stayed on the maximum-size law, saving the dealers countless thousands of dollars that otherwise would have been doled out to fishermen for great studs.

Dow and other scientists tried without success to explain through supposedly irrefutable data that the world catch of lobsters fluctuated more or less with Maine landings, and that the cyclic rises and declines could be attributed to seawater temperature and overfishing. If, explained the biologists, no other section of the world protected large lobsters and they were, indeed, the saving propagators, then why were not the Maine landings slowly rising in comparison with other areas? The fishermen countered by claiming the fishing effort in Maine was greater than in Canada or Europe. The scientists came back with convincing figures to refute this. Maritime Canada, for instance, had more than 20 separate seasons, twice the lobstermen, and no maximum limit. The Canadian catch was staying on a par with Maine's.

An interesting item concerning large lobsters unfolded in upper Penobscot Bay in 1980. Two large West Coast sablefish (black cod) traps, four feet square by eight feet, were fished on an experimental basis by a field agent of the Maine Department of Marine Resources. The trap was purposely set in shallow water, about 25 feet, on an underwater ledge known to be a haven for lobsters. It was a favorite spot for local fishermen. The trap was baited with fresh herring, and the first haul was a four-day set-over. A few sublegal lobsters and crabs were caught. A longer set of a week was tried and the haul produced 10 lobsters, all of them over 10 pounds and two of them 16 pounds. All of the lobsters were male. They were banded and released. The trap was baited and hauled in conjunction with other gear research projects on the bay that summer. Some of the banded lobsters were recaught. Many unmarked oversize male lobsters were also taken. Field records indicate that 44 oversize lobsters were taken from that one shallow-water area with one trap during that period. The smallest was just over the legal limit and the largest was 21 pounds. Not one female was caught. Several smaller lobsters, usually legal, were caught, and from the parts of lobsters observed in the trap, it was apparent that the large lobsters were eating the smaller ones. The puzzling thing was, of course, why no females were taken. It is possible that the egg-bearing effort of mature females consumes the energy that would otherwise be available for growth, but this is speculation.

Maine does not have any data on oversize lobsters because they are illegal. It is difficult to paint a picture of a subject covered with a shroud. Maine fishermen do take large lobsters outside the three-mile state waters. The lobsters are kept in large submerged lobster cars, and when enough poundage is accumulated, they are run into New Hampshire or Massachusetts. All very legal. Offshore lobstermen, however, have no responsibility to report their catches.

Even if the maximum gauge were lifted, it is doubtful that large-lobster landings would significantly alter economic or biological standings. In 1981, for instance, the DMR sampling data showed that the catch of lobsters just below the 5-inch maximum numbered 20,746, or about one-tenth of one percent of the state's total catch.

Maine's unique maximum-size law was given the cold shoulder by the proposed Lobster FMP, which states, "The FMP does not include a maximum size limit such as enforced by the State of Maine. The Council is not convinced that such a measure would serve any valid conservation and management purpose. Nonetheless, the Council does not intend that the State of Maine should be precluded from enforcing this measure against vessels licensed to fish for lobster by that state." The plan has conceded political weight to Maine, which is, of course, the dominant force in American lobstery.

Thus is created the great oversize-lobster impasse. The scientists claim that any increased production of lobsters in the North Atlantic is due to climatic, economic, and technological factors, and has nothing to do with prohibiting the taking of lobsters with carapace lengths over five inches.

The lobstermen, and yes, the politicians, say, "Goddamn it, them's the breeders."

Although our good friend *Homarus americanus*, it is agreed, is the only lobster worth its salt, some stimulating science has been directed toward lesser cousins. Michael Berrill is an associate professor of biology at Trent University in Ontario, Canada. His lobster theories have been published in *Natural History* magazine and other publications and he has some interesting suggestions concerning the territorial ranges of the homarids—our northern, coldwater, large-clawed lobsters—and the palinurids—the clawless spiny lobsters caught in warm temperate, subtropical, and tropical waters.

In 1981, 6.6 million pounds of spiny lobsters were landed in the United States, with 94 percent of these harvested in Florida and the rest in California and Hawaii. The ex-vessel price for spiny lobsters is somewhat higher than for *Homarus*—$2.90 per pound versus $2.09 per pound in 1981.

But it's the comparative biology more than the price of the two species that catches the imagination and fancy of lobster watchers. Berrill and others say the spiny lobsters make harsh rasping sounds by rubbing their antennae against a shieldlike portion of their carapace below the eye. These rasps have an antipredatory function; researchers claim they are used primarily for communicating degrees of aggressiveness to other lobsters and to predatory fishes. In the adult spiny lobster the antennae are quite formidable and are used to sweep their private spaces, pushing smaller lobsters away. The palinurids are definitely a gregarious animal, not aggressive like the homarids. They live together in crowded conditions that the northern clawed lobster would not tolerate.

A lot of publicity surrounds one of the palinurids, *Panulirus argus* of the Caribbean. Their autumn migrations into deeper water are conducted in long, single-file formation, a behavior that cannot be explained by scientists. No other lobster is known to behave in this manner. Berrill released several *P. argus* individuals on open stretches of sand, and they walked away in single file, the antennae of one individual touching the body of the next in front. Apparently any individual could be the leader, and the queues continued until the lobsters encountered the protection of grass beds or other hiding places. They then dispersed and hid themselves separately.

Juveniles contained in a large tank exhibited what Berrill called a bizarre queuing behavior. There were caves along one side of the tank, and in Berrill's words, "When one lobster was jostled or evicted from a crowded cave and began to walk away, the evictor usually left the cave as well and hooked on behind the evictee. As the procession of two walked by the mouths of other caves, the resident lobsters were drawn out as if by magnet and another queue was born."

Such behavior would be totally foreign to the northern lobster with his solitary lifestyle.

Palinurids don't tunnel because they don't have the equipment to do it, as do northern lobsters. The spiny lobsters hide among seaweeds, grasses, and in caves. They readily share their hiding places with others of their kind. Like their northern cousins, however, they are solitary while foraging for food, and mating is not a communal affair.

A large lobster of any kind can hold its own with a predatory fish, but the palinurids share the warm sea bottom with a guy who knows his way around—the octopus. The palinurid's spines and raspy antennae are not much of a deterrent to the snaky suction-cup tentacles of the octopus. However, a bunch of spiny lobsters presents more of a challenge. Berrill and other spiny lobster scientists postulate that the daytime habits of spiny lobsters, coupled with their gregariousness, may be an antipredatory adaptation against octopods. And, say the scientists, this gregariousness could only have evolved as much of the mutual antagonism of the lobsters diminished and more complex communication mechanisms developed.

The distribution of lobsters and octopods on the eastern and western shores of the Atlantic is very interesting. *Octopus vulgaris*, the dominant octopus species on both sides of the Atlantic, likes relatively shallow, warm water; on the western shore its range is from North Carolina to Brazil—identical to the range of the spiny lobster. North Carolina marks the southern end of the American lobster's range. Perhaps the octopus has adapted its range to prey upon its favorite food; it does not mess with the powerfully clawed northern lobster, who could probably defend himself quite well.

If the lobster biologists tell us that spiny lobsters form single queues with antennae touching elephant-fashion and march down the Florida Keys in migrating columns, they admit to very little usable knowledge of the migration patterns of the northern lobster.

Jay Krouse of Maine's DMR has been involved with migration studies in recent years, and his research indicates that what migration exists along the Maine coast is to the southwest. The first tagging studies on the American lobsters indicated this movement in 1898. This first attempt to determine lobster movement was conducted by Herman Bumpus of the United States Fish Commission when he released about 500 tagged mature females near Woods Hole, Massachusetts. Later, in 1902-03, A. Mead and L. Williams of Brown University tagged 400 lobsters in Narragansett Bay near Wickford, Rhode Island. There were about 110 recaptures in these early efforts, and it proved for the first time that lobsters did migrate considerable distances. Some of these recaptures were 16 miles from point of release. And in both studies, the lobsters moved in a south or southwesterly course.

It was nearly half a century before tagging studies were resumed. In 1950, Don Harriman of Maine DMR began a tagging study in the waters off Monhegan Island. This island, about nine miles off midcoast Maine, is the only area in the state with a closed lobster season. Lobstering is permitted only from January through June. Harriman and his crew released 1,093 trap-caught lobsters with plastic disc tags attached to the middle flipper of their tails. Over a two-year period, 24 percent of the lobsters were recaught. The Monhegan lobsters apparently like their home, since only 10 of the recaptures had moved two miles or more. And the movement was random. This study seemed to clash with earlier and later migration work; it may be that too few lobsters were used for definitive conclusions, and the Monhegan area is an isolated ground with a nonmigrating lobster population.

In 1957, C. Owen Smith, then editor of the *Maine Coast Fisherman*, suggested in an editorial that further migration studies be conducted. The Maine Department of Sea and Shore Fisheries obliged with a program headed by Bob Dow and several volunteer commercial lobstermen. One hundred sixty-two lobsters were tagged and released. Unlike the 1950 study, no legal lobsters were tagged, the researchers hoping that illegal lobsters would be allowed to continue their migratory habits, if they had any. There were four classifications of lobsters released. Those with extruded eggs, those under the minimum (shorts), lobsters over the legal size, and those that had a V notch cut into the tail, the traditional mark of Maine lobstermen showing that the female had once been caught with eggs on her stomach. Seventy-four lobsters were released in Penobscot Bay in 1957 and 88 in Sheepscot Bay in 1958. Seventy-five out of the 162 were oversized, and the 18 of these recaptured represented 78 percent of all the recaptures. Four of the large lobsters that were liberated from Penobscot Bay traveled 75 or more nautical miles. Another, a 4½-inch (carapace) sprightly female was tagged near Tom Rock, Sheepscot Bay, and was recaptured seven months later near Race Point Light off Provincetown, Massachusetts. Those four Penobscot Bay travelers showed no common destination. One released near Little Green Island was recaptured near Timber Island, Cape Porpoise, Maine two months later. Another tagged at Little Green Island was recaptured 14 months later near Gloucester, Massachusetts. Another starting out from Little Green in September 1957 was recaptured 19 months later near Cape Ann Light, Massachusetts. The champion

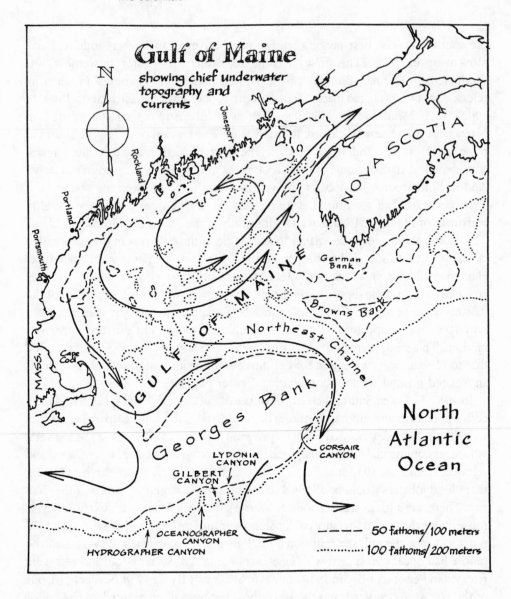

long-distance crawler was a 5-inch (unidentified sex) lobster released in Penobscot Bay and recaptured 13 months later at Nauset Light, Massachusetts—an estimated straight-line distance of 138 nautical miles. The smallest lobster recaptured traveled less than six nautical miles.

It was apparent from this study that the large, mature lobsters were more prone to major migration than were smaller lobsters. Maine lobster biologists were quick to flaunt this migration study in an effort to discredit two of the Maine lobstermen's strong convictions, that of retaining a maximum measure and the practice of V-notching berried females when caught. The scientists said the 1957-58 migration report only confirmed that Massachusetts lobstermen were expressing great appreciation for Maine's unique oversize and notching laws because those Maine illegals were eventually traveling to Massachusetts, where they were perfectly legal.

The largest and most recent migration study was conducted by Jay Krouse in the spring of 1975. The large-scale coastwise project took place at three tagging locations—Kennebunkport, Boothbay Harbor, and Jonesport. At each site, the researchers contacted dealers and made arrangements to purchase about 1,000 boat-run lobsters native to the area they were bought. The lobsters were, of course, all legal size. A sphyrion tag was used, not the button tag of Dow's study. The sphyrion consists of a slender yellow PVC tube 2¼ inches long attached by a thin polyethylene thread to a ¼-inch-long stainless steel anchor. The tag's anchor was implanted with a hypodermic needle through the thin membrane joining the tail and the back and into a band of muscle tissue. This is the location at which the shedding lobster exits from his old shell, and it was hoped that the tag would remain in the lobster through molting periods.

On May 6, 1975, 957 tagged lobsters were released about two nautical miles seaward of the mouth of the Kennebunk River. On May 17, 942 lobsters were freed 10 miles south of Boothbay Harbor. The final phase of the operation took place 12 miles southwest of Jonesport when 983 tagged lobsters were liberated on May 30.

Within days of each release, tag returns inundated the project headquarters at DMR's West Boothbay Harbor headquarters. There had been considerable publicity about the tagging study through news releases and reward posters. Fishermen received $5 for tag and lobster. To say that lobsters from all three areas were recaptured at an extremely high rate would be an understatement. Four months after release, 65 percent of the lobsters had been returned, and a year later, 75 percent had been recaptured. By January of 1978, of the 2,882 lobsters tagged, a total of 2,188 had been caught.

The Kennebunkport lobsters were caught mostly close to shore and within a five-mile radius of the release site. Only 14 recaptures went more than five miles and 10 of these lobsters moved in a southwesterly direction. The most noted marathoners were a 3½-inch male that traveled 63 miles to Boston Harbor in 369 days, and a robust similar-size female that was caught 199 days later some 185 miles southwest at Tiverton, Rhode Island.

The Boothbay Harbor lobsters moved inshore between the mouths of the Kennebec and Damariscotta rivers. Only one return came from the Damariscotta River itself, while not a single return was recorded for the Kennebec River. But the lobsters liked the Sheepscot River estuary. Twelve lobsters moved more than 10 miles upriver. The general movement of the Boothbay lobsters was toward the east, with some minimal southerly travel. Some exceptions were a capture at Monhegan (14 miles), one at Cape Porpoise (42 miles), and one at Jeffreys Ledge (16 miles).

The Jonesport lobsters showed a more easterly movement, but still, like all the lobsters from the three areas, they headed inshore. Long-distance crawlers were lobsters caught at Kennebunkport (134 miles), Schoodic Head (20 miles), and Great Duck Island (29 miles).

In apparent contradiction to the earlier 1957-58 migration study, Krouse and his associates did not detect any differences in movement between the smallest and largest lobsters. It should be noted, however, that the project involved all legal-sized lobsters, and the largest one tagged was 4.6 inches in carapace length.

The Krouse project, in summary, said that the lobster fishery is being subjected to extremely high levels of exploitation, that most coastal Maine lobsters within the legal size range are generally nonmigratory yet undergo extensive localized movements, and finally, that long-distance migrants, over 20 miles, follow a south to southwesterly course in response to the counterclockwise coastal currents.

The migratory results were still hot off the scientific press when they were lambasted by a group of Casco Bay lobstermen. Don McVane of South Portland and about 30 other lobstermen had been conducting their own lobster research and made it abundantly clear that the state migration study was, in lobsterman's language, a "crock of shit."

There was nothing right about the state study, they yelled. In the first place, the tagging was accomplished with all legal lobsters, and they were too quickly removed from the water to determine any believable results. How in hell, they asked, can you have any conclusions without realistic data? Furthermore, the state study was not late enough in the year. "Christly," they said, "lobsters don't migrate in May, even a tourist knows that."

While they were at it, McVane and friends laid into the entire state lobster research program. McVane put it quite, quite bluntly. "DMR biologists spend most of their time sitting on their asses. They have been doing the same thing for 20 years. Not one new innovative lobster management proposal has come from the state in two decades. Why, we have asked them and asked them to ride our Casco Bay lobsterboats and observe the catch. To date, they haven't."

These southern area lobstermen are also not great boosters of the Maine Lobstermen's Association, a 1,000 member organization made up primarily of midcoastal and downeast lobstermen. They do not subscribe, for instance, to the state- and MLA-backed program of buying and releasing female lobsters. They might accept the principle, but they say why pay through the nose for a two-claw prime lobster when the state could purchase cull and one-claw females for much less money? McVane & Co. claim the one-claws are just as sexy. They are adamantly against raising the minimum measure, saying this will leave more lobsters in the water and there are enough there already. They want the oversize ban lifted, claiming these

126

"big 'uns haven't a goddamn thing to do with increasing the lobster population." Incidentally, they have also found that all—and they state every—very large over-legal lobster caught by their group has been a male. This coincides with the upper Penobscot Bay findings.

In their Casco Bay in-house migration study, which the biologists call down and dirty, the lobstermen band only illegal lobsters. These are shorts, V-notched, eggers, and oversize. They use a spaghetti tag around the claw. The bay lobsters migrate offshore, south and west. They can move out. One lobster was tagged in the morning and 24 hours later was caught six miles away. How long it had been in the trap was speculation.

Every fall the Casco lobstermen have a census day. In 1978, for example, 22 boats participated. The fishermen hauled 7,360 traps and caught among the others 1,090 V-notched. Of these, 163 of the notched lobsters had eggs on their stomachs.

Several years of Casco lobstermen's records were forwarded to the University of Maine, where a Sea Grant worker agreed to computerize the figures. The state DMR biologists were also given a copy.

The results? Let Don McVane answer. "Why, Jesus Christ, when the computer stuff came back we couldn't tell if we were raising turnips or catching lobsters. Never saw such a goddamn mess. How in hell could they screw up like that? Oh, t'hell with 'em."

McVane also phoned the state DMR and told them to return his figures or he'd send a nose-poking platoon up from Portland.

Other migration studies on *Homarus americanus* have been conducted in other states and offshore waters. Taken together, they weave an interesting mosaic of the life and travels of *Homarus* over his briny north-south range. Krouse and other lobster researchers basically agree that their work supports certain apparent conclusions about the migratory patterns of lobsters. There is a south-to-southwesterly movement of predominantly large, mature lobsters along the Maine coast. There is a directed movement of egg-bearing lobsters along the eastern shore of Cape Cod and into Cape Cod Bay during summer months. There is a seasonal inshore-offshore migration of lobsters inhabiting Corsair Canyon southwest to Baltimore Canyon. Lobsters intermix between offshore canyons. And there is a seasonal movement of some lobsters from eastern Long Island Sound and southern Rhode Island to the middle and outer ridges of the Continental Shelf, while there are few, if any, extensive migrations of lobsters living in Virginia and North Carolina waters.

(The offshore canyons—canyons such as Corsair, Lyndonia, Gilbert, and Oceanographer—are steep valleys between the 100 and 500 fathom lines southeast of Georges Bank, which lies east of Cape Cod, Massachusetts. Like fingers, they reach their tips up into the shoaler waters of the bank, which is probably the richest fishing ground in the world.)

Tagging studies are comparatively popular with fishermen—Casco Bay fishermen excepted, maybe—because of the mysterious nature of the movement of sea creatures. Lobstermen are fascinated with the long journeys of creatures that walk, not swim, hundreds of miles. Scientists recognize the one "bug chasing" thing that fishermen accept, and a considerable amount of recent lobster research monies have been channeled into migration studies. It is doubtful, however, that the tagging projects have added to any measurable management or conservation plans. The differences and similarities between the inshore and offshore populations have been identified more from serology, or blood, studies.

If the tagging studies have not resulted in new management laws, then two research projects in Maine definitely fathered the existing trap-vent statute. The first was started in the summer of 1971 by the Maine DMR's Bob Dow, who was then the department research director. Bill Sheldon, a DMR extension division scuba diver, assisted Dow. It was labeled the "ghost trap" project.

Prior to the 1950s and the widespread use of synthetic materials in the lobster-trap industry, fishermen built their traps with twine heads of natural fibers, usually cotton dipped in tar or some other preservative. Even the best preservative would not extend the head life more than a few months. As the two kitchen and one parlor head began to rot and disintegrate, the trap would lose its catching characteristics if old heads were not replaced. Although this was one of those damnable fishermen curses, it did have a decided conservation aspect in that when a trap was lost, any trapped lobsters would soon escape because of the rapid rotting nature of the twine. Also, prior to the 1950s, there was widespread use of softwood laths such as spruce. Marine worms made short order of these, sometimes eating a trap to uselessness in a couple of months. The laths nearest the sill or bottom of the trap were the first to go, releasing any lobsters contained in lost gear.

With the advent of nylon heads and the more general use of oak laths in trap construction (to say nothing of wire traps, which came along in the 1970s) the "ghost trap" ball game changed considerably. It was presumed by biologists and fishermen alike that thousands of pounds of lobsters contained in these underwater prisons were being lost every year. Even if no bait was in the lost trap to attract lobsters, it was known that they would crawl into the traps as places to hide, especially during shedding season. If the lobster molted inside the trap, there was a very good chance that it would be cannibalized by other lobsters. Also, in areas which were not infested with boring worms, some lost traps might continue fishing for years. Scallopers have dragged up traps that had been lost for two to three years and were still fishable.

Dow and Sheldon set out to gather some facts surrounding these "ghost trap" theories. On July 22, 1971, Sheldon placed 98 tagged lobsters of various legal and illegal sizes, including both sexes, in 35 unbaited conventional wood-lathed square traps with 1¼-inch spacing in an area of Moosabec Reach at Jonesport. The study area site, with depths of 30 to 65 feet, was considered by area fishermen to be unsuitable lobster habitat because it had a muddy bottom with no rocks that could be used for cover. It was purposely selected because it would not interfere with commercial fishing, and the traps would be protected from storm damage.

Traps were checked on 26 occasions, either by diving or hauling, during the following two years. The results were quite interesting. During the first summer-fall season, 43 percent of the tagged lobsters could not be accounted for; 25 percent remained captive; 20 percent escaped and were recaptured; and 12 percent were cannibalized. During the second summer-fall season, 126 percent recruitment occurred; 22 percent could not be accounted for; 18 percent of both tagged and recruited lobsters were cannibalized; 55 percent remained in the traps; and 5 percent of tagged lobsters escaped and were recaptured. A minimum of 67 wild lobsters were recruited by the traps. Two tagged lobsters that departed their original traps entered other experimental traps, which they in turn left before entering two of the commercial traps surrounding the study site. One tagged male that escaped from one of the study traps was caught in a commercial trap about 800 feet from the study site; it had remained in the study trap for 22 months and had molted from sublegal to legal size prior to its escape. Four traps failed to recruit any lobsters, nine recruited one, six recruited three, two recruited four, and one recruited six. Only five traps recruited more lobsters than were initially placed in them, while six recruited a like number.

Dow wrote in his study conclusions that unbaited, unbuoyed traps definitely continue to catch lobsters for an indefinite time, with most of the catch being made between June and December. He said that restrictive lath spacing prevents some lobsters from trap escapement, and the traps do not disintegrate as quickly as thought. And, he stated, only 12 percent of the traps were sufficiently damaged by lobster claws to permit escape. It was apparent from the study that cannibalism occurs during the summer and fall, coincident with molt. Dow had some dire predictions for the industry concerning "ghost traps." During the two-year period of the investigation, the annual Maine lobster catch was 14.2 million lobsters caught in 1¼ million traps. And between July and November, when the peak of cannibalism occurs, 77 percent of the annual catch, 10.9 million lobsters, was made. With this in mind, Dow predicted that approximately one-third or more of all lobsters entering unbuoyed traps would be lost to the fishery from cannibalism or retention.

Dow's doomsday words and the Jonesport project might be tempered somewhat by another Maine DMR research study in upper western Penobscot Bay in 1978–79. The objective was to determine the abundance of *Pandalus montagui* shrimp, but incidental catches were dutifully recorded from the small otter trawl tows. These included "ghost traps." A total of 36 traps, or parts thereof, were pulled from the bottom of the bay, the tow depths being generally in the 90- to 150-foot range. Of these, 20 were undamaged and capable of holding lobsters, but not one lobster was found, only crabs.

In 1976, a formal vent study was commenced by Jay Krouse of Maine's DMR. There were several arguments for an escape vent besides the "ghost trap" theory, the most important being that the commercial lobster fishery was catching an excessive number of "shorts." Considering that Maine lobstermen haul their traps 20 million times a year, even the handling logistics of throwing the shorts back overboard was time-consuming. Another problem was that many shorts were damaged in the handling, causing the loss of one or both claws. These immediately enter the "cull" category. A study in 1974 by DMR estimated that the catch that year lost about $500,000 due to the lower value of culls. And a third negative factor in handling all those shorts was a belief long held by fishermen and shared by many scientists that when short lobsters are thrown back overboard they fall prey to predatory fish while descending to the ocean floor. This is a pretty tough cookie to document, and the argument is offered when it suits the occasion. It is likewise hard to refute, and so it lives quite safely in the life, times, and myth of the Maine lobster.

Devising a trap vent seemed a logical conservation project, but it became apparent to Krouse that just any old trap vent would not do. The two main concerns of fishermen and scientists alike were the optimum size and shape of the vent. The size because any egress had to retain legal lobsters, and shape because of crabs. It was known that rectangular vents would work quite well, but this configuration would not retain rock or Jonah crabs where either or both of these are important commercial species caught incidental to lobsters in the same gear. Krouse and his colleagues, with much important assistance from Boothbay Harbor lobsterman Charlie Begin, undertook an investigation to assess the situation with several independent approaches: a trap escapement study; an analysis of certain body dimensions of lobsters; an evaluation of the size composition of lobsters caught in commercial traps with escape vents of various sizes; and a comparison of the lobsters caught by lobstermen using traps with different lath spacings.

Through the course of the project, the researchers discovered some interesting things. In selecting the right vent size, it was the width of the lobster carapace, not height, that was more important; lobsters trying to escape between laths would twist on their sides. They also found that only a very small percentage of legal-size lobsters might escape through a 1¾-inch vent, but such a rectangular vent would not retain all the marketable size crabs. (Although there is no legal minimum size for crabs caught in Maine waters, market selectivity imposes a 3½-inch minimum. And market-size crabs are virtually all males, since the females are much smaller.) And so additional work was done with circular escape openings.

The extended and comprehensive work done on escape vents resulted in a law that became effective on January 1, 1979. It states that all Maine lobster traps, wooden or wire, must be vented in one of five methods: a rectangular or oblong vent not less than 1¾ by 6 inches; two circular escape vents not less than 2¼ inches in diameter; a gap caused by raising both ends of a bottom lath in the parlor section by 1¾ inches; a gap caused by separating both ends of two vertical laths on the end of the parlor section by 1¾ inches; or a gap created by cutting wires in a wire trap in such a manner as to meet the minimum requirements. The escape vents have to be installed in the parlor sections of the trap, on side or end but next to the sill, which is the bottom of the trap.

The indomitable free market arrived on the scene even before the research study was complete, and plastic panels with the legal dimensions began to spew off forming machines in southern Maine. Today, about half the fishermen use the precut plastic vents, while the remainder lath space. The latter view it as a matter of economy. When the plastic vents first appeared on the market, they sold for 20¢ each. Today, a precut vent for a wooden trap is 50¢, and 40¢ for wire. That's between $200 and $300 for a lobsterman with 600 traps. Lath spacing, however, does have some disadvantages. The wood wears, especially when just-under-legal lobsters start working on the spacings. The commercial trap builders, both in wire and wood, include the vent installation as part of overall cost.

Because of the work done on escape vents, primarily in Maine, the American Lobster Fishery Management Plan, which was effective, in full, January 1, 1985, contains an escape vent law. Although this plan pertains to federal waters, it is expected that all states, and their waters, will be in compliance after 1985.

Not all lobster scientists agree, as was the apparent case with the trap vents, in all matters. There seems to be a mystery for instance, involving lobster larvae. This work

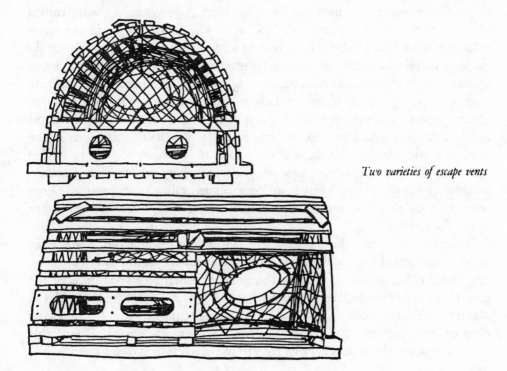

Two varieties of escape vents

has been comparatively recent considering other lobster studies. In 1980, there were five larval studies in progress in New England. Strangely, all five of these concerned potential impacts that nuclear power plants would have on the larvae. Two earlier lobster larvae studies also involved power plants, one study (1974-77) being part of the ecological evaluation of the Pilgrim Nuclear Power Station at Plymouth, Massachusetts, and one (1976) in Penobscot Bay, Maine, for Central Maine Power Company. One thing is quite certain from these past and ongoing larval projects—that the lobster larva is elusive and unpredictable, and scientists are quite baffled by its ability to disappear. Large areas where larvae should be found are often devoid of them. And the matter of larval migrations is a real question. What larval sampling has been completed indicates that larvae (before the fourth stage), when found, are concentrated in surface waters, with abundance declining rapidly at depths of less than three feet. When it comes to discussion about how little lobsters get from one point to another, the plot mystifies and thickens.

If the larvae are totally moved about by surface wind currents, as many biologists claim, it would seem that lee shores (for prevailing wind patterns) should become saturated with larval lobsters to the detriment of other sites and that the "spreading out" of the lobster population would have to take place after the fourth stage, or when the lobster has taken up residence on the sea floor.

Another theory was born when the results of the two early larval studies were compiled. They showed that when winds were onshore, many larvae were caught in the surface neuston nets used for larval catching. As soon as the wind turned offshore, they virtually disappeared. Nor were they found deeper in the water column at those times, either. One school of lobster theory suggests that larvae do not just passively drift with the wind and currents but rather have the ability to move up and down in the seawater column, selecting the right current to get them where they want to go. Fish biologists believe that herring larvae do this also. Oceanographic observations offshore suggest that wind-driven currents fall off rapidly below a certain depth. So, say some scientists, if a larva wants to stay in one place in a wind-driven current, it doesn't have to go down too far to remain stationary. But where do they go? Laboratory tests have suggested that larval lobsters would not go down through a very sharp thermocline, or drop in temperature. Other researchers say they have made tows on the edges of these thermoclines and not found the larvae.

Lobster scientists treat the Gulf of Maine as a "system." Within this system, some see the migration of large, and particularly berried, lobsters southwest and offshore. Eggs laid by offshore lobsters are carried onshore by counterclockwise currents in the gulf. Other scientists dispute this, and there are certainly a hundred variables in Maine and Canadian lobster populations that complicate the theory. A few biologists disagree that females make any "directed" movement toward a favorable environment, one that would improve the survival of larvae by allowing them to drift toward shore.

What is apparent through all the research on the lobsters is that nobody seems to know much of anything about them from the time they hatch until they appear in the commercial traps at just under legal size. The Canadians have attempted to construct traps that will catch very small lobsters but have had poor results. Some of these experimental traps have caught lobsters down to a carapace size of about 2 inches, but few smaller than that. The larval and juvenile wanderings are of tremendous importance, however. The studies done by power-generating companies are notable for the small number of lobster larvae found. Yet, if they are there, and a standing population of millions of adults does indicate it, then nuclear plants and other industries located in the marine environment and entraining and discharging millions of gallons of salt water a day could have, eventually, a terrifying consequence on the lobster industry.

Scientists also delve into fishing gear research and have come up with a rather prosaic conclusion: The lobster trap can't be appreciably improved. There has been virtually no research, however, on what scientists call "trap saturation." This is when a lobster trap fills up with crabs, or—in the very unlikely event—with lobsters. Some data obtained from crab studies indicate that crabs, if present in large numbers in a trap, release a strong "odor" that will repel lobsters. However, the dearth of information leaves begging the question of how much scientists can achieve by pursuing the study of what they call "interspecific behavioral responses."

The fishermen have an answer. They bait differently for lobsters and crabs, modify their traps to top openings if they want crabs, and set their gear on different grounds for each critter. Damnable simple fellows.

There are pro and con arguments from fishermen about lobster research. There is a general adversarial layman-science tangle that is universal and confrontational. Freewheeling independent fishermen see the scientist as someone ready to restrict his movements and profits for no valid reason. There is the "educated" fisherman who agrees in principle with biologists but is generally against specific programs. And there are the majority, who do not get involved one way or the other. They view the scientist as some never-never person, seldom seen, working behind secretive, closed doors—an abstract to reality except during the inevitable public hearing when new prohibitions are threatened.

In a sense, the lobstermen have a point. Maine lobster research is conducted from Boothbay Harbor only and is not visible in other areas of the coast. The Boothbay fishermen have personal and professional contact with lobster science, and the laboratories of DMR are open to them. The Cutler and Eastport lobstermen are not so fortunate.

The lobster scientist has his point, too, and the financial facts bear out his lonely existence. In fiscal year 1980, the total budget for Maine's DMR was about $4 million. Of this total, $1,026,000, or 26 percent, was allocated for all research. Maine had two lobster scientists and three technicians. They had a 1980 fiscal-year budget of about $110,000, or 10 percent of the department's research funds—or, in other figures, about 2 percent of the department's total operating funds. At the same time, lobsters were the state's top fish crop, bringing the lobstermen $47,237,000 in ex-vessel prices. The added value is estimated from two to four times the ex-vessel price. The state support of lobster research is a little more brazen when considering that the federal government pays half of the lobster budget. As a comparison, over 50 percent of the total DMR budget is expended on law enforcement.

Lobster biologists worldwide, and certainly in Maine, are a frustrated bunch. They know, and most deep-thinking people involved with the lobster industry agree, that lobster regulations are enacted for marketing rather than biological purposes. Perhaps it's because lobster is a luxury product, but legislators have a very sympathetic ear to regulations that reinforce the dealer monopoly. Most of these laws have nothing to do with conservation, which is the vehicle used to justify the means. Size restrictions are imposed for the purpose of supplying the market with the size of live lobster that is wanted. Closed seasons in Canada, for instance, have little to do with conservation; rather, they are a marketing device "justified" on grounds of protecting the breeding lobster. Scientists have shown time and again that there is no relationship between the number of eggs hatched and the eventual lobster population, yet fishermen in Maine almost totally support the "seeder" program, claiming the more spawn the more lobster, and they cannot be convinced otherwise. Lobster regulations, the biologists sigh dejectedly, are emotional rather than rational.

But the "bug chasers" keep plugging away at the fisherman dogma. Even though the odds in Maine tally 8,500 lobstermen and two biologists, the scientists get little help from their own department. There is scant interbureau aid forthcoming, unless one could call a coastal warden arresting a fisherman for short lobsters as help. At one time, the Maine DMR had the first and perhaps the country's most unique marine-extension program, later adopted by most marine states and the federal Sea Grant program. Maine extension agents assisted lobster pound owners in disease detection and environmental monitoring; they helped lobstermen with gear and other programs; they were ombudsmen between the state and the industry and were well respected. The DMR commissioner in the late 1970s abolished the extension program as a viable force for some reason, and a valuable service was lost to both the state biologists and the fishermen.

As the venerable Pit Ginnis used to say when confronted by lobster science, "The way's I see it, once upon a time there was two things crawling around in the ocean. One waded ashore, went up t'the university n'became a biologist. The other stayed where he was n'became a lobster. They ain't had a goddamn thing in common ever since."

But then, what did Pit know, anyway?

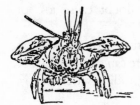

The Government

Anything, be it wardens or weather, impeding a lobsterman in his work is the fault of the "goddamn gum-mint." The "gum-mint" can be a coastal warden checking for a valid license, a judge handing down a stiff fine for short lobsters, or even the legislature passing a law. They are all lumped into the pot called "gum-mint."

Lobstermen have plenty of allies in their adversary relationship with the government—just about the whole fishing community. One time four clam diggers were returning from a day of island clamming in their 16-foot skiff with the usual big-horse Mercury outboard bolted to the stern and running wide open. The body weight plus 10 bushel of clams plus pet hound dog (barks when wardens approach) plus a couple of cases of empty beer cans (returnable) left little that any prudent person could call freeboard. The just-awash apparition was sighted by a marine patrol boat, which eventually overtook the clammers. Coming alongside amidst blue flashing light and wailing siren, the patrol boat's chief badge threw a line, which was ignored by the clam diggers.

"Hey, you, you in the boat there, let me see your registration," shouted the warden, not taking the prima facie valid boat decal's display word for it.

The throttle handler dug around in his muddy pants and eventually came up with an equally soggy piece of paper that passed as a current boat license. The other clam diggers sat looking like a pack of dogs denied their supper.

"Your license is OK," said the warden, passing the wad back to the operator, "but you're overloaded. I'll have to terminate you right here," added the warden in learned but unfortunate terminology.

"Jesus Christ, he's gonna shoot us!" said the bow ballast.

"No, sir," said the warden. "However, I cannot allow you to proceed in your precarious position."

"We been clammin' like this for forty years," said a forward thwartsman.

"I must terminate you at once," replied the warden.

"You go first, Willy," said the bow, "you ain't got kids."

The warden explained the terminal operation. Half the skiff would get out on that there ledge while the boat operator took the remainder ashore. Then he would return and pick up the rest of the motley crew. This would prevent the dangerous overloading condition, which would otherwise without a doubt cause loss of life.

The aft thwartsman had a question—make it an observation—for the warden. "That there ledge is a half-tide rock, cap, and before Willy here can get t'the harbor n'back we ain't gonna be standing on no rock, we gonna be treading water, that is, them's that can tread."

There was a large huddle in the patrol boat cabin over an area chart, which took some 10 minutes. When the final play was called the chief badge emerged and said rather sourly that all the clam diggers should come aboard and they and the clam skiff would be escorted to the town dock. When the patrol boat approached the dock, the pile sitters and sunny lee slouchers all yelled and applauded. The clammers waved and yelled back like returning heroes.

The fisherman concept of the government shooting first and making it a law later persists, but beating the "gum-mint" is so sweet.

Maine lobstermen have been regulated since the mid-1800s. It started with the canning industry but spread gradually, so that by 1895 the size of the minimum legal lobster was defined as 10½ inches (head to toe). From the beginning of this century, hundreds of laws have been enacted, usually under the guise of conservation, to regulate the lobsterman. An outgrowth of that regulation has been the adversary roles of regulator (gum-mint) and regulatee (fisherman).

The most readily available and conspicuous government representative confronting the lobsterman is the warden. The first wardens came into part-time being in the early 1900s as laws became more stringent. They were part-time because lobsterfishing in winter months was a rare occurrence. The "fish wardens," as they were then called, were mainly concerned with the lobster canning industry.

The job was highly political. "Fish wardens," stated the 1939 Sea and Shore Fisheries Laws, "shall be appointed by the commissioner and shall be removable by him at pleasure."

It's also interesting to note that in the pre-World War II days, the fish wardens were required to post a $2,000 bond to ensure "the faithful performance of the duties of their office." They also had to make a monthly report of their activities to the commissioner, a requirement that will cause a few smiles on the faces of present-day wardens, who report in detail their daily person, boat, and vehicle operations.

Old-timey wardens were sometimes the ex-poachers and law breakers, with the government working on the theory, tried and true, that it takes a thief to catch one. Nevertheless, the wardens of yesteryear commanded great respect among the fishermen, probably because they came from the same ranks and were looked upon as fair game, something the wardens themselves understood and sometimes took great pleasure in. The old fish wardens were uninformed and unarmed and had no communications or fast boats or vehicles, yet they somehow kept law and order within an emerging industry. "Law and order" of yesteryear, however, cannot be compared to modern-day enforcement.

From "clam cop" status to present-day marine patrol officer is a quantum leap, not only in professionalism but in expenditure. The decade of 1970 to 1980 is an example of the rise in the cost of marine law enforcement. In 1970, the warden service represented $348,700 of the Sea and Shore Fisheries Department's total $1,331,400 annual budget. This prorates to about $7,700 a warden. In 1980, law enforcement was 36 percent, or $1,361,900, of the department's $3,900,000 expenditures, representing $32,400 per marine patrol officer.

The lobsterman has a tough time relating his existence to armed officers in speedboats and automobiles frothing up the coastal waters and shores embarked on practically the same duties that the old-time fish wardens performed 40 years ago. The lobsterman sees the fisheries little changed over the decades, and certainly not to the extent of justifying the expense of about 40 full-time wardens policing a fishery that nearly shuts down from December to April.

The government, of course, sees it differently. Wardens once were concerned primarily with short lobsters, night hauling, and a valid license, but over the years the warden's duties have increased dramatically. They have always had the powers and duties of sheriffs, but with the transformation of the Sea and Shore Fisheries into the Department of Marine Resources in the mid-1970s, a lot of things happened. The new wardens were expected to enforce not only strict fish laws but also shoreland zoning, pesticide control, boat safety, boat registration, shellfish sanitation, closed and conservation areas, marine mammals, pollution, and navigation, among many others.

In the late 1970s, another duty was assigned to the marine patrol officers, as they are now known. Wearing sidearms was no longer voluntary, but compulsory, and the once fish-law wardens were now drug enforcement officers, something that the young wardens really relished as true excitement compared to the mundane chores of measuring a basket of lobsters.

The 1970s saw the beginning of considerable drug traffic along the Maine coast. Given the pyramid of law enforcement organization, this surveillance fell first to the federal authorities and then to the Maine State Police. But what better enforcement ally than the eyes and ears of the coast, the marine patrol officers?

The Department of Marine Resources administration cooperated fully, in part because of the potential rewards in the form of confiscated gear. (The present DMR research vessel is the former *Jubilee*, an ex-Southern shrimper-turned-drug-runner.) Many lobstermen say, and with justification, that the warden service changed dramatically at this point from being fishery oriented to "just plain cops." Certainly, the concept of "conservation officers" was lost when the wardens strapped on firearms and waited excitedly in the night for "pot smugglers" to invade their turf. The DMR administration also saw the political value when the media ran every iota of a drug bust on Page One but relegated the short-lobster fines to local court news.

The wardens soon discovered, however, that there is a bureaucratic order to drug busts, with the state police highest in the pecking order. Confiscated vessels were stripped of electronics by the police even though the gear had only marine value. Trucks and land vehicles went to the state police on a first priority, as did small speedboats. The wardens were often reduced to the role of mules off-loading 60-pound bales of marijuana from confiscated drug vessels. Even expensive crystal, silverware, and pottery disappeared from one of the first drug vessels, the *Onalay*, seized in the midcoast Maine area. Whatever the warden role is within the drug surveillance order of things, he has little choice as long as the federal and state bureaucracies assign that role.

In the winter months along the eastern half of the coast there is little activity. Many weeks, the clam flats are frozen over, preventing digging, and lobstering is an offshore occupation with only about a two-to-three-day-a-week hauling frequency. Wardens really have little to do and resort to teaming up with their colleagues in other branches of law enforcement and widening their enforcement scope in such activities as traffic violations, chasing deer jackers, and other nonrelated (or so the fishermen figure) law enforcement. This raises the ire of fishermen, who believe that wardens should stick to the fisheries.

If the 1980 cost of $32,400 per marine patrol officer continues to increase at its present rate, the fishermen in Maine will be looking at $60,000-per-year clam cops in 1990. Whatever the costs, however, lobstermen demand that wardens be assigned to their areas. Vinalhaven is an example. There is no way that one warden can police an offshore, 32-square-mile fishing community whose living heritage is lobsters. It is self-policing. Yet, the inhabitants insist that a warden be stationed on the island "to show the flag." One is, at extra-pay duty. The station is not exactly sought after and has been used by former chief wardens as the St. Helena for insubordinate clam cops. A tour of duty as the lone badge on an island with 700 aloof lobstermen can be a sobering experience.

All in all, the warden/lobsterman relationship has survived despite the new and inexperienced people entering both professions. A strange bond of respectfulness does prevail. The warden and the lobstermen are about as close as two opposite poles can be and still have substance in the middle. Perhaps because of this, they do coexist.

If the lobsterman tolerates the warden, he absolutely scathes the politician.

In Maine, any legislator may introduce a fisheries bill, either through his own conviction or by request from a constituent. All marine-related bills are referred to the Marine Resources Committee, consisting of 13 members—three from the senate and 10 from the house of representatives. The committee is appointed by the majority leaders of both houses, and depending on who runs what, the committee can be all Republican or all Democrat—and most certainly the house and senate chairmen come from the party in power. Of Maine's 16 counties, eight are coastal, and generally, but not always, the committee is composed of legislators from these coastal districts. Some shining examples to the contrary emerge when political favors are granted. It certainly is a committee to which coastal legislators aspire, for the fishing community can be quite vocal and energetic when it comes to voting.

Since all proposed fishing legislation is referred to this committee, it recommends or kills most legislation. An unfavorable committee report—ought not to pass—is usually accepted by the whole legislature when deliberating. Likewise, a majority ought-to-pass committee vote will, nine times out of ten, sail through the body politic as a whole with flying colors.

The problem in this seemingly democratic process arises because of the length of the Maine coastline and the different methods of fishing coupled with area special interests. The lobster trap-limit proposal, for instance. This is a proverbial hot potato and the legislators know it. The western area lobstermen traditionally have more gear in the water because of the bottom topography—sand. The eastern fishermen lobster on rocky, ledgy bottom as a rule and use single or pair traps. The gear type limits their fishing effort.

The DMR supports gear restrictions and, through a legislator on the Marine Resources Committee, usually sponsors a "trap bill." The committee, not wanting to be caught in the political whirlpool that surely follows, holds hearings along the coast. As expected, the east-west pro-con arguments persist, and the committee report states that lobsterman opinion is divided and the issue "needs further study." The politicians once again have evaded the sharp hook of controversy.

There is, of course, much subterfuge in getting a bill into the legislature. Only a legislator can present a bill, but they rarely do so on their own. There is a provision on bill printing that allows a legislator to have the legislation labeled "by request," but there is also an unwritten law among legislators that such a proposal is "unbrotherly" and unworthy of debate. These bills are quickly canned. The real sponsors of fisheries legislation are the special interest groups and the Department of Marine Resources. The Maine Lobstermen's Association will have a score of bills before each biennial legislature, as will the DMR.

All proposed legislation goes to public hearing, by law, and fishermen often make the most of this opportunity to have their say. It is difficult, however, for a lobsterman attending a public hearing to determine a bill's real sponsor. When the

DMR, MLA, and several coastal legislators rise and speak in favor of a certain piece of lobster legislation, the audience usually smells something fishy.

Lobster-bill hearings are generally held in Augusta (some say for committee protection) and are, to say the least, colorful. The media always cover lobster hearings.

Years ago there was a very controversial legislative bill proposed that would prohibit lobstering on Sundays during the months of June, July, and August. It was an out-and-out shot at "cottage owners" and "part-timers" who, in those months, would come to the shore for vacations and "set out a few traps." The MLA sponsored the bill with concurrence from DMR (which saw the political handwriting on the waters) under the broad banner of conservation—the catch-all argument for most legislation. Since most full-time lobstermen, the state, and the MLA were behind the move, there appeared to be no legitimate opposition. On the day of the hearing, however, leased school buses started arriving quite early on statehouse grounds.

The Marine Resources Committee chairman nervously gaveled the hearing to order, wondering what on earth could have gone wrong. It seems they had failed to do their homework. In the lobstering communities of downeast Maine there is a variety of strong religious beliefs. One of the larger faiths is Seventh Day Adventism. And for the followers of this faith, Saturday is their day of rest and religious observance. As pastor after pastor rose to speak at the rostrum, explaining that a Sunday closing would, in effect, restrict their parishioners to five days a week of fishing, the committee squirmed in total dilemma. When the divided committee report of ought-to-pass finally came out, the implication, although conspicuously absent in wording, was that the proponents hung their sou'westers on the ageless proposition of separation of church and state. The bill passed the full legislature and has been law for several years. The Seventh Day Adventists have rolled with the 90-day restriction quite well. The part-timers are still mad as hell.

Because of the controversy and political fallout of practically every lobster bill proposed as law, the politicians and bureaucrats conceived and gave birth to an answer to their problem—the Lobster Advisory Council (LAC). This buffer group was established in 1980.

Although the appointments are made statutorily by the governor, they are actually chosen by the DMR commissioner, who forwards the names of persons (obviously favorable to the state's positions on lobster management) to the chief executive, who routinely agrees with the choices of his appointed commissioner.

There are 11 members on the LAC. The political makeup is a paragon of how to cover political asses. One person (who must hold a lobster- and crab-fishing license) is appointed from each of the eight coastal counties. Two persons who hold wholesale seafood licenses and are primarily dealers in lobsters are members. And filling out the council is one member of the general public (human race?) who doesn't hold any marine licenses. The members are appointed for a period of three years and meet at least four times a year. They receive no compensation but are reimbursed for expenses equal to that afforded state employees for travel and lodging. This privy council of the DMR commissioner has no statutory powers, but it "may" investigate lobster problems and it "may" review current lobster research and submit recommendations to the commissioner. The role of the LAC is clearly advisory, and from the council's early makeup, it's apparent that self-interest groups are well represented. For instance, the executive director of the Maine Lobstermen's Association is a member, apparently falling under the provision of a lobster license holder in Hancock County or "a member of the general public." In fact, the MLA executive director was chairman of the LAC in 1983.

With all the councils, committees, and other bodies meeting to discuss proposed legislation, the notices of public hearing are well confused. Ditto the lobsterman. Under the state's administrative procedures act, when public notice is required, it is in a newspaper of "general circulation" in the county or counties affected. DMR almost always publishes in one or both of the two daily papers serving the coastal areas. Of course, many fishermen do not subscribe to daily papers, and the matter of public notice is for them academic. Lobster council meetings are only publicized as news items by interested media. The same applies to Marine Advisory Council meetings, at which many lobster rule changes are discussed. This is another council, in effect chosen by the DMR commissioner and approved by the governor, consisting of nine members "adequately representing commercial fishing activities."

Increasingly, more authority is being vested in state department heads under "rules" rather than statutes. Bureaucrats forever complain that their hands are tied by legislative edicts, and changes can only be effected by legislators on a biennial timetable. In 1983, "Notice of Agency Rule-Making Proposal" notices began appearing weekly in daily newspapers in the classified section. Much of what changes in the DMR laws is included in these notices, but they are rarely read by lobstermen. The trend from statutes to rules usually reflects the philosophy of the current DMR commissioner, since this person is the sole administrator of the rules. Some lobstermen feel that the ability to take immediate action is necessary, for example to close an area to dragging if the lobster habitat is in danger. Others see a czarist trend in the DMR commissioner's office that may or may not be beneficial to the lobster industry.

For those lobstermen not brought up in the business, just complying with present laws presents quite a task. A lobster license must be the last state license unaccompanied by any pamphlet or other written instructions on the laws governing the permit activities. Boat laws, hunting and fishing statutes, and even driving license rules are provided the respective applicants. No so marine laws. By statute, the DMR is required to compile marine resources statutes into a "convenient reference for Maine's fishermen" every two years, but these 4-inch by 6-inch spiral-bound booklets containing about 200 pages are not distributed. Persons aware of the publication may write for a copy from the DMR, State House, Augusta, and may or may not receive one, depending on availability.

Some fishermen claim that there are more laws on lobsters than on humans in the state. Not quite, but fishing laws are extensive, so much so that at one public hearing a fisherman suggested that DMR bind the laws in Styrofoam and issue them as life jackets.

State "gum-mint" regulations say that a lobster license (including crabs) can be issued only to a resident. The residency requirements over the years have diminished. At first there were none, because nonresident lobstermen were unheard of. In 1939, a person applying for a license was required to have lived in Maine for 10 years. In 1970, that applicant must have been a resident of Maine for eight months of the year for a period of three years. In the late 1970s this residency law was challenged, and the law courts determined that a requirement of "longevity" was unconstitutional but that the state (under the banner of conservation, again) could regulate the lobster industry by issuing a resident lobster license only (or so the decision was interpreted). That is the position of the State of Maine today. The applicant, if he has not held a license before, must show proof of residency by property tax receipts, driver's license, or other supporting evidence.

The lobster and crab fishing license is also only issued to an individual, and this has effectively maintained the individual status of the industry. Corporations, companies, co-ops, and any other groups are not allowed permits. Although it is true that most full-time fishermen "fish for" a co-op or dealer (which can supply capital, among other things), these organizations operate under a dealer or wholesaler license, another breed of cat. One could easily imagine the chaos if the law were changed and General Motors was allowed to purchase 5,000 licenses and institute the sharecropper plan.

Most of the laws governing lobster harvest have been mentioned—the minimum and maximum size limits, berried females, conventional traps, escape vents, gear molesting, V-notched females, designated areas for trawls, sunrise and sunset hours, summer Sunday hauling, and even the $100 fine for anyone caught in the dastardly act of scrubbing eggs from a lady female's tummy.

Other licenses are required once the lobster has been landed ashore. Wholesalers must have wholesalers' licenses, retailers of lobsters must have retailing licenses, and one cannot transport lobsters in a vehicle (except the lobsterman with his personal catch) without a lobster transportation license. One license, one vehicle; multiple vehicles, multiple supplemental licenses at $65 a crack. And there is the lobster-meat permit, which authorizes a wholesale seafood license holder to remove lobster meat from the shell under these conditions: that meat is removed only in the establishment named in the permit; the tail section is removed whole and intact and maintained in that state; and containers of lobster meat shall be clearly marked with the lobster-meat permit number. Cooked lobster meat does not escape the minimum size law.

Cooked tail sections less than 4¼ inches or more than 6½ inches "when laid out straight and measured from end to end" are illegal. Maine law allows restaurants and hotels to cut up tail sections for serving, but it must be done immediately prior to serving. Cutting up a bunch of lobster tails for salad the night before tomorrow's luncheon special is a no-no.

Maine's virginal lobster reputation was in danger of being soiled when, in the mid-1970s, coastal wardens were checking restaurants (another added duty) for valid retail licenses and those sneaky cut-up cooked lobster tails, and found, oh my God, a few crawfish mixed with good old *Homarus americanus*. The DMR hierarchy went into its inland-war bunker and outlined a plan of action. Obviously, outlawing a perfectly edible food was a bit much, if not downright illegal, so a brilliant offense was executed. Tax the bugger. And so for a $25 permit, retailers can sell crawfish. There are some restrictions. Just a few. In the first place, crawfish, according to the State of Maine, means "all species of the family Palinuridae including the representative genera *Panulirus, Jasus, Galatheas* and *Palinurus*." For those not steeped in marine biology, these are (but not limited to, of course) rock lobster, spiny lobster, sea crawfish, red lobster, thorny lobster, langoust, langoustini, crayfish, Sidney crawfish, kreef, Cuban rock lobster, African lobster, and African crawfish.

Now that the state has the restaurant chefs' attention, how can the imposter be served? It/they cannot be comingled with *Homarus*, not one ounce worth, Mr. Chef. Lobster is lobster and crawfish is crawfish and never the twain shall meet—in Maine anyway. So what if a wholesaler wants to make a few pesos selling crawfish? OK, buy license, make record of all crawfish purchases (including country of origin), how processed, weight sold, and name of common carrier transporting the product.

Crawfish sales in Maine are plainly on the wane.

The lobster as a special-interest animal is no better exemplified than in special laws for specific islands, which effectively close lobstering to all but inhabitants. The offshore island of Criehaven (Ragged) lies about one mile south of Matinicus and was long held in ownership by families involved in the early lobster industry. A law was lobbied through the legislature, and passed, that carved a neat triangle around the island and proclaimed that "a majority of the lobster fishermen at Criehaven" could petition the commissioner to open or close these waters. As land ownership changed the option was not exercised, probably because the scant population of Criehaven would come out second best in a legislative fight with the more populous northern neighbor Matinicus, which, with state ferry service, a dirt airstrip, U.S. mail, a general store, and about 75 full-time fishermen, wouldn't cotton to a closing of rich Criehaven waters.

Another special lobstering area is famous Monhegan Island. This island, sitting like a lost duck nine miles south of Port Clyde in the approaches to Penobscot Bay, has long been one of the richest lobstering areas of the Maine coast, if not the world. Over 40 years ago, Monhegan lobstermen petitioned for and received a special law prohibiting lobstering between the 25th of June and December 1 (now changed to January 1). Politically and financially it was a move of genius. Because of island geography, no one could lobster within the two-nautical-mile closure in open season except those persons living on the island. And social, unwritten rules determined who those winter residents might be, quite neatly keeping the prolific lobster grounds for the hometown boys. The other consideration was the timing—winter lobstering only. This time of year the lobsters bring the highest prices, and because of its offshore location the island lobsters do not migrate to any extent, leaving the fishermen with a captive catch of fresh, unpounded lobsters at premium prices. They are close-mouthed about catches, but first-day hauls—the day after trap day, the first of January—can reach one ton per boat. That translates into $7,000 in a day.

The other genius stroke in closing the island to summer lobstering is that the tourist trade has grown tremendously in recent decades, with artists and craftsmen arriving at the island in droves throughout the summer aboard the mail and passenger boat, the *Laura B*. Island lobstermen capitalize on this summer business between overhauling gear and setting an occasional gillnet or making groundfish tows.

In late 1984, Swans Island lobstermen were granted special legislation setting trap limits in waters adjacent to that island.

Special waters for special groups have tough going, as aquaculture lease applicants are discovering. Mussel growers especially are requesting bottom leases, which preclude any lobstering, and they are being confronted by irate lobstermen. In fact, the Maine Lobstermen's Association has gone on record, in 1982, as opposing any and all aquaculture leases in state waters—bar none, whether bottom leases or not.

When lobstermen run upon the ledges of the law, they appear before a bar of justice that is in general quite sympathetic to the plight of fishermen, much to the consternation of perplexed wardens. Although this story does not involve a lobsterman, it could have, and it illustrates the sympathy of the court and the reputation and mystique of fishermen—or maybe a smidgeon of all three.

A clam digger appeared in a coastal community's district court charged with digging clams in a closed area. It was not the first time, and the judge and the digger were not total strangers.

"Aubrey," said the voice from the bench, "you are charged with digging clams in a closed area. Do you have anything to say for yourself?"

"Yes, your honor, I was not digging clams."

"Aubrey, the warden states that he observed you on the flats with a clam hoe, digging here and there. Is that correct, warden?"

"Yessir, your honor, and Aubrey hadn't had time to find a good bed of clams and I thought I'd better stop him before he did," answered the badge man in green.

"Well, Aubrey?" asked the judge.

"Mr. Judge, you see it was this way like I tried t'tell the warden here, fall's coming on, ya' know, damn, this mornin' I had t'build up a good kindlin' fire for the missus, well, anyways, I ain't got the money f'high price firewood, judge. Christly, they want all getout f'a cord nowadays. I 'member when slab edgings was $5 a dump body. Well, they ain't now f'sure. Like I said these nip mornings turned my thoughts t'my wood plight n' I 'membered all that driftwood in the flats, been hunkered in f'years, all water-logged, so's I took a piece home week or two back n' dried her out n' goddamn if'n it wa'nt the best firewood I ever burnt. So's come yesterday on low water I headed f'the flats t'stock up on winter firewood. I wa'nt moseying around more than a few minutes when Warden Norm there comes a frothin' down over the bank n' pinches me f'clamming. Hell, judge, I was woodin'.''

"Warden?" came the one-word query from the bench.

"Your honor," said the warden, gaining his composure, "that's the most preposterous story I have ever heard in my life."

"I'll be the judge of absurdity, officer, just tell me if it was possible that Aubrey could have been collecting firewood."

"I would say, your honor, that the odds would be somewhere around one in a million."

"But there is that possibility, isn't there, warden?"

"But sir, Aubrey had a clam hoe, a clam hod, and was poking around where clams live on an illegal clam flat."

"I get your point, warden, but it seems to me there is reasonable doubt in this case that Aubrey was, in fact, digging clams. It is coming on fall, and just this morning I said to the missus, 'Martha, we have to get a couple cords of firewood.' Anyway, I am dismissing this case with a warning to you, Aubrey. If you do any more fire-wooding, make it a high-tide venture."

"Thank you, Mr. Judge," said the clam-flat woodsman.

"Jesus H. Christ," muttered the warden, ripping a page from his summons book.

The courts were so lenient in dealing with fishermen that the state eventually had mandatory sentences passed, which puts a little more starch in the game. In keeping with modern-day justice, the fines are on a sliding scale. The court "shall" impose a base fine of $25 for each offense involving illegal-size lobsters, with another $10 per short lobster up to five and then $30 for each short in excess of five. A bushel of short lobsters could run into a fairly long court cash-register tape. But probably the penalty that does more to curtail short lobsters is that upon conviction a lobsterman can lose his license for three years. It rarely happens on first offense, but the option is there. A few license losers tried to circumvent this penalty by transferring their gear to a wife and fishing in an "advisory" role, meaning the lobsterman would do all the work until a warden appeared and then he would sit back and read the paper while his wife fiddled and faddled and did a lot of make-work until the warden sped off down the bay. Alas, the loophole was closed, and license losers must now take their gear out of the water.

Full-time and thoughtful lobstermen rarely took shorts anyway. Just ask them.

"Hey there, cap, tell me something I been meaning to know for years. I'll keep a secret. But who catches all these short lobsters they talk about?"

"Well, sonny, if'n you've a hankering t'know, it's those Frenchmen from over Lewiston way."

"Really now, well, how do they do it?"

"Tell ya', sonny. They buy a license 'cause nobody can stop 'em. Then they buy a couple lobster traps in some antique place. Foller me so far? Then they take their yellar perch boats n'come down here t'the nice launching ramp the state Frenchmen legislators built for 'em. They honk out back of the islands, set their double wad, n'leave 'em until next weekend when they repeat the run only it's usually 'bout dark. They get 'bout five bushel of shorts a trap. Seen 'em myself."

"Thanks, I'll keep it close to my vest."

The Frenchmen do come down from Lewiston, but they have a lot of company. Some lobstermen take shorts home just to test their own ingenuity. In the last 50 years there must have been 20,000 gas tanks built with false bottoms. Fishermen carrying 5-gallon gas tanks back and forth are more common than the twice-daily tides. Wardens are taught in school that scratchy gas is grounds for closer inspection. It is amazing, though, how many different ways a 5-gallon gas can can be taken apart and reconstructed. One warden, hearing the rustling of lobsters in a can, despite the lobsterman's plea that it was ice (in July), tried for an hour to open the thing with no success. The can, lobsterman, and warden all ended up in district court, where the judge dismissed the case for lack of corpus delicti. The warden offered to ventilate the can with his .357 magnum if the judge wanted a corpse, but he was denied his request.

Carrying shorts ashore bound to the body by bandana strips can cause severe wounds, but the sacrifice has been made. Hiding shorts under old bait is a common ruse, because most wardens dressed in pressed go-to-meeting uniforms don't really care to paw through rancid herring. After all, they have to ride with themselves all day long. Anything carried ashore can be utilized as a short lobster vehicle. For years, fishermen have lugged old life preservers back and forth like St. Bernards. Short lobsters come ashore in lieu of kapok. The life preserver gimmick is still one of the best against new wardens, especially if the fisherman is wearing it. His whole attention is consumed by the law-abiding demeanor of the wearer, given that most fishermen would rather give $2 to the church sewing circle than wear a life preserver.

The old burlap-bag-overboard trick is highly successful. A good-sized rock is deposited in a grain bag of shorts, and the fisherman kicks the contraband overboard halfway to shore in his punt. There it lays in salt contentment until the tide uncovers it a few hours later. This trick has to coincide with the tide phase, but what's lousy this week will work like a charm next week. Anyway, a good short lobster stew once every couple of weeks is good enough.

There are a couple of stunts that haven't yet reached the interception course at warden school. One is the birch log sting. This trick originated on Eggemoggin Reach, of all places, but quickly spread coastwise. The original log is still in existence. It was made with a 4-foot section of 6-inch plastic pipe, an obvious leftover from somebody's plumbing job. The entire pipe was covered with birch bark, which the inventor masterfully removed whole from a living tree of the same diameter. The adhesive is of unknown make but amazingly sticky. The ends of the pipe are plugged with butts sawed from a real birch tree. Assembled, the fake log would fool an Indian. It will hold about a dozen shorts, enough for a respectable cookout. The log can be cast adrift for the tide to carry ashore, or it can even be taken to land in a punt. Picking up driftwood for firewood is a common custom. So common, in fact, that up to this time not one person has been caught using the birch log short lobster sting.

Another is the fire extinguisher ruse. A 15-pound CO_2 extinguisher is cut in half, and the two halves are threaded with tap and die. This trick takes a little doing. Anyway, after the alteration there is only a very thin scar to reveal the surgery. This is covered with a piece of Coast Guard orange tape, which actually makes the extinguisher look better than it did originally. When a short lobster stew is going down, the perpetrator simply unscrews the two halves, inserts the illicit crustaceans, and reseals neatly as a brain surgeon. A warden might be suspicious of a fisherman carrying his fire extinguisher ashore every week for recharging, but who would be stupid enough to suspect anybody could get shorts into something that resembles a thermos bottle? There was one reported close call at Camden when two wardens confiscated a doctored extinguisher and gave it the drill instructor's inspection. But even these veterans could find no false bottom or top, and nobody, just nobody, fools around with Coast Guard orange certification tape. Like the birch log sting, the phony CO_2 short lobster carrier has a perfect record.

A few lobstermen eat shorts for lunch, especially when they have company aboard. This is accomplished in a couple of ways. In the first, the lobster is split down the middle, wrapped in tin foil, and placed on the engine manifold. If the lobsterman has a lot of company, the engine will look like a Christmas tree full of tinsel balls. About half an hour later the lobsters are removed from the waste-heat pan and served with cold beer. If a lobsterman refers to Chevy, Olds, Caterpillar, or John Deere lobsters, this is what he's talking about. The second on-board lunch is called short lobster stew, same as ashore, but is prepared atop the small gas stoves that lobstermen keep in the fo'c's'le for making hot buttered rum. A large kettle, a gallon of milk, butter, salt, and pepper are carried aboard by the guests. After all, the fisherman supplies the main

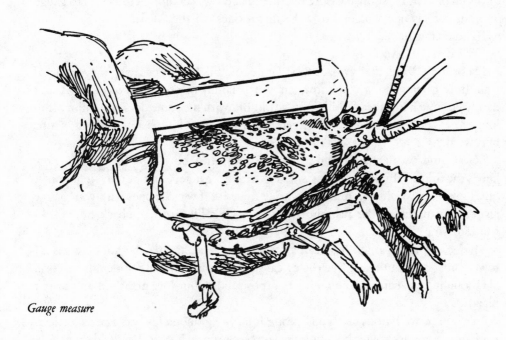

Gauge measure

meal. When enough shorts have been caught to leave little space between four quarts of milk, the procedure begins. It takes three people to make an on-board short lobster stew. The fisherman runs the boat in a normal, nonsurrepticious manner (as viewed by anyone with binoculars). One person is on watch like a crow. The other boils the lobster, shells the meat, cuts it up, and makes the stew. The crow sentinel is extremely essential, and many otherwise excellent stew makers have been busted for leaving this ingredient out of the recipe. The reason is that wardens have an uncanny ability to sneak up on working lobstermen, who can't hear them over the engine noise and whose eyes and hands are on their work. This is where the crow comes in. Any fast approaching small boat should arouse suspicion. Any fast approaching small boat with a moose-and-pine-tree decal on the side is disaster. However, the crow can alert the stew maker in enough time so that the whole illegal mess can be heaved out the fo'c's'le companionway and overboard. Without the crow, a warden would be standing in the doorway and would get milk and short lobsters all over his uniform. Leftover stew can be taken ashore very lawfully, although wardens rant and rave and curse knowing full well the source of the chunks in the stew. So far, there hasn't been one short lobster stew presented in a Maine court as prosecution evidence.

What happens when a fisherman is caught red-handed with the little fellas? Well, again, this stimulates the undercover psyche that all lobstermen are born with. Some of the more common responses after being caught with hands in the short pail are:

"Well officer, I lost my measure overboard and I was taking these ashore to gauge 'em but sure as hell would throw the illegal ones off the wharf."

"These ain't mine."

"Warden, you won't believe this, but . . . ."

"Short huh? Well, that's what I thought but old Bill here kept saying they was legal n'all. Bill's getting along you know, ain't got a family or nothing. No money. Ain't hardly got much life ahead of him. I take old Bill with me some days n' pay him off in lobsters so's he can at least get one square meal a week. Bill's lobsters are really short, huh warden?"

"Goddamn, warden, am I glad t'see you. I was settin' out t'look for 'ya. OK, now here's the thing. I think something's wrong with my gauge. Can't put my finger on it, but, look here, would you mind measuring up these few close ones with your gauge just t'set my mind at ease? Just put the shorts aside n'I'll throw 'em back. Sure glad I run into you, warden."

"Judge, sir, this warden has been after me ever since the day he ran outa gas n'I towed him home but made five passes 'cause there was so many people on the dock. He thought I was hangin' him high on purpose, judge, but I wa'nt. Wind wa'nt right t'land."

"Ya'honor, we Eatons are God-fearing folk. My granddaddy was a peace officer. An Eaton don't go 'round breaking the law on purpose. No sir, I really didn't think them were shorts. Yes sir, I was in here a couple weeks ago."

There are other lobster violations as serious as the taking of shorts. Possession of an egg-bearing lobster brings a fine of $30 a mama, and if a lobsterman scrubs the eggs from mama's tummy to be cute, then, as mentioned, the fine is $100 for each scrubbed lobster plus a mandatory one-year loss of license. It would seem rather difficult to prove that a clean female lobster's tummy was laundered, but the biologists say they can tell—but are not telling how. Mutilated lobsters and those with a V-notch in the right tail flipper bring a $30-apiece fine. The most severe punishment is reserved for "molesting" another person's lobster gear. That is defined as fooling around with a lobster trap, warp, buoy, or car not one's own. Conviction means a mandatory loss of license—if the violator is a lobsterman, of course—for a period of three years. In addition, the commissioner "may" actually suspend the license or certificates of anyone convicted of violating any marine-resource law. Duration of the suspension is six months for the first offense, nine months for the second, and one year for the third collar. In the real world, the commissioner rarely exercises this option, since to do so could be poor politics.

It would be unfair to leave the warden force without noting that marine-resources laws usually state "he" when referring to marine patrol officers. In truth, the marine patrol is the most sexist law enforcement group in state government. As of

September 1983 there had never been a female coastal warden, although many females have attempted to join. The reputation of a good ol' boy outfit is intact despite some recent pressures to integrate the service. Although state personnel procedures do not preclude females as wardens, unwritten DMR policy does. Through state civil service a female may place high on the available register of qualified candidates, but the department has the option of selection from the top of the list. It's doubtful, however, that DMR can hold out much longer in the day of women guards, female state troopers, and lady game wardens. One seemingly qualified female said she was ridiculed by interviewing officers and told that night stakeouts and chasing beer-drinking clam diggers through the spooky woods were "tough jobs for a girl." To which she replied that she'd been doing this for 10 years.

There are other nonregulatory happenings that the lobstermen call "gum-mint" and that do have short- and long-range implications to their livelihoods. Certain science workshops can formulate policy. An example was the Canada-United States Workshop on the Status of Assessment Science for Northwest Atlantic Lobster. Although less than a handful of working lobstermen in Maine ever heard of the meeting, their prey and subsistence was the star of the show. Attending were 19 representatives from the National Marine Fisheries Service, state scientists from 10 states, 26 Canadian federal and provincial biologists, and two European lobster experts. The symposium consisted of 23 papers discussing everything from statistical reporting systems to larval studies to lobster growth rates. Since these were key people within the world lobster industry, there was bound to be some regulation spinoff, and indeed, much of this science did manifest itself in what would become the federal American Lobster Fishery Management Plan. A well-known lobstercrat was asked once why such professional meetings never included a bona fide lobsterman who just might offer some different perspectives and probably some revealing eyeball data.

"My God," he said, "we'd never get anything accomplished. They just don't understand the language."

Money sources, whether private or public, are also considered "gum-mint." Unless one inherits a lobsterfishing business by working through it from age five, the entry fee for full-scale give-her-hell lobstering can be frightening. The sum of $100,000 for a boat and gear "to make a living" isn't too far out of the ball park. There are several sources that underwrite lobstermen, or say they do, but when it comes to fish or cut bait, the prospective lobsterman is usually cutting bait.

Federal loans are practically nonexistent, although they are advertised through the Production Credit Association made possible by the Farm Credit Act of 1971 (not a government function, but created by one), as well as through the National Marine Fisheries Service, the Economic Development Administration, and the Small Business Administration. Maine state assistance programs include the Maine

Guarantee Authority, the Small Business Loan Authority, and the Maine Small Business Loan Authority. And then there are local banks, private investors, and credit unions.

The federal programs are not geared to small fishermen, even when there is money available. Fish processors and fleet operators, through political pressures and lobbying, seem to gobble up what bucks flow through these bureaucratic labyrinths. And lobstermen are opposed to them, especially the Small Business Administration, because, they say, the loans (from taxpayers' dollars) give them more competition on the water. ("Christ, my taxes are setting up people to threaten my livelihood.") In fact, because processing small loans was such a pain, especially in view of the lack of support from within the industry, the federal government declared the lobster industry a "conditional fishery" several years ago. That translates to too many fishermen so no "gum-mint" bucks. And so, voila! The feds are off the hook under the banner of conservation—again.

The Maine Guarantee Authority statutes and intent state that the program permits a loan guarantee for any documented fishing vessel, but the red tape surrounding such a loan (creating a local nonprofit development corporation, for one) makes such a route torturous, with little light at the end of the wharf.

The state's two small business authorities were created just because of this problem. Many banks found that the paperwork required for processing loan guarantees of less than $25,000 was excessive. The two small business programs, which are administered under the same roof, provide that 80 percent of a maximum $30,000 loan may be guaranteed. Veterans may apply for assistance under both programs, raising the maximum loan to $60,000. And these loans seem to be the most popular for lobstermen.

Lobstermen, incumbent and prospective, shy away from "gum-mint" loans, however. Collateral is stiff, often requiring the mortgaging of houses. And government agencies have little heart when the lobsters aren't crawling.

Local banks seem to be the prime moneylenders, although it has taken a very long time for bank executives to understand the strange vagaries peculiar to the fishing industry. This seems odd, because banks have been dealing with farmers and crop failures and fallow land and independence since the country was founded.

One bank president expressed it well. "Look, I don't know anything about fishing, it's true, but I do know the fishermen that come in here for loans. They are the most hard-working, conscientious, honest members of this community. But Jesus, his equity and my assets are one inch away from zero 24 hours a day. One faulty seacock, one sprung plank, and that's all she wrote. I can go repossess a farm or a tractor, but I'm no good in the marine salvage business."

The gap in understanding seems to be narrowing. The banker is getting more collateral (and interest) for his money and the lobsterman is finally learning something about business and financial records.

Private investors are a well-used source of loans. "Putting a little money" in a Maine lobsterman is a comfortable tax dodge and a lovely conversation subject. The lobsterman or investor first forms a corporation or partnership (more and more lobstermen are becoming corporations anyway). Return on investment may be small, but it's well cared for.

Fish and lobster cooperatives have credit unions for members only. Anything from a new boat to engine to traps is a reason for obtaining a credit union loan. As with all CU's, the interest is lower than commercial loans and the applications are handled by loan officers of the co-ops who know exactly how and where and if the loan is needed. Loan demands are high from fishery co-op credit unions but are rarely denied.

Whatever source the lobsterman gets his loan from today, and they all seem to get one sooner or later, he is looked upon as a businessman, a recognition a long time coming.

"Years ago," said a Winter Harbor lobsterman, "when I went into the bank and asked for a loan, they sent me to the rear of the line of people buying a new refrigerator at 18 percent interest. Nowadays, they jump right up with a fine how-d'ya-do."

That the lobsterman is self-employed goes without too much saying. This independence precludes any unemployment compensation, in direct contrast to the lobsterman's counterpart in Canada. The U.S. fisherman considers unemployment compensation as "gum-mint" and wants no part of handouts if they involve being accountable. The Canadian lobsterman works on quotas, a system that allows him automatically to get unemployment during off-season. The U.S. lobsterman says to hell with it, although many politicians have pushed for legislation that would make the lobsterman's life a little easier during the winter months. It falls for lack of a second.

Outside of a loan here and there, the lobsterman has always operated on a cash-only basis, and when it came time to pay his income tax, he figured up what he had for income and what it cost to get that income, and then he paid the "gum-mint" what he thought was a fair share. All those IRS tables and rules were for other people, he figured, those nine-to-fivers. Not that the lobsterman paid no income tax at all; he merely changed the rules in that he decided "fair share," not the IRS, which didn't understand the fishing game. As one lobsterman expressed it, "The IRS goes about collecting taxes like a fart in a mitten."

Up until the mid-1970s, there were some feeble attempts by the IRS to audit lobstermen. The federal auditors came away from these sessions as if they had had a lobotomy—just staring off into space.

After one encounter in Rockland, a young IRS accountant said, "These guys keep their records on the head of a match." Maybe not quite that minimum, but the matchbook cover has been a standard ledger sheet in the Maine lobsterman's bookkeeping scheme for decades. Other favorites include envelopes, hat bands, any clear surface in the pickup's cab, pilothouse woodwork, and skin of the wrist. To audit a lobsterman might require leasing a moving van, as the Internal Revenue Service was soon to find out.

Some say it began with complaints from fishermen themselves. Others claim the record-keeping practices were so arrogantly flaunted that the IRS was bound to take some action—if only to save face. Known variously as the "Great Gum-mint Strike Force," the "Invasion," or the "Gestapo," among other unflattering titles, a surprisingly large IRS contingent did, indeed, show the flag in 1975. Gathering information as only the IRS can, they called lobstermen to audits all along the coast, mailing out notices to come and bring "seafood receipts for the past three years." A refusal to honor the invitation, some lobstermen discovered, produced a "G-man" at the door in the form of a United States Marshal—shades of the Old West.

The auditors began by showing each lobsterman a copy of his license, which had been obtained from the Maine Department of Marine Resources (and the DMR has been trying to convince the industry that it maintains confidentiality ever since), and would then proceed to heap upon the desk wholesale lobster receipts, bank statements, credit card duplicates, and other financial records that tended to show that the fisherman was spending about twice as much money as he had reported making. Many lobstermen got sand-bagged by their own doing. Wholesalers—persons or co-ops buying lobsters—were a little more record-oriented than the harvester, and usually insisted on a receipt being given. At the sale, the lobsterman would say, "Aw, make the slip out to Brown." It could be Smith, Jones, or Mickey Mouse and Donald Duck—anybody but the rightful seller. No name, no record. Well, when a Brown, Smith, or Jones walked into the auditor's office and was confronted with sales he could not possibly have transacted, he yelled "railroad" with conviction. The word got out in a hurry that the IRS was there to frame, man, frame. One auditor actually took a pretty good shot on the nose from a Smith clansman.

A part-timer with 10 traps and a very common last name got notice to appear for an audit. He took along his wife, who did what bookkeeping was necessary in the household. The auditor proceeded on prescribed course with duplicate license, seafood receipts . . . . "Whoa, there, how many pounds did you say I sold last year, mister?"

The young accountant flipped through four sheets of figures and calmly said, "It looks like, er, right here on the bottom line, $34,500."

"Jesus Christ, I never sold a one. Shit, I only got ten traps."

"Ten?"

"Five and five—ten."

"Well, it doesn't seem that you could catch that many, does it?" asked the auditor. "But just how many lobsters do you catch a week?"

The wife, who had taken a no-pay day off from work to attend her husband's honor, had had it by now. She jumped up, grabbed her shoebox of "receipts" from the auditor's desk, and said in a loud voice, "He gets about two and we fight over them!"

"Guess there's been a slight mistake here," said the auditor to himself as the highliner and his wife slammed the door.

The more the IRS lanced the Maine lobster industry, the more they got covered with gurry. "Unprecedented problems" arose, according to the IRS district director. They sure did. The main one being that the auditors had no knowledge of the workings of a lobsterman. An example was lobster bait. If a fisherman purchased bait from a recognized bait dealer, that was fine and a traceable, accepted business matter. Lobstermen, however, get their bait in various ways. One of them is the spring run of alewives that ascend Maine rivers and streams to spawn. Lobstermen, come April, begin to drive to their favorite "dipping" brooks. When the tide, moon, and factors known only to fish all are in alignment—then the alewives are running. The lobsterman, obviously, couldn't tell just what specific night the alewives would run, but he would deduct as a business expense all the times he traveled to the brook and came back empty-handed. Of course, the auditors saw things differently. No fish, no deduction. And besides, the "gum-mint" men would say, the lobsterman usually went shopping or to the movies if he didn't find fish. "Well, shit, sonny," they would reply with Maine logic, "I didn't want to waste the gas."

Another expense that baffled the auditors was Clorox, the same household product used in the wash. When one lobsterman claimed 50 gallons of Clorox as a business deduction, the auditor just shook his head.

"You state here that you bought 50 gallons of Clorox. Why, my wife wouldn't use that much in 20 years."

"Your wife gut a bot, sonny?" asked the cap'n.

"Well, no, but what's that got to do with it?"

"Well, sonny, if'n your wife had a bot, she'd have a bottom, n'when your bot's bottom gets slimy, she's got t'be cleaned n'when she's cleaned, she's cleaned with Clorox. Got me so far, sonny?"

"Fifty gallons?"

"Big bottom, sonny."

Some auditors, in exasperation or desperation, would finally concede to things such as Clorox and alewife runs, but there was no table of IRS organization guidelines that governed procedure. So the auditors began to stamp the receipts, be they on envelopes or matchbook covers, when they were approved. And so what did the lobsterman do? Well, he would just let his neighbor use his receipts saying he had seen another auditor and had had them approved.

The whole thing was turning into a royal mess. The feds turned to the state for help, and the DMR sent a man down to hastily compile a "Lobsterman's Dictionary."

This now-rare, out-of-print primer (copies burned by feds after task force left state) listed common lobsterman's terms not found in general usage anywhere else in the world. There were "niggerhead" for winch; "Clorox" for bottom cleaner; "horse turds" for tears; "snots" for bad kids; "pounded thumb" for number than a . . .; "whore's egg" for sea urchin; "shitpoke" for blue heron; "brim" for bait; "asshole from appetite" for doesn't know the difference between; "finestkind" for quality; "flat ass calm" (FAC) for no swell; "flat ass flat" (FAF) for no swell and no wind; "gurry" for guts; "shags" for cormorants; and "fucking" as a noun, verb, adjective, adverb, preposition, and period. All these and many more were included in this crash-course guide to better understanding the Maine lobsterman. Armed with this new insight in their briefcases, the IRS regrouped and made another foray into the trenches of financial fishing records.

It was not long, however, before the IRS discovered what they probably had known all along—that it would be impossible to change 300-year-old habits, and throwing any Maine lobsterman in the slammer would be political suicide. The IRS director, who was to retire following the industry audit, admitted that leaning on lobstermen was like pissing on apple pie. "God," he kept saying to his staff, "I'll be goddamn thankful when this is over."

When it was over in about 18 months, a handful of civil fines went out to individual lobstermen who admitted to "a couple of mistakes," and there was just one criminal indictment, which was later changed to a civil offense when the fisherman agreed to pay taxes on $22,000 rather than the $367 income he had previously reported. "An oversight," he called it. The IRS left seemingly happy that its integrity, honor, and watchdog image had been preserved.

The "gum-mint" includes anything threatening a lobsterman, as shown when a lobsterman appeared quite unexpectedly at a 1974 public hearing at which the state was proposing to spray insecticides on 3.8 million acres of Maine forests because of spruce budworm infestation. The paper companies own more than half the Maine real estate, and their political power is considerable. The Romeo-footed, green Dickies-clad fisherman stood out among the three-piece suits and leather briefcases like a conifer at Brooks Brothers. Acknowledged and invited to the rostrum, he pulled the paper envelope from his hind pocket and used the writings for reference during his speech.

"Now this here $12 million project ain't just right. There's $3 million of that coming from us Maine taxpayers—that's me. Now I'm a lobsterfisherman n' I ain't smart but I know that all that spray stuff has got to run inta the sea someplace. That's where I come in 'cause I work on the sea. Now I know that spray stuff ain't too good f'lobsters. If you kill the lobsters I ain't gonna make a living, am I? Now, I read in the paper the other day where this paper company man said a cord of pulpwood is worth $29 delivered t'the mill. He said you gotta spray 'cause those loads of $29 is what would be lost if'n you don't spray that stuff on them trees. Well, I been figgering here [envelope brought closer to glasses] n' this is what I come up with. Now, as I said, I ain't bright but I figger a cord of lobsters eight feet by four feet by four feet weighs about 3,840 pounds. Now, last year them was worth $5,242 to the fisherman. Now, I checked over at Sea and Shore n' some bright guy there says that by the time that cord of lobsters reached the customer they were gonna be worth $26,213. Now, I don't know, that's just what the man said. He's gotta be smat, ain't he, working for the gum-mint? Anyways, I also figgered up how many lobsters been caught in Maine between 1945 and 1973, and it comes out to, let's see here, yep, comes out t' 'bout 582 million pounds or 151,000 cords, which boils down t' about $4 billion at today's prices. Now, that's all I gut t' say. You can spray as you want but there's gonna be a lot of lobstermen headin' f' the woods if you go killin' off our business."

Well, the state and feds did spray that year but on a much smaller scale. And today, neither the state nor feds contribute to forest spraying in Maine. It might just be that the lobsterman had a small voice in that policy.

Like the kid with freckles, the lobsterman knows he has the "gum-mint" and doesn't like it but can't do much about it. It's an affliction he can live with and sometimes takes pleasure in, as when confrontation leads to victory. But most of the time he ignores regulation if it doesn't suit his own fashion.

Old Pit Ginnis once said that "gum-mint people are like a good case of the shits. They don't know when t' stop."

The community supper

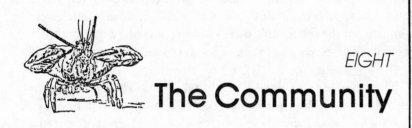

EIGHT

The Community

Maine lobstermen, for all their fiercely independent image, do not walk alone. Like the rest of us less fortunate mortals, they have families and live in communities. They exist within normal social mores, and except for the hours spent upon the water, lobstermen and their brother fishermen are ordinary citizens—contrary to many rumors.

It was not always so, but today the anthropologists consider the lobsterman a really fun guy to play around with. These social scientists consider the lobsterman and his longevity rather remarkable in human terms. Some even say these crustacean catchers are a species not unlike native tribes found a few decades ago in remote jungle areas—with a few refinements, of course. Science is often self-serving, and education and government grants are more readily given to "study" the lobsterman than, say, a garage mechanic. And so perhaps the lobsterman's image as one who walks alone on water is the result of an oversell job.

In the long-ago lobstering days of hand-hauling 25¢ lobsters from Friendship sloops, the fisherman and his family and community were exceedingly close-knit. The fishermen were sons of fishermen, the wives were daughters of lobstermen, and children were intricately wound within the struggle of family life.

A lobsterman's wife had a harsh life in the late 19th and early 20th centuries. In the New England fishing ports of that era one can imagine her lifting her eyes from the overwhelming drudgery of existence and through the window of her home watching a magnificent sailing vessel clearing port for the far reaches of the world, and aboard, waving from beneath a filling spanker, the captain's wife in ribboned bonnet and sailing best. The nearshore fisherman's wife was as land-bound as the farmer's wife. She rose with, and often before, her fisherman husband and kindled the wood fires and warmed the wool socks on the stove rods. She made the oatmeal and fried the bacon and salt pork, man's food for a man's day. She packed the tinned dinner pail with bread and meat and dried fish and apple pies and cakes made the night before on the sideboard beside the soapstone sink, and then cooked and browned them by maple and oak wood heat coaxed through the cast-iron cookstove.

And when her husband fisherman left in the early morning darkness, her day had just begun. The children were wakened and breakfast was begun once again. The school children were wrapped in their homemade woolens, dinner pails were filled, and books and lessons were gathered in cloth pokes or belts. The small children were a comfort and company for the fisherman's wife. The long days of waiting and work were helped by a baby's kiss or cuddle and a cup of tea and reading a story to the near-schooler.

Lobstermen's wives did not live by baking bread alone. They helped their husbands with their shore work. They painted the skiffs and punts, carved the buoys, knit the lobster-trap heads, and did those hundreds of shore errands that the husbands could never fill working all the daylight on the water.

Her rewards were few. The unexpressed love of husband maybe. Discipline in the old fisherman households precluded much affection shown by children, also, and the often extreme hardship of the family's mere existence did not spawn family laughter or playfulness or basic joy. Yesteryear fishing was a dangerous occupation, and many lostermen never returned to those warm kitchens and dutiful wives and children they left on those early mornings. The family loss would be learned from a knock on the door and a group of silent, standing fishermen. No words were necessary. Children clinging to aprons seemed to sense the tragedy. The community would respond, of course, with sympathy and food and visits by the pastor and wives, doing what they could, doing all they could. There was little security bequeathed in the death of a fisherman. His house, maybe, some fishing gear, a boat. Scarce enough to sustain a widow and children. The community accepted the loss and responsibility. It was to happen, as before, over and over again. As a part of the community, the survivors were entitled to its assets without humility or shame. Eventually, and usually, the young widows remarried and a foster family was born. Widows, childless, would often not remarry but instead become the community seamstress or store clerk or quilt maker. Children, not gaining a stepfather, would be taught the needed fishing-family doctrines and heritage by the uncles and aunts and grandparents and community at large.

These were times of hardships and sorrows, but also of prosperity. Not in the financial sense, but in ideals and spirit and brotherhood of man. These humanitarian traits have been passed along to the fishing families and communities of today. Although the times have surely changed outwardly, the lobsterman of today still carries the determination and humility of his life that sustained his father and grandfather before him.

Who can say who laid down the rules and duties of a fishing family? Whoever sealed that package did most certainly leave the daughter's role caught in the seam. Poor missy, sometimes the daughter feels that she was predestined by the gods of the sea forever to sweep floors, do dishes, and knead a million loaves of bread into food for the men in her life. Unfair, unfair, she says in her prayers, when dad takes brother to the island for clamming and to town to buy new pot warp. Modern missy is not quite so jilted as her grieving predecessors, but it's tough being a girl in the lobstering world.

Daughters can also be the object of much love from their father lobstermen. Being out in the boat all day with Junior doesn't leave much for man-to-man conversation when the supper dishes are cleared. That's when dad takes a keen interest in his daughter's activities of the day, although father fisherman doesn't know much about the women's world of things like knitting and kneading dough. Sometimes, daughters demand to enter the lobsterhood. And succeed. They can knit lobster heads, lath a trap, and fill bait bags with the best of brothers.

There was an instance involving one downeast family with brother and sister about a year apart in age. Susie was born a lobsterman and a girl all in one. A terrible dilemma. Brother Eben could not leave the house with dad alone from the time the siblings were four years old. Dad realized he had a problem. And as the youthful years rolled by, dad accepted reality and shipped two sternmen, Susie and Eb, aboard his lobsterboat.

When the "guys," a term that Susie insisted be applied to her also, reached the mature lobsterman's age of 10 years, the father decided that competition and entrepreneurship would weed Susie from the first team. After all, dad grimaced, he did have his reputation to keep standing. And so he bought two semi-dory skiffs, those clinker-built, lapstraked, copper-clinched, rocker-bottomed boats that loved a load and could handle a sea chop like a canvasback duck. He purchased enough trap materials—laths, heading twine, rings, nails, warp, buoys—to build 20 traps. He then laid down the rules. On the word "go" each sibling would build up his "string" of 10 traps. When finished, dad would provide bait for a week's fishing. From the sale of their first catch, they were on their own. Each, however, would have to pay the old man $10 per week for his original grubstake of boat and gear. At the end of the summer, coinciding with school opening of course, the total pounds of lobsters landed, plus capital improvements such as new traps, would be tallied, and the best "man" (father was a diplomat) would win. The trophy was not discussed, but it was quite evident to the participants that the winner would be dad's sternman—*the* sternman, period.

The day after school closed in early summer, the gong "go" was rung, and how the laths did fly in the shared fish house. Father, the tutor, had taught well. Twenty shiny, new-woody traps hit the wharf at about the same hour. Ten minutes later, two five-trap loads, driving the dories down to their first strake Plimsoll marks, were headed to a lobster rendezvous within the confines of the harbor, the predetermined battleground. Eb, the stronger rower, was first to return dockside for the second load of traps. Susie was not far behind.

Eb hauled the next day, Susie set over. Score: Susie, five pounds; Eb, three pounds.

Days and weeks passed, and Susie's and Eb's philosophies became quite apparent. Eb, the worker. He hauled more frequently; baited heavier; moved his gear more often. Susie, the tactician. She found the holes in the ledges and dumped her traps as neatly into their voids as putting on a pair of gloves. She left her traps to fish on three- and four-day set-overs—until her instincts told her that five lobsters lived in that hole and she had caught four of them. She then scouted out, on the low tides, the big rocks and kelp beds. And she shifted her enterprise accordingly.

At midpoint in the summer experiment, it was a close race. Eben had made a down payment on a small outboard, which got him around the harbor course with more ease. As the shedder season came on, Eb was hauling twice a day. Susie had invested in more traps but retained her oar power, meaning that her per-hour labor costs were higher. Eb wasn't foolhardy in purchasing the outboard. With it he could venture outside the shallow harbor to fish for flounders and dogfish on a middleground sandy bottom beside the island that guarded the harbor entrance. Susie was still buying bait at the lobster cooperative, and redfish racks were nearly $5 a bushel. Although most fishermen don't use dogfish for bait, Eb had learned from his father that if he headed and skinned them and cut them into pieces and put them in bait bags, they fished pretty well. Dogfish also caught crabs very well. Both Eb and Susie were catching crabs, but they differed in utilizing them. Eb sold his to crab pickers for 15¢ a pound. Susie picked her crabs at night and sold the meat to the village market for $5 a pound.

Susie was beginning to run out of time in a day. The fishing alone took half a day. Then there was selling the lobsters and getting bait and salting it down. At night, she was picking crabmeat and building traps. Eb had the same logistics to contend with, but he could haul and set his growing trap string much faster with the outboard. The industrial-age lobsterman. Susie did not have motor payments to make, and instead moved her capital into hard assets—more traps.

A week before school began, father gave fair warning that the summer accounting would take place within five days. There was a flurry of the things lobstermen do best. Last hauls were made, lobster gear was put on the bank, boats were hauled and cleaned (father would buy back the boats and pay according to condition), accounts were paid, receivables were collected. And then one Friday morning at 8 o'clock, the deadline arrived. The troops, all present with ledgers and gear, ready for inspection, sir!

It was, as the horse players say, nearly a dead heat. In cold cash, Eb was the victor. In capital equipment (despite the outboard), Susie was clearly the winner with her to-hell-with-motoring, buy-me-some-trap-stock theory. Susie had 18 fully fishable traps that could be sold for nearly their full value, compared with 14 for Eb.

The old man took his new dilemma under advisement. Obviously there was no clear sternman. Splitting a few dollars would not solve the family structure. He assembled the combatants in the kitchen next morning and told them just that. Expecting tears, rage, or even the silent treatment from his daughter, father waited for the blow.

Susie rose from the wooden kitchen chair and got a banana from the fruit bowl that mother never seemed to let run dry. She opened the silver drawer and took out a small, plastic-handled paring knife. Sitting down, she peeled the banana in a deliberate, teasing four strokes and sliced it into her bowl of Rice Krispies.

"Well, Dad, I know you got a problem. I know you want Eb to fish with you. But I wanted that job, too. So, what you did was fair enough only we're pretty close, ain't we? Too close to call, right? Well, I been thinking 'bout what I want t'be when I grow up. Probably you think it's a lobsterman, huh? Well, so did I. Did up until last spring when I wanted to really stay ashore and be with Betsy n'the girls but didn't how how to tell you. Then you came up with this contest thing n' I just had t'prove I could of been a lobsterman, didn't I? And I couldn't let Eb beat the pants off me, could I? Boy, I never would of lived that one down. So Dad, seems to me that if'n you buy my traps n'give me credit for my boat payments n'promise t'take me lobstering whenever I feel like it, well, looks like my brother Eb is the next lobsterman in the family."

The father came about as close to crying in front of other people as he ever had. "Susie, you can ride in my lobsterboat until the tides stop turning," he said, giving her a big bear hug.

Boy fishermen turn into father and grandfather fishermen as surely as the tides turn. In the early years of establishing lobstering as an occupation distinct from handlining and seining and trawling, it was expected of a son that he would become a lobsterman, too, that he would continue the tradition, the profession of his father. With that mandate, small boys started very young to learn their trade. The transfusion of knowledge was subtle yet exceedingly effective. The psychological weaning of the son from his mother was not a deliberate and conscious power play by the lobsterman father, but one of subsistence and survival that had uncanny resemblances to the natural world of animals. Just as a mother seal trained her pup to select the right fish to eat by diving with the infant and ignoring the bad fish, so did the father lobsterman take his son to sea and teach him the differences between survival and death.

The fisherman of a few decades back ignored the rules of social and community order if those rules conflicted with his own. School was a good example. Many lobstermen viewed school as something for their sons to attend when not needed in fishing. When a time conflict arose, the father, now the very dominant parent, would simply ignore the laws of schooling and use his son to fulfill the family obligations—the world according to father.

Even when the son did attend school, there was no such thing as extracurricular activities. To school and to home was the daily ritual. Straight home. The son had the importance of time instilled within him from a very early age. The fisherman's life is predetermined in great measure by the tides of the day influenced by the phases of the moon. The lobstermen of the future learned before they were five years old of the earth, sun, and moon effects on their watered life. They heard their fathers speak of the moon cycles, and that the tide follows the moon, and the ranges of spring and neap tides. The colloquial language of the sea was established almost before the alphabet.

One lobsterman tells in uncanny clarity how his grandfather read to him at night from a special book. A very special book that was kept in his grandfather's sea locker at the foot of his bed. At night, when the day's chores were over, the grandfather would say, "What say we read from the book." And the fisherman-to-be would climb into his grandfather's lap and rest his head on Gramp's chest just below the billowing calabash pipe filled with cut tobacco.

The book was covered in brown leather, and scarred as only old brown leather can be scarred. And wrinkled old. There was no title or writing on the back or front, only on the binding spine. There was just a small red strip outlined in narrow gold borders. It said, "Blount's Coast Pilot, Seventeenth Edition." But the book required no title. It was the world inside that mattered. And the grandfather read the inside title page every night before starting an adventure. The boy remembered a half century later. "The American Coast Pilot; Containing Directions For The Principal Harbors, Capes and Headlands On The Coast of North and South America. Describing the Soundings, Bearings, of the Lighthouses And Beacons From The Rocks, Shoals, Ledges, &c. With The Prevailing Winds, Setting Of The Currents, &c. And The Latitudes and Longitudes Of The Principal Harbors And Capes; Together With A Tide Table. Published By Edmund and George Blount, 179 Water Street, Corner Of Burling Slip, New York, May, 1854."

If there ever was an introduction to the adventures and mysteries of life promised to a boy fisherman, this was it. He learned of his own harbors and ports and the vagaries of tides and currents. How, if you were running into Penobscot Bay at night, you had better not attempt going through Muscle Ridge, that your best way is to go by Two Bush Island, which you must leave on your larboard hand keeping the course E.N.E. And Gramps read how Two Bush Island is round and barren but has only one bush on it. Formerly it had two bushes. The boy fisherman thought about that missing bush for many, many nights lying awake in his bunk bed.

There were faraway places only realized in dreams. They became real in Gramps' book. The Manheigan Light, the Penmequid Point Light, Long Island Sound, and Plum Island Light. There were Charleston Harbor and the main bar of Cape Fear

River. There were the shoals named Rebecca and grounds called Gingerbread and keys like Gun. There were islands named Serpent and Sapello and hooks called Sandy. And breakers, breakers, everywhere.

The best adventures were rounding, rounding this point and that river mouth and the best rounding of all, passage round Cape Horn. His favorite reading, and grandfather's too—Gramps never tired of the recitation. The boy remembers the beginning. "Ships bound from the Atlantic to any of the Ports of the Pacific will find it advantageous to keep within 100 miles of the coast of Eastern Patagonia as well to avoid the heavy sea that is raised by the westerly gales."

Later, many readings later, Gramps and boy would each take a ship around the Horn. One night Gramps would take his ship through the Strait le Maire and the boy would take the alternate route around Staten Island. They would meet once they passed the meridian of Cape Piller—probably meridian 82 degrees—and have a mug-up to discuss the passage. And then it was to bed to dream the passage once more, once more.

That lobsterman of today recalling his grandfather's bedtime readings refreshes his memory at times because grandfather left him that leather-scarred book in his one-page will when he died. With it was the advice that he pass his love to another generation.

It is difficult in this day and age to imagine a preschool boy experiencing such a family occurrence, much less trying to fathom that a small child could comprehend those readings. But they did. Along with the discipline and drudgery fostered upon a boy child, there was always a dose of that adventure of the sea, that secrecy of the unknown, that puzzlement of ships disappearing over the horizon. It was no wonder that by the time boys gained the strength to tackle hard labor, they were definitely dedicated to the water.

Boy lobstermen began hard work about the time they entered their teens. Fathers did make holes in school curriculum, but they couldn't make the schoolhouse disappear. Education has built-in voids called vacations, and fathers usurped these in short order. Holidays and midwinter times were taken up with the teachings of trap building and boatbuilding and a hundred maintenance chores required around fishing gear that takes a salt bath half of every year.

The teaching method then and now is a show-and-learn affair with the father showing his son, quite methodically, the ways "things" are to be done. The boy is then on his own, and father will rarely offer advice unless the lesson is hopeless. Boys, for instance, are never shown twice how to knit a bait bag. "Is this it, Dad?" Or, "I got it right this time, Pop?" is invariably answered with a "nope" or "yep." Knitting 50 wrong-way bait bags can do something for the powers of concentration when the next lesson rolls around.

How soon a boy goes fishing "for himself" depends on factors in the family order. One of these is the mother. Although relinquishing her son to her husband as a

Knitting bait bags

working companion is one thing, the mother usually has a "say" when her child goes alone down to the sea. More often than not, in days gone by, it was a silent protest in keeping with the role of a lobsterman's wife, but subtle pressure and influence were virtues inherent in most fishermen's wives. And although most sons left the nest and willingly accompanied their fathers to the sea school of learning, some preferred the shore life, and these sons would turn to their mothers for help. The controversy was almost always solved or debated within the confines of the home, for being a "mama's boy" was an image unbecoming any member of any family living in a fishing community. But mama had her say, one way or the other, and many a young boy has been saved from spending a tortured life, a hated life, in his watery prison.

The teen lobsterman begins with the inevitable skiff and small outboard, but the starting gate is jammed with all manner of craft. A few young men jump into lobstering with complete financial abandon, going for the big-time inboard boat and lobster gear to match. Dad is usually the backer or at least the cosigner at the community bank. Other, less reckless young fishermen buy used boats and gear or "buy out" a fisherman who is "putting it on the bank" either because of age, lagging enthusiasm, or money woes.

Whatever his entry level, the young fisherman, because of his community status and having spent a few years with the old man, does not have the territorial problems associated with a stranger. Waters and ground fished by the father are inherited by the son, who may or may not expand his fishing territory to include some ledges and kelp beds and "ground" of his own. Once on his own, however, he is treated with the same competitive tolerance as any other lobsterman, even by his father. Setting traps too close, dumping excessive gear on good common ground, or, heaven forbid, molesting gear, is dealt with as if the family did not exist. "Every man for himself" is hardly a meaningless cliche in lobstering. Lobstering anecdotes are common concerning father-son friendships turning downright ugly and even causing lifelong intrafamily splits. And in most cases, it is the mother who suffers disproportionately from the harsh, unbending rules of lobstering. Not that the rules are absolute, and many an evening ashore is consumed in the father-to-son lectures on lobstering responsibilities.

Young lobstermen in recent years have joined the moving-out generation when it comes to speed on the water. Outboards up to 200 h.p. are used by teenage fishermen on seemingly ridiculous boats. Imagine those power plants bolted to the stern of a 19-foot boat. With the throttle only half open, nothing but the prop touches the water. You could set up camp under the hull, there is so much room.

"Sufferin' Jaysus," said one old-timer watching the kids return to the harbor after a day's lobstering. "They're gettin' back 'fore they're goin' out."

Fathers rarely interfere with a son's gear purchases once they start fishing on their own. Dad may wince when Junior bolts that Mercury mill on his transom, but there is no "take that goddamn thing back or else" attitude. One reason is that fathers have almost absolute faith in the seamanship of their sons. Two hundred horsepower or three, father lobstermen have a pragmatic mind set that sons have the inherent knowledge to recognize the moods of the sea and handle their boats accordingly. After all, who taught them?

Although the young lobsterman is an integral part of the family life until he finishes school or is old enough, usually 18, to drop out, his finances are his own. Incidentally, many young islanders are faced with a schooling problem when they reach the secondary school level. It happens about the same time they are beginning to lobster alone. A few islands on which lobstering is the only income of consequence have only primary grade schools. No high school. Three examples are Frenchboro (Long Island), Matinicus, and the Cranberry Isles. The state subsidizes these students to attend mainland high schools, but they must board and live on the mainland. There is usually a traumatic shock within the family when a teenager leaves for the mainland to live during his academic months. These are the first times away from home for close-knit, sensitive kids, and even though some reside with relatives, the parting is difficult. Also, the spring and fall months are good lobstering times as well as school-keeping times. These sons of fishermen forfeit a head start and are confined to the vacation lobstering of June through August.

Through the period up to, perhaps, about 1956, a young fisherman contributed his share of earnings to the family financial pool. And a lot of them still do. But increasingly, the beginning lobsterman is an enterprising entity with a bank number of his own. He is an unquestionable saver—saving for a boat, saving for a pickup, saving for a 140 h.p. Merc. It would seem that the cash-only nature of the lobstering industry would be too great a temptation for so young a mind. But frugality is also taught by fathers along with knitting bait bags. They are not selfish, these emerging lobstermen, and the industry is one of the very few where teenage boys—young, developing professionals engaged in hard, manual, proletarian labor—regularly give their mothers new washing machines or living room sofas and their fathers new TVs and sets of snow tires and their sisters new sleds and fluffy Snoopy toy dogs for bedroom companions.

Bank managers in small fishing communities will confirm that there is hardly any risk in giving a young fisherman reasonable credit. One said, "I remember cases where youngsters took days off from fishing to come in and see me about one problem or another. That's unusual. Even adults find that difficult."

The subject of drugs is a legitimate point of discussion when analyzing the Maine lobster industry and the teenagers and adults that comprise the workers. The Maine coast, for all its independence-loving inhabitants, is not immune to the use and trafficking of narcotics. The geography alone lends itself to smuggling. The coast was a haven for "rumrunners" during the years of Prohibition. Maine fishermen were undeniably entwined in the logistics of moving contraband alcohol from the offshore waters into the tidal coves and mysterious inlets that puncture the coast like saltwater fingers. After all, what better people to ensure safe passage of illicit goods than those who know the waters and tides and secret ways of the mighty ocean where it meets the immovable land? There is hardly a coastal community in Maine that does not display material edifices from those rumrunning days. Historians write of churches and parish buildings constructed and maintained by demon rum, as the pious congregated flocks called the distilled spirits of molasses.

Rumrunning, however, was a specialized vocation. Some called it a sport. And it's doubtful that the bona fide lobsterman was that involved with smuggling. For several reasons. Their boats were small and slow, hardly capable of running to, and waiting on, the three-mile-limit boundaries where transfers usually took place. Even if the occasional lobsterman did venture to sea, and it was the big sea to him, his boat could hardly carry much of a load. The big boats were favored. Also, in rumrunning, the intrepid smuggler did not just steam out to the territorial sea and hail a rum boat. Contacts were made, sources confirmed, middlemen consulted—all very business-like. Conveying the coveted alcohol into the Colonies became a very professional industry.

Lobstermen were no more virtuous than the rest of the fishing flock, and many, seeing more profits in a night than they earned all year dunking traps, said to hell with fishing and went full-time smuggling. A rumrunner sternman seems a little comical, but that's what a lobsterman usually became if he left his fishing heritage. Few had the boats to compete, but then again, many, in a rather short time, did accumulate enough money to buy a rumrunner that could stay away from the "revenooers." Sternman to captain was a commonplace, rapid advancement. Government records seem to confirm that rumrunning was an exclusive adult occupation, one that fathers rarely exposed their sons to. It was not ethical, albeit the local pastor never turned an eyebrow when unexpected large sums of money appeared in his collection plate soon after a lovely, calm, moonless night. Sons were ignored in the smuggling business. The lobsterman was a pragmatist and knew that rumrunning was a short-term adventure and offspring should be versed in an occupation that had a bit more stability and longevity to it. Also, wives and mothers emerged from their passive roles in the community and forbade their sons any participation with the criminal elements.

The role of rumrunner, therefore, was usually occupied by the ex-fisherman, the ex-lobsterman. These men were not the unsavory characters of the community, but leaders, the pillars in some instances, such as selectmen, merchants, and even school overseers. Their rationale, and usually the acceptive philosophy of the community as well, was that strong drink was nothing new to the world's human inhabitants and certainly not to the small fishing villages on the coast of Maine. The immorality of smuggling alcohol was not apparent or relevant, the laws of the country to the contrary. It was not like stealing. Or uprooting fence posts. Or cheating the shoemaker. Rumrunning was not within the sphere of badness. One old-timer who remembers those exciting days said this:

"Some of us never drank, the missus would've skun me anyway, she could smell rum a mile away. But she didn't say nothing when we left just after dark n'returned home just 'fore daylight. And on Sundays the preacher always said a prayer we could all understand, maybe not a stranger, that asked the Lord t'keep us safe in the night. Hell damn, there wa'nt nobody out there in the night but us rum boats—less it was revenooers n'he sure as hell wa'nt praying for them. They didn't throw nothing inta the plate. We started a library on rumrunning money, we all kicked in, the thing t'do. We always took care of the poor, too. Kicked in there, too. Once a widow, I ain't saying no names, of course, fell on hard times n'was gonna lose her house n'we all chipped in n'bought out the mortgage so's she could pay us anytime she got a chance. She never did, of course, but that's no matter. If'n anybody got caught, n'some did, then we stood by him no matter what. Paid his fine, goes without saying, n' on the rare time that somebody went t'jail, well, we all chipped in there, too. Helped the family along. There wa'nt no club or organization or anything, we all just got together n'talked it over n' anted up. Hardest part was when someone got caught n'lost his boat 'cause the revenooers took away the boats there at the last of it. First, they didn't, just fined us, but later it got a little rougher. Got shot at sometimes, we did. My brother got shot right in the ass. T'was funny at the time. He couldn't sit down for a month. Government man came around n' asked my brother's wife how come he was limpin' around 'cause they knew that he was in that shootout. We didn't shoot, no guns, just the revenooers, n'my brother's wife said the billy goat nailed him. Federal man said, sure, sure, but they never proved nothing. Sure we made pretty good money. Depended on the trip n'the mother ship n'brand of stuff, but it was generally $25 a case. Once, for some high-class Scotch, I got $75 a case. When Prohibition was over in '33, me n'my brother went back lobstering. He still had a sore ass n'quit after a couple years. Said he couldn't stand the salt damp. Went to Florida, finally, where the sun helped his ass quite a bit. I lobstered right up 'til I couldn't haul much then gave it up. But you know, up in the attic there in my father's sea locker I got a bottle of demon rum—the missus don't know—that I saved from those rumrunning days. I figger when I'm about done in, I'm gonna go up and get that bottle n'swig it all down in one afternoon just t'see what in hell that Prohibition was all about."

Discounting adventure, which one shouldn't, it's easy to see the financial attraction for smuggling versus lobstering. In 1930, at mid-Prohibition, there were about 3,000 licensed lobstermen. They averaged 75 traps apiece and the average yearly catch per trap was 38 pounds—2,850 pounds per man per year. The lobstermen were paid 26¢ a pound in 1930, so the average annual income for lobstering was $740. A lobsterman could get the same payoff in one night running 30 cases of booze.

It's interesting to note, however, that in 1934, a year after Prohibition ended, there were almost the identical number of licensed lobstermen (3,000) landing less (886,955 pounds) for just 16¢ a pound. That year's landings were the lowest since

1899—the only time in this century, between 1900 and 1983, that lobster landings fell below a million pounds.

Statistically, it is apparent that Maine lobstermen did not rush into the profitable rumrunning business between 1922 and 1933, and obviously what did not enter could not leave.

Smuggling returned to the Maine coast in the 1970s in the form of narcotics and drugs, specifically marijuana and hashish. Harder drugs such as cocaine followed in the 1980s. Lobstering, of course, was an all-new ball game. In 1979, Maine's 8,361 licensed lobstermen landed 22,133,235 pounds for a value of $40,987,472. In the Maine coastal lobster fishery there were 7,478 vessels, each with an average of 326 traps aboard.

Nevertheless, the financial scale of temptation to smuggle illicit goods still paralleled the rumrunning days of the 1930s. Lobster fishermen had standing offers of between $25,000 and $50,000 for a one-night marijuana run with a 30- to 50-bale load—and that wasn't hay to a lobsterman netting about $15,000 a year. These lucrative smuggling opportunities continue into the mid-1980s. And yet, rarely is a working lobsterman caught smuggling dope. The reason can be traced back to the generic roots of lobstering families. In Maine fishing communities there is a strong resentment toward drugs. Not that the narcotic culture has bypassed coastal Maine, because one can find kids rolling joints behind just about any fish house. But the connotation of drugs versus alcohol strikes some puritanical strain that seems to run through Maine's provincial coastline. A bottle of beer and a slug of rum are accepted, albeit reluctantly in some households, but joints and roaches and pills and cocaine are not the stuff that fishermen are made of.

Drug smuggling on the Maine coast is commonplace, with truthful authorities admitting that less than 3 percent of dope runners are caught. And these are the stupid ones. Imagine steaming a foreign flag yacht up a small Maine river in the winter and trying to be coy and stealthy about it? Happens all the time. In these drug busts, there are men arrested with connections to the fishing industry, but invariably they are on the fringes, such as the fish trucker from Deer Isle who was busted in 1983, or the larger dragger-type boat owners and operators going bankrupt for one reason or another. Big-vessel mortgages run into the tens of thousands a month. No fish, same mortgage.

Lobstermen are approached, obliquely, and perhaps because of this roundabout procedure, lobstermen rarely turn in the inquisitors to the authorities. Coastal wardens are forever asking lobstermen about inquiries from strangers. And lobstermen shrug their shoulders. Their nature is not one of speculation about other people's motives. But perhaps the second greatest deterrent to joining the drug trade—after, and simply, roots—is the nature of the fishing community. Whatever one does in these small villages, which most lobster ports are, it is almost immediately known by everybody. And just about everything is tolerated. Extramarital affairs, drinking, even an occasional theft. But the rules and the laws of the sea are inviolable. Gear molestation is not tolerated, and invasions of historical territories are scorned. Trespasses are severely dealt with. If any person in a fishing community is running dope, the whole place knows about it. And reacts. In the case of the Deer Isle man accused of smuggling dope, a relative's pickup truck received several bullet holes in the night.

It is very doubtful that a lobsterman consistently participating in drug trafficking would be allowed to stay in that community. There are ways to persuade him to leave, including scuttling his boat on its mooring. It has happened more than once in the last few years. One lobsterboat was sunk not once, but twice. By innuendo and then by outright physical actions, the community as an enforcer will expel the lobsterman who abdicates his profession for illegal profits. Moving to another community will probably prove fruitless because of the communications network of the industry. What happens in Stonington this morning is known in Boothbay at noon.

Drug running has not been integrated into the Maine fishing community, but only time will tell if the future can handle the temptation. In fishing states to the south of Maine, there has been more and more involvement by fishermen in this practice. Maine fishermen, however, are primarily small-boat inshore fishermen, versus, say, the offshore fishermen of Massachusetts. The Bay State fishermen assume much larger mortgages, and perhaps, temptations. In Maine, the illicit drug trafficking is self-policing no matter what the law enforcement authorities claim. Without the participation of fishermen, it is doubtful that the colossal drug running problem encountered in other states will prevail on the coast of Maine.

The last real socioeconomic study of the Maine lobsterman was done by the University of Maine in 1970. Because of money restrictions and the time allotted (six weeks), it was decided not to tackle the industry as a whole but to concentrate on three lobster fishing communities. These were Corea, representing a highly specialized, isolated economy where lobstering was the predominant activity; Beals Island, again because it is a highly specialized lobster community, although less isolated than Corea; and lastly, Phippsburg, a lobstering port with a more diversified economy and a close proximity to alternative job opportunities. Each of the areas had one thing in common—the lobster fishery was the major economic activity.

Of 277 licensed lobstermen in those three communities, 131 were surveyed in the study using a questionnaire and personal interviews. The response rate was better than 90 percent.

The survey results indicated that the average age was 42.6 years and the average income was $6,213. Two-thirds of the fishermen said they went lobstering for the money. The rest wanted lobsters for home consumption only, or they lobstered out of a preference for the particular way of life. There was a scattering of other reasons such as "the old man made me." The average years of education was 9.8, and approximately 40 percent had less than a ninth year of education. However, 41 of the 131 fishermen indicated that they received some type of formal vocational training in such areas as carpentry, metalworking, and mechanics. When the questionnaire asked about preference for receiving vocational training, only a small fraction expressed any interest. Perhaps the fishermen thought they were being asked whether they could, in fact, "do" carpentry and mechanics and woodworking. Most lobstermen are jacks-of-all-trades.

There has been no socioeconomic survey comparable to the 1970 study done since then. The current lobster license application does not require the applicant to declare completed years of formal education, but in nearly a decade and a half the average school years most certainly have risen above a high school sophomore.

There aren't many fishermen around nowadays like Pit Ginnis. Pit was asked one time how far he went in school.

"Far's I could, sonny, far's I could."

"Whatcha mean by that, Pit, mean you went right up through college n'everything?"

"Goddamn right, sonny. Tell ya how it was. Began in the grammar school of spankings, woodbox fillings n'dory cleaning. Learned good. Went right on up t'the high school of fetchin' f'father, punt building, trap heading n'staying dry. Took an extra course there, gettin' wet. From there went right up t'the college of hard knocks. Been knocking around ever since. Get my sheepskin every night I make it home safe and sound."

And there are some still, who like Pit, live by their wits.

A lobstering community is comprised of both full- and part-time lobstermen. There is no absolute handle on who's who. There are some educated and uneducated guesses as to the percentage makeup, and the spread is considerable. One study found that only about 17 percent of commercial lobstermen surveyed in four Maine communities fished over 150 days a year. According to statistics compiled by the National Marine Fisheries Service in 1983 for inclusion in the American Lobster Fishery Management Plan, Maine had 3,409 full-time and 4,952 part-time or casual lobstermen. In other words, 41 percent of lobstermen are full-time. Whether NMFS defines "full-time" as fishing 150 days or more a year, or just what criterion does designate that category, is not revealed. In Maine, however, inshore lobstermen who do not work outside their profession, at any other job, can hardly support that 41 percent figure. The very nature of the inshore fishery predetermines that a lobsterman could not physically fish year-round. The lobsters are not there. The weather is. And so shore jobs are sought.

One of the coveted jobs along the Maine coast is that of caretaker for the "summer people." Hundreds of sou'westers have been permanently hung up on the hallway peg when an opportunity for a caretaker job came up. They are coveted for many reasons. Although the jobs are not particularly well paying, neither is the work that strenuous. It consists primarily of opening the "cottage" in the spring, maintaining the dwelling(s) and grounds in the summer, and closing in the fall. Summer folk are usually in residence for about a month only. The rest of the time the caretakers work on pretty much puttering-around schedules.

The best positions include a house within the "compound," the utilities expenses going with the job. Handed the amenities of a prepaid roof over their heads, plus cash for being there, it's a wonder that fishermen don't queue up by the miles for caretakers' jobs.

Another reason is that the jobs, once landed, are generally passed down through families like a precious heirloom. Father caretaker, son caretaker. It's a rare son that turns down the opportunity to take over the big house and opts instead for filling smelly bait bags and hawking lobsters. Sons do, however, apprentice into this position, and during school vacation they will work with their fathers and even run a small string of traps. The catch is usually sold via fathers to their summer employers. Lobster cars are kept tied to floats and landings and stocked with fresh lobsters for the inevitable tens of lobster feeds at the "big house" during the summer occupancy. Caretaking jobs sometimes include entire families. Father in permanent employ, son helping dad with the maintenance during vacation, and mother and daughter working as cook and maid and getting the cottage "ready" in early summer and closed in early fall.

The ex-lobsterman-turned-caretaker oftentimes runs the estate boat as part of his duties. And in other situations, ex-lobstermen convert to exclusive boat captains. The summer folk do not generally stray far from their compounds either by land or by sea. But they sometimes have rather large and expensive craft to ply the home waters. Enough of a vessel to require a captain who assumes fitting-out command plus seagoing expertise when the folks take their daysails around the islands and bay. The logistics of a summer-folk daysail command professional help for a range of tasks from lightering aboard refreshments and people to providing a running bus-tour commentary for the guests. What better character for the position than an ex-lobsterman?

In the communities that are made up of local and summer folk, there is a distinct and accepted dividing line. There is a peaceful, passive, respectful cleavage between the two types of dwellers. Lobstermen do frequently take out summer folk on day lobstering trips, but the association does not extend to any social friendships or even infrequent visits between "those from away" and those that work and stay. There are two defined sanctuaries, both privileged and honored. The lobsterman and his wife do not attend the summer folk cocktail party, nor do the vacationers sit and drink coffee by the native kitchen Clarion.

Children from both sides of the fence are taught this at an early age. The lessons were learned well in the decades up to the 1950s, but there have been some problems with the loose social structures of modern times. One of the worst horrors that could be imagined by a summer-folk father wa that his Wellesley freshman daughter might be deflowered during summer vacation in Maine by the local teenage lobsterman. Summer dads have always realized that daughters have a fascination for young lobstermen in their damned independent ways flitting about like oversexed mosquitoes. But there are fewer and fewer whole flowers among Wellesley freshmen these days, and summer dad's lecture to offspring takes on the newer tack that falling in love with Eben the lobsterman and living the rest of your life among bait bags will be purgatory.

Home and away loves that do manage to bloom among the rich downeast humus generally fail to consummate in anything but tearful love letters going on until Thanksgiving, with solace from parents who have returned from shore to city life that, "Honey, this will all be over and you will forget about him soon."

There are occasional case stories from the lobstering circuit involving intersocial sexualizing between home and away adults, and the consequences are far more disastrous. It is rumored, just that of course, that a rather massive shingled summer cottage burned to the ground in less than 10 minutes when the summer owner-gentleman began to pay considerably more attention to a lobsterman's wife than was called for in the rules of summertime fair play. The volunteer fire department, in fact, never responded, despite the fire chief having been ashore resting for the day.

There is common and acceptable cruising ground for the home folk and the aways. One is the public supper. All Maine communities, be they marine or meadow, have public suppers. Some are "put on" apparently for no good reason. Others are a benefit to prop up the financial ruins of a member of the community who may have been burned out, drowned out, or plain tuckered out. There isn't much in the way of advance notice of a public supper except word of mouth, and that's probably just fine with everybody.

Summer folk plainly love local public suppers, although they are never, but never, included in the solicitation of food. And although there may appear to be chaos in the public-supper spectacle, it is in fact run with the precision of a Marine brigade.

The person soliciting the food and handling general operations is the Commander-in-Chief, a position that is inherited. This victual General will know each local woman's capacity for cookery. She does not call on a sour-apple-pie maker for pastries or a runny-casserole concocter for scalloped dishes. Each housewife is tapped for her best. If a housewife had a mealy potato harvest in her garden, the General knows it, and mashed potatoes do not come from that quarter. And a housewife would not be asked, for instance, to provide a scalloped clam dish if her husband dug water-belly clams.

The General also commands the kitchen corps, and there is status associated with this seemingly routine KP operation. It is organized along the lines of an army platoon. There is the Top Sergeant, whose duty is to wield a big spoon. She nibbles the meat, slurps the soup, pinches the rolls, and dispatches condiments to her personal satisfaction.

The turnip masher and potato whipper are long-standing areas of experience. Not

everybody could mash a turnip for a public supper. Left-handed mashers are more in demand than right for some strange reason.

Head-of-Pies is almost a commissioned officer. Her performance is often the critical stroke that saves a drowning supper. She is a sculptress possessed with an uncanny eye for measurement. Unassisted by any foolishness such as mechanical pie cutters, her miter-box sight cleaves wedges to the sixteenth of an inch. Allocation is within her authority also. The kids at the end of the table do not get chocolate cream, nor does the first selectman or prominent summer folk get even a slight glance at a crumbling graham cracker or sagging squash.

The Meat Slicer is just below Head-of-Pies in rank. She must possess many of Pie's assets plus more or less of a blacksmith's knowledge of stone and steel.

176

The waitresses are the privates of the public supper. They come under the jurisdiction of the Chief in the table of organization. Often recruited haphazardly, they are treated with tolerance by the Chief. Only when gross bobbles are committed will the Chief intervene. A patron receiving a lap full of gravy from a private waitress will not usually have time to utter a syllable before the Chief is by his side with a four-foot Turkish towel and a select wedge of Boston cream pie.

The Ticket Seller comprises the Chief's entire financial section. Not especially a position of importance, the Ticket Seller is usually a busted Meat Slicer who left the string on the roast beef. She sits with countenance demure behind a shaky card table at the portal to the public supper, dispensing reusable hand-printed meal tickets.

Meshed among the positions of trust, the Commander-in-Chief has numerous fledglings such as napkin runners, coffee refillers, sugarers, creamers, dropped-fork replacers, and pie fetchers. All these proletarian categories are filled exclusively from the native labor pool. There has not been a documented case of a summer folk ever regularly staffing at local suppers. A couple of guest appearances, maybe.

When the last supper patron has loosened his belt a peg or two and departed, the Chief supervises cleanup maneuvers. Pot wallopers swing into sudsy action. Floor sweepers and table cleaners know their appointed tasks. The hall now shipshape, the Chief allots leftover grub to the worthy, pulls the puckering strings on the canvas sack containing the "proceeds," and follows her troops out the door to their respective billets.

Summer folk absolutely marvel at the local efficiency talent displayed at public suppers.

Only one other home-and-away confrontation of any importance occurs. This is the annual volunteer firemen's fund drive, which conveniently coincides with the time in summer when summer folk occupancy is greatest. There are two types of solicitation. One is cold cash, and summer folk fall all over themselves writing out checks, usually generous. The other is goods for the firemen's auction. There have been goods donated to local firemen's auctions by summer folk that would make an antique dealer turn forever green. Local fishermen families are not much taken with such collectibles as period wicker furniture, for instance, and what would bring $500 on the New York market goes for $5 at the local fire department sale.

For any coastal Maine lobsterman there is a hiatus. Even the hardy few that fish offshore take a break. The inshore fisherman usually has his gear on the bank by December, and setting out does not commence until April, sometimes May. When scallops were fairly abundant, the lobsterman would re-rig his boat with winch, wire, and scallop dredge. Throughout the winter months—scalloping is legal from November 1 to April 15—inshore scalloping could be quite lucrative. That industry started to decline in 1970 and has gotten progressively worse since.

Lobstermen also turn to shrimping in the winter. The Northern shrimp, or *Pandalus borealis*, comes inshore to colder waters to spawn starting about December, and lobstermen convert to dragging with small otter trawls. In recent years there has developed a substantial shrimp fishery using wire traps that are somewhat similar to the lobster trap. The boat need not be converted because the traps are hauled with the same hydraulic hauler. Lines, or pot warps, are taken from the lobster gear and used on the shrimp traps. Shrimp-trap fishermen were receiving about 70¢ a pound in the winter of 1984.

One problem with shrimping, however, is that it is either offshore or confined primarily to the midcoastal area. The Boothbay-Sheepscot River area is the center of the shrimping industry, probably because of the large river systems that feed fresh water to these coastal waters, giving them a lower sea temperature than many other

178

parts of the coast. Whatever the reason, there is little shrimping in the Washington or Hancock County areas, which could use an alternative winter fishery.

The lobstermen, except those in the mosquito fleet, rarely turn to clam digging or worming. It is somewhat beneath the status of a lobsterman to dig in the mudflats. Besides, clammers and wormers are a breed apart and they probably wouldn't allow lobstermen into their exclusive brotherhood.

If a lobsterman doesn't switch fish, then he either gets a shore job or works his gear. Most work their gear. Because of the weather and outside winter storage, boats are usually left for springtime. But there are traps to be built. Fish houses become brotherhood lodges. "Fish house" is a generic term meaning any place with a stove, workbench, and just enough room to store some trap-building materials. Fish houses can be on wharves, in the barn, in the garage, or even the kitchen.

The role of the cooperative is very important in the lobsterman's life. In 1976 there were about 20 cooperatives along the Maine coast. They were almost all lobster co-ops. The oldest was the Pemaquid Fisherman's Cooperative Association organized in 1947, followed by the Stonington Co-op in 1949. Stonington was the largest with 164 members. The smallest was in Winter Harbor with 19 members. There has been a considerable increase in membership in all Maine co-ops during the early 1980s.

The co-ops are incorporated, with officers, a board of directors, and a manager. Some are affiliated with the Maine Lobstermen's Association and some are not. Either way, they usually have a credit union, group life and sickness insurance, and considerable clout when it comes to boat insurance. P&I insurance for commercial fishing vessels is quite expensive, but an agency looking at the premium of, say, 95 boats (in Stonington's case), can offer a more attractive rate than for a single fisherman.

The larger co-ops sometimes operate more than one buying station and market their own lobsters, sometimes out of state via their own trucks. All have some kind of storage facilities, either inside tanks or outside tidal pounds. Inside tanks are desirable because the lobsters can be graded to size and sold in categories (chicken, halfs, etc.) adding to the overall price. Without tanks for "culling," the lobsters are sold "boat run," which means less per overall poundage.

As a business corporation, the fishing co-ops buy in quantity, which includes just about everything marine from trap-building supplies to gloves. Merchandise is sold to members only at enough of a markup to cover expenses. The lobsterman is morally obligated to sell all his lobsters to the co-op, which pays, in cash, near the going price. At the end of the year, however, after business expenses are paid, the co-op members receive a bonus of so much per pound that they sold to the co-op. It can be as small as 2¢ a pound and occasionally more. In bad years, or with unforeseen capital expenditures, there is no bonus.

A fisherman is not obliged to join a co-op, and more do not than do. They prefer their independent marketing freedoms and sell to private buyers, which are usually set up right in the same harbors as the co-ops. The private buyers usually pay more per pound, but there is, obviously, no year-end bonus.

The key to a viable co-op is the manager, and they have a working longevity equal to a combat Marine platoon leader. Shepherding a flock of 50 independent lobstermen all with separate ideas on what gloves the co-op should buy, what trap nails, what brand of boat paint or even candy bars, has driven co-op managers literally crazy after only a few months on the job. And like a wounded animal, once down, the manager is defenseless. Aldo Ciome ran the Stonington Co-op for many years. His success seemed to be in allowing free discussion from all quarters and then he—and only he, goddamnit!—made the decision. If they didn't like it, they could get a new manager. Respecting Aldo's business sense made the Stonington Co-op probably the most successful in Maine.

Some co-ops are low key, preferring it that way. A clubby self-help organization banded together for selfish business reasons and caring hardly a whit if the co-op makes money or not. Others, like the Boothbay group, even expand into a retail, summertime take-out and picnic-table-lobster-bake-on-a-wharf outfit.

But the road of lobster co-ops is not paved with golden coins. In a word, almost every co-op is undercapitalized. They have little operating capital and no prospects for getting any. Starting up today is almost impossible. Shore property and wharf sites, which are imperative, start at $250,000 in any cove or harbor worth its salt. Co-ops need buildings and supplies and bait—all the investments of business establishments—which means borrowing money. The trouble is, lobstering is seasonal, and making bank payments in January is tough. Sometimes inter-co-op fights gets downright dirty, and lobstermen jump ship and "sell across the harbor." Losing a captive membership can be curtains.

Besides co-ops, fishermen join other self-help organizations. There are two lobstermen's associations in Maine—the southern or western group and the Maine Lobstermen's Association, which is, by far, the larger, with about 1,000 members.

The MLA has a full-time executive director, a former lobsterman, who handles the lobbying and other daily tasks. Incidentally, the MLA board of directors allows the executive director to fish 50 lobster traps, apparently to "keep his hand in." The MLA dues are $35 a year, for which the MLA lists several benefits of membership: representation in Augusta, legal counsel on retainer, fishermen's credit union, group health and life insurance, disability income insurance, and hull insurance. The executive director lives and works from Stonington, but the MLA has a midcoast office in Damariscotta staffed by a secretary.

The MLA offers nothing that a local co-op couldn't supply to its membership except perhaps full-time lobbying at the state capitol and before legislative hearings. The MLA is very active in this field and authors several self-interest legislative

Rigged for scalloping

proposals each session, sometimes in concert with the Department of Marine Resources and sometimes in opposition to DMR. A recent cooperative effort in special interest was the formulation of a program of limited entry into the lobster fishery by requiring a mandatory apprenticeship course for all new persons entering the fishery.

As noted previously, the MLA is primarily an organization with an eastern-area fishermen's base. Membership figures indicate a large majority in the Washington-Hancock area, the birthplace of the MLA. The group strongly supports trap limits, which the southern-western lobstermen do not.

Coastal communities in which fishing is the primary economic factor are "quite religious," a downeast designation meaning that the fundamentalist denominations—Nazarene, Church of God, Pentecostal, Baptist, and Seventh Day Adventist—are the dominant congregations. But there are Roman Catholics, Episcopalians, Congregationalists, Unitarians, Mormons, Christian Scientists, Jews, Lutherans, Greek Orthodox, and members of some sects peculiar to Maine such as the Bullockites, a society of primitive Baptists. Another sect was the Higginsites of Carmel, named for its leader the Rev. Higgins. The good reverend was accustomed to driving the devil from the children of his sect by whipping them. Alas, finally his fellow citizens applied tar and feathers and escorted him from town. The colony expired. Then there was Cochranism, named for a Scotch-Irish preacher whose followers gathered in the woods each Sunday, joined hands, and sang songs and performed dances. Perhaps Rev. Cochran was a little ahead of his time. He eventually packed up his free-love religion and headed west, leaving the puritanical Mainers back where they belonged.

A really bizarre religious group is connected with one of Maine's most famous lobstering villages, Jonesport. In 1866, a rogue and discredited Mormon named Adams formed the Palestine Emigration Association. And in that year, he and 156 followers—men, women, and children—left Jonesport for the Holy Land. According to recorded history, he "proposed to commence the great work of restoration foretold by the old prophets, patriarchs and apostles as well as by our Lord Himself." Darned if the group didn't actually found a colony near Jaffa. Leading a Mainer to Israel was one thing, surviving in that harsh land was another. They encountered nothing but grief. The leader, Adams, "took up strong drink," and within a year the group straggled home as best they could.

The Israeli experience didn't faze the Sandfordites, who sailed in three ships to Jerusalem. Their leaders told the flock that the Lord would provide for them. After sitting around for many weeks waiting for the Lord to provide, the very hungry Sandfordites returned to their temple, Shiloh, in Durham. The sect's leader, Parson Sandford, a rather convincing evangelist, was jailed and convicted of exploiting his flock, who were found in dire misery and poverty. Nevertheless, the sect, "Church of the Holy Ghost and Us" flourished at the turn of the century.

Maine was the first state to have a radio parish. It was founded in 1926 by the Rev. Howard O. Hough for "shut-ins," and it was interdenominational in character. And the widely known Seacoast Mission headquartered in Bar Harbor operates the vessel *Sunbeam*, which brings religious, educational, hospital, and recreational facilities to the coastal communities, especially those on the offshore islands.

There are large populations of Catholics in Maine, but these are located not along the coast but rather inland in cities like Waterville and Lewiston and in Aroostook County. The predominantly Protestant coastal people did not start out that way. The first Christian missionary was the Jesuit Nicholas d'Aubri, who preached to the Indians at Douchet Island in the St. Croix River in 1604. Jesuit churches and schools were built, and most Abenaki Indians were converted to Christianity by the early missionaries. Almost all present-day Indians are Catholic.

It is a fact, however, that there are 1,500 churches representing 26 denominations in Maine. And it's probably fair to assume that fishermen and their families are represented in all of them.

Fishermen are also in the mainstream of service clubs in the state. There are about 200 of these, including the familiar Rotary, Lions, Kiwanis, Elks, Knights of Columbus, Odd Fellows, VFW, and American Legion. It seems that one community will have a very active, say, Odd Fellows, while another will involve just about everyone in American Legion activities. It's safe to say that the clubs that meet at noontime, such as the Rotary, have mostly retired fishermen. It's tough to schedule viable lobstering around docktime every Wednesday noon. The VFW and Legion dances, usually held on a Saturday night, are the liveliest game in town in many places.

Another surprising focus of community participation is the Granges, which one usually associates with farming families. However, there are 600 local Granges throughout the state and no dearth of these organizations along the coast. Although the first agricultural society was formed in Maine in 1818, the state did not become a part of the national Grange movement until 1867. Probably because there was no comparable social society for fishermen (and there is none today, either), and fishermen of that era were also part-time farmers, the Grange appealed to the community as a whole and not just to agricultural interests. It's entirely conceivable that the Grange Masters and Lecturers and Stewards and Pomonas and Floras in their ritual openings of the Grange meetings on Friday nights filled the halls with the earthly togetherness smells of manure and lobster bait. A homogenous mug-up.

Another "secret" order gaining much favor with fishermen is the Masons. This fraternity founded on a belief in God as the father of all men and the spreading of universal brotherhood is a distinctly British institution, although 18th century English writers in their convoluted efforts at historical midwifery have nearly obscured the birth of Freemasonry. But probably in some form the Masons were such about 1717. Considering the English and Irish ethnic components in the heritage of the Maine coast, it's not at all surprising that fishermen join this order. Masonry has had an interesting history in Maine. It was an exceedingly strong order, because of its English influence, well into the 19th century. When the cornerstone for the state capitol in Augusta was laid on July 4, 1829, the ceremonies were Masonic. But reformers emerged on the political scene about 1830, and one reform movement was anti-Masonry. The movement was so successful that Freemasonry nearly disappeared in Maine. In 1831, 1832, and 1833, anti-Masonic candidates entered the elections for governor. The political activists and their anti-Masonry crusade are mentioned in many histories of Maine communities. In one of the finest, *History of Belfast* by Joseph Williamson, there is this pertinent paragraph:

"The reputed murder of Morgan in the year 1826 near Ft. Niagara, N.Y. for divulging secrets of the order (Freemasonry) implicated the whole fraternity and for several years suspended its growth. So strong a current of feeling prevailed that it was turned to political purposes. A numerous anti-Masonic party was formed which sought ascendency, not only to several states, but in the general government."

Today, Masonic Lodges are alive, well, and claim among their membership a goodly representation of lobstermen.

Maine lobstermen are quite superstitious, although not to the degree of one character a few years ago who, seeing a seagull drop a clam from a height to break it open, would not go to sea that day fearing he would crash upon a ledge.

Some lobstermen seem always to stay ashore on Fridays, a traditional bad day among ancient sailors. The roots of the tradition, according to some historians, can be traced to Catholic priests who, out of respect for the day on which Christ was crucified, once urged seamen and fishermen not to sail until Saturday's dawn. When asked about this, one local modern-day lobsterman said, "Hell, no. I just get an early start on the weekend."

An old fisherman's superstition was that any bird following a boat was an ill omen. Obviously that fear has disappeared, if one can judge by the number of gulls in the wake of lobsterboats picking up old bait. However, a fish crow landing on a lobsterboat is something else again. These birds rarely do, but fishermen consider this unnatural and a very bad sign. One lobsterman sold his boat after watching this happen for a week. Perhaps the guy had read *Moby Dick*, in which Melville said it was an ill omen for ravens to perch on the masts of a ship at the Cape of Good Hope.

Animals play a part in fishermen's superstitions. Cats are reportedly always considered feminine and a breeder of bad weather. Every cat's action has significance. Her tail carries the wind, playing is provoking a storm, scratching a carpet is summoning a tempest, and crying in the night is calling for the witches. Cats are never a ship's mascot. If one happened to be on board, it was always someone's cat, never the ship's. Cats hang around fish houses and subsist on fish, but they never seem to belong to anybody.

Dogs are the opposite. Lots of lobstermen take their dogs along on their boats, especially the skiff fishermen. Dogs love to ride as far into the bow as they can get, usually standing up. Dogs meet their masters at the dock and walk home with them. Along the Maine coast a "dog navigator" is one who follows the sound of familiar dog barkings onshore when running in the fog.

Knots and hitches are superstitions. Moorings are tied the same way each day. Lines are made to a cleat in identical fashion year after year. Fishermen's wives tie their clotheslines the same way. And some detractors of lobstermen say that their children never learn to tie a bow in their shoelaces because there is no place in fishing for such a knot. Never learned to tie one.

Lobstermen rarely take women on their boats when working, although this is probably not superstition so much as a pragmatic avoidance of supercargo. After all, what use would a woman be aboard ship unless she was a working crew? There is, however, some basis for not carrying women aboard boats. In the days of yore and sailing ships, women were considered kittle cargoes—"kittle" meaning anything hard to handle. Sailors were very reluctant to sign on any vessel that carried the captain's wife. Such a ship was known as a "hen frigate," and supposedly the wife often countermanded the captain's orders, especially when it came to personal appearances.

Women might take some solace that sailors also considered ministers and lawyers as kittle cargoes; lawyers were especially hated by sailors, who usually only met them ashore and on the wrong end of some litigation.

Maine coastal communities are as varied as the weather that engulfs them. The ports with lobsters as an economic base share that common financial denominator, but each harbor and cove has its definable characteristics.

A sampler of these lobster communities from east to west:

Bucks Harbor is located about eight miles south of Machiasport on the west side of Machias Bay. This fishing area would also have to include Machiasport and Starboard Cove. Machiasport has a population of some 900 people. Bucks Harbor is the focus of the lobsterfishing with about 75 men involved in the fishery. There are about 40 lobsterboats in the 25- to 35-foot range and 20 outboard-powered skiffs in the lobster fleet. The two lobster buyers in Bucks Harbor include one fisherman's co-op. Each buyer has dock facilities, fuel, and supplies. There is also one tidal lobster pound in the harbor.

Jonesport and Beals (Island) are generally grouped together by the statisticians, a fact that doesn't sit too well with the two separate communities. But they are close. Jonesport is located about 32 miles west southwest of the Canadian border at Lubec. The town is on a peninsula some 10 miles south of U.S. Route 1. Jonesport is on the north shore of Moosabec Reach, and Beals Island is a separate township on the south side of the reach. The two towns are connected by a bridge that was built in 1957. In 1980 the population of Jonesport was 1,509 and Beals Island had 695 citizens. These two towns are located in one of the most isolated parts of the Maine coast, and fishing is the primary occupation of the area. There are an estimated 160 lobsterfishing boats in Jonesport-Beals, with about 100 owned by full-time lobstermen. The area fished by these lobstermen is large and productive, one of the best lobster-producing areas in the world. The fishermen range from 25 miles offshore to the ledges and rocks around Great Wass Island. There are five companies that buy lobsters, the largest being the Jonesport-Beals Fishermen's Cooperative. There is a Coast Guard station located here, as well as a few draggers and gillnetters.

Winter Harbor is a hamlet in the township of Gouldsboro on the west side of the same peninsula that shelters Corea and Prospect Harbor, also lobsterfishing communities. Winter Harbor is about three miles from the Schoodic Point segment of Acadia National Park. The 1980 census was 1,115 people. There are no individual plants in the town, but some residents travel to Prospect Harbor to work at the Stinson Canning Company plant. There is a detachment at the small Navy base. There are four stores, three restaurants, and a few "take-out" stands in the summer. There is only one commercial dock, which is operated by the Winter Harbor Fisherman's Cooperative. About 25 lobstermen fish from Winter Harbor, half of them full-time. Since no other buyer exists, all the lobsters are purchased by the co-op. In later years, the larger boats have been rigged for winter otter trawl fishing. A couple of boats re-rig for scalloping after lobstering season. This area, incidentally, supports about 140 clam diggers. The co-op is very active with about 22 members. In addition to purchasing lobsters from members, it also buys clams and fish and contracts to have the seafood trucked to Boston for sale.

Bass Harbor and Bernard are neighbors facing each other across a harbor that serves both. Both are part of the Town of Tremont, population 1,221, on the southwest corner of Mount Desert Island. The whole island, including Bass Harbor, has a large influx of tourists in the summer. The Tremont area, however, does not have many motels, restaurants or other facilities to serve the public. Bass Harbor has no large stores. It does have a state ferry terminal for the ferry running between the harbor and Swans Island and Frenchboro Long Island. The important industry in Bass Harbor is lobsterfishing. There are about 65 lobstermen, and most own inboard boats in the 30- to 45-foot range. There are three lobster buyers in the harbor. One of the companies purchases crabs from lobstermen and operates a crab-picking plant with an estimated 500,000 crabs picked annually yielding about 50,000 pounds of meat. It is one of the largest crabmeat operations on the coast.

Stonington/Deer Isle is an important lobsterfishing port. The towns are located on Deer Island, which is connected to the mainland by a high suspension bridge. Stonington is the commercial fishing center. Deer Isle is located at the northern end of the island and includes the towns of Little Deer Isle, Sunset, and Sunrise. The 1980 census of the island was 2,758. There are many wharves and piers available to fishermen. The Stonington business district is located on the waterfront and includes many small stores and shops. It is a decidedly proletarian town of fishermen and boatyard, fish-plant, and other "blue-collar" workers. There are probably about 300 lobstermen on the island. There is a lobster co-op, the largest in the state, and many other lobster buyers. There are tidal lobster pounds on Deer Isle plus a large boatyard and several boatbuilding shops. Although somewhat isolated—it's a 70-mile trip to most any town of any size—the people who live on the island are fanatical about their environment. Consequently the island has never been commercialized for the tourist industry, and it is probably Maine's only truly all-fishing community accessible by road. The range and diversification of fishing activities using the Port of Stonington make it unique in a unique industry.

Vinalhaven is a large island, about 32 square miles, located in the center of Penobscot Bay. It is 6½ miles due east of Owl's Head, the closest place on the mainland. The island is mostly independent of the mainland, however, with a small medical clinic, four grocery stores, two hardwood stores, a variety store, an electrical and plumbing shop, and two lobster trap stock mills. There is a company that supplies gas and heating oil. The island has both an elementary and high school with about 250 students regularly enrolled. The population is served with a 17-car state ferry making three runs a day in the summer and two in the winter. It has 10 miles of paved state-maintained roads and about 34 miles of road maintained by the town. There is also a private airfield. Vinalhaven has five anchorages, the most important being Carver's Harbor, which is bordered by the island town. About 150 lobstermen are located on the island, and a majority have inboard boats between 30 and 38 feet. There are large-skiff fishermen who have adapted their outboards with "power takeoffs" via the flywheel and hydraulics so that they can haul surprisingly large numbers of heavy traps. The island fishermen stay generally within the water confines of the island and rarely "mix fish" with lobstermen from, say, Stonington or Rockland. There are three lobster buyers on Vinalhaven, including the Vinalhaven Fishermen's Cooperative of about 25 members. Historically, Vinalhaven was known for its granite quarries and contributed to many beautiful buildings in the country. The 120-ton monoliths on three sides of the choir altar in the Cathedral of St. John the Divine, New York City, were quarried here. Strangely, the man for whom the island was named, John Vinal, never set foot on the island, but brought the petition of 1785 to the General Court of Massachusetts asking that the island and others in the Fox Island group be granted to the then-present settlers.

Rockland is a "big town." It is also a working and fishing city of 7,918 people. It is the fifth largest port in New England. Located on the west shore of Penobscot Bay about 80 miles northeast of Portland, the city has a very large harbor protected by a granite breakwater seven-tenths of a mile long. The harbor can get very rough, however, and the inner harbor is shallow away from channels. The port houses several large fish processing plants, a Coast Guard base, and a state ferry terminal. Surprisingly, there are only a few lobstermen—about 36, with fewer than 10 full-time. There are no lobster dealers buying from fishermen and no lobster cooperatives in Rockland. The fishermen of this port are almost totally engaged in trawler fishing, herring fishing, or other large-vessel enterprises such as supplying menhaden to the fish reduction plant in the summer months. Rockland was once widely known as the "Lobster Capitol of Maine," but the title has gradually eroded.

Port Clyde and Tenants Harbor: These two fishing communities are located south of Rockland in the township of St. George, and fishing is the largest single occupation in both places. About 600 people live in Port Clyde and 375 in Tenants Harbor. Both have well-protected anchorages. There are 72 active lobstermen in the two ports, with over half full-time. Lobstermen from Tenants Harbor and Port Clyde each have their own lobstering areas. Fishermen from Port Clyde have an area that extends out to Allen's Island and Burnt Island but does not extend west to McGee and Gay islands, which are controlled by Pleasant Point fishermen. Tenants Harbor lobstermen fish the area between Martinsville and Rackliff Island. There are four lobster buying companies in the two harbors, and Port Clyde has a lobster co-op.

South Bristol is an 800-person town at the end of the Pemaquid peninsula, a few miles east of Boothbay Harbor. One who has traveled through it cannot forget its fishing character and the small swing bridge that operates right in the middle of the village, where one could step from the road right aboard a boat going through the Gut. There are about 60 lobstermen here, with a lobster co-op and three lobster buyers. The famous Harvey Gamage shipyard is located in this town, but the majority of local men are engaged in the fishing trade. Several lobstermen re-rig their boats in the fall and go groundfishing or scalloping.

Boothbay Harbor is a must stop for tourists who make annual pilgrimages to Maine. A peninsula town, it is a separate municipality from all the rest that surround the area. The whole economy of Boothbay Harbor is based on tourism, fishing, and boatbuilding. The town has an excellent large and protected deep-water harbor, and is a port of call for just about every Maine coast cruising boat. As for lobster fishermen, there are some 60 with about 25 of them year-round. Many of the lobstermen convert to shrimp trapping in January. There are a fishermen's co-op and three lobster buyers. The co-op has been very successful over the years and has a large retail seafood business in the summer months. The harbor is home to several large groundfish vessels that fish out into the Gulf of Maine. On the harbor, but in the town of West Boothbay, is the state's Marine Resources Laboratory and research boats. The old National Marine Fisheries Service complex adjacent to the DMR facility has been leased to a private marine biological laboratory, Bigelow, which employs some 75 scientists and technicians. There is also a Coast Guard station on McKown Point with 23 men and two 44-foot patrol boats.

Bailey Island is in the town of Harpswell at the northeastern end of Casco Bay. It is connected by bridge to Orr's Island, which in turn is connected by bridge to Great Island, which, again, is linked by bridge to the mainland near Brunswick. Bailey Island itself has a population of about 400 year-round residents. The excellent harbor is named Mackerel Cove. There are about 40 large lobsterboats berthed here, with about the same number of skiff fishermen in the summer. There are two lobster buyers, but there is no fishermen's co-op.

Portland is Maine's largest city and its largest fishing port. It is the transportation hub of the state, the largest manufacturing center and medical focal point. It has a magnificent setting on Casco Bay, which extends for 20 miles and encompasses about 200 islands, many of them inhabited year-round. Although Portland itself has only about 62,000 population, the greater Portland area encompasses about 184,000 people. The port infrastructure is large and varied. Portland is not, however, home to that many lobstermen. There are only about 75 full-time lobstermen, with another 150 or so skiff fishermen in the summer. Of course, the surrounding areas, including the inhabited islands, increase the Casco Bay lobstermen ranks considerably. As in other Maine localities, there are lobster "territories" within Casco Bay. Portlanders fish the western side of the bay. Men from Harpswell keep to their waters, and the lobstermen of Chebeague, Long Island, and Jewell Island have their own fishing zones. There are eight places in Portland where fishermen can sell their lobsters, not including direct sales to restaurants. There are no so-called lobster dealers in

Portland—that is, dealers who buy lobsters exclusively and supply the lobstermen with bait, fuel, and other supplies. Probably because of the many businesses and overall competitiveness, the lobstermen prefer to trade where they can get the best prices.

Cape Porpoise is located two miles northeast of Kennebunkport and is part of that town. The entrance from the ocean is a narrow dredged channel, which the U.S. Army Corps of Engineers tries desperately to keep cleared of lobster buoys. The most important fishery is lobstering, with about 75 summertime fishermen. Half of these are in the skiff mosquito fleet. The harbor has six lobster buyers, although they are small operators. With one exception, they do business from floats anchored in the harbor.

As can be seen, the lobsterfishing ports are as different in character as the men who sustain the industry and the families who live on their shores. Yet the people of lobsterfishing communities have a common bond, although their independence belies that fact. They like where they live and defend those roots with uncommon tenacity when their life is challenged by encroaching civilization or "from away" meddlers. Their idiorhythmic hamlets, large or small, are their business, and nobody should pry from without or prattle from within. And yet, their communities are too rich in love to ignore.

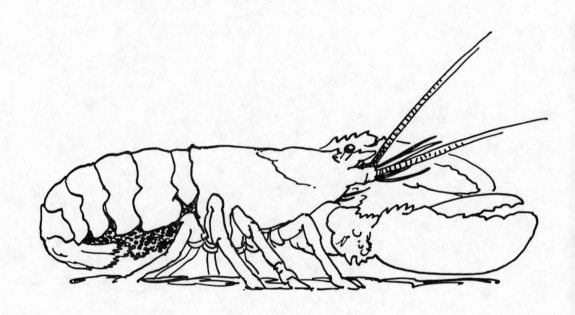

NINE

The Eating

There must be 10,000 recipes for cooking and eating lobster. Every chef from Paris to Kansas City has his best method for separating the true lobster flavor into unrecognizable parts. You name it—they got it. The Galloping Gourmet, Graham Kerr, suggests Langouste Flambe. Imagine sitting down at a quaint Maine dockside restaurant and the waitress serves your lobster covered with brandy and flaming like a brush fire.

Out in California in a restaurant named Bernstein's on Fisherman's Wharf, where they should know better, a dish called Lobster Princess is served. The formula should stay there. The ingredients include salt, pepper, cayenne, butter, shallots, sherry, prepared mustard, cream sauce, eggs, artichoke heart, and grated Parmesan cheese. The lobster, obviously, hasn't got a chance.

The flavor mutilation of lobster is not strictly a modern-day ritual. In the 1914 edition of Fannie Merritt Farmer's *Boston Cooking School Cookbook* there is a recipe for Lobster a la Muisset. In this French exercise, lobsters are cut into parts (shell and all— and alive!) and the parts are simmered in this: shallots, chopped carrots, butter, sprigs of thyme, bay leaf, red peppers, brown stock, stewed tomatoes, and sherry wine. Remove the concoction to platter, pour brandy on top, and sprinkle with finely chopped olives. F'shame, Fannie.

Even an "official" Maine seafood cookbook gets into lobster assination, suggesting lobster casserole with mustard and white bread crusts. And continuing with state gourmets, the summit of humiliation for a Maine lobster, a newburg recipe calling for a teaspoon of the commercial flavor enhancer, Ac'cent.

Even the prestigious International Marine Publishing Company has a Maine seafood cookbook with such head turners as lobster stuffed peppers, lobster cutlets, a lobster loaf (with canned corn and chopped pickles, for heaven's sake), and mock lobster salad containing no lobster at all—two haddock fillets are supposed to pull the seaweed over the eater's eyes.

Oh, dear.

Well, there is only one best way to cook lobsters. Even lobstermen, if their backs were pushed to the absolute wall, would choose this method. We must remember that lobstermen can have lobsters anytime they choose. And 8,500 fishermen can't be wrong—can they?

A kettle of sufficient size, at least twice the volume of the lobsters to be cooked, is used. About three inches of water is poured into the kettle. The very best water is that from the seas from which the lobster came. For a reason. The same chemical makeup such as salts and minerals (taste) are in both the lobster and the water. There is no interchange. Exact same fluids. If seawater is not available, then tap water will have to do and in some places tap water is simply horrible. It might be better to cook the lobster in bottled soda water; the sugar imparts a somewhat sweeter taste. It's a helluva lot better than chlorine. Cookbooks almost to a one say to use salt in the cooking water. If you use seawater this is obviously not necessary. If you use fresh water, it really isn't either. In cooking, actually steaming, the steam does not permeate the lobster meat. It cooks by convection. The skeleton of the lobster is on the outside, remember?

The lobsters should be fresh, and that brings up a rather complicated subject. Just because lobsters are alive, and they should be, doesn't necessarily mean they are fresh. Lobsters that lie around in holding tanks and the like take on a musty flavor from their waste accumulations at the bottom of the tanks. Lobsters traveling for four days in refrigerated whatnots for transportation are not fresh. But these are the lobsters that most people are confronted with, unless they happen to live in Maine or other lobster places where fresh means getting them off the lobsterboat.

Back to the pot. The covered kettle should be brought to what is called a "ril'n br'l." This is when the steam is trying to blow the kettle top to the ceiling and the whole cauldron is hissing like a nest of angry snakes. Wait five minutes after you think you've achieved a "ril'n br'l." The lobsters are put into the steaming kettle very carefully, head first and making sure the tail is tucked beneath their stomachs. The reason is that lobsters don't especially care for this last swim and they sometimes quickly react by flexing their tails. If not headed downward, head first, into the kettle, you could get a tail scoop of third-degree water in your face.

Lobsters plunged and kettle cover on, there will be a few thumps and knocks and strange noises from inside the kettle, and squeamish guests will leave the room. Nobody knows for sure whether lobsters "feel" this cooking business or not. They have a brain the size of a split pea, so probably pain to them is not like pain to us. Some people say lobsters experience excruciating pain. They suggest putting them in a kettle of cold water and bringing it to a boil. The same folks would probably kill a stockyard steer by pulling out all his hair strand by strand.

While the pain theory is discussed around cocktails, the lobsters die very quickly and begin to turn red. Six lobsters should have turned red and be ready to eat in 10 minutes. Most cookbooks say to boil them 20 minutes. That's because instructions say to fill the kettle half full of water. Dumb. Steam cooks quicker than water. The quicker you cook anything, the better.

Lobsters are eaten with "drawn" butter—a strange and mysterious designation for melted butter that has become very much associated with lobsters. Butter is also clarified—that is, melted and kept quite warm for a bit, allowing the salt to settle to the bottom. Some people, usually from away, like lemon in their butter, and some people, those at home, like a splash of vinegar in their butter. A few homes and aways don't like butter at all. More the pity.

Lobsters should be eaten with all rules barred. Cracking, breaking, sucking, slurping, spilling, and questioning are all perfectly accepted etiquette in lobster eating. The best advice given to a lobster eater is—don't give up. There is just one more morsel hiding there under a piece of shell. Everything in a lobster is good to eat. City cookbooks warn of eating the lobster head and brains. They eat calf brains, don't they? If you can find a lobster's brain, eat it, it won't harm you a whit. Lobster bodies are full of little surprises. The green stuff, called tomalley, is liver, and it's sumptious. That stringy white stuff is blood and fat and is delicious spread on a cracker if the host didn't forget to place a bowl of saltines on the table. The red stuff is "coral" or eggs. Every leg joint has a sweet socket of meat. Every small leg segment should be sucked like a straw. The biggies are, of course, the two claws and the tail. Maine folks tend to save the tail for last. It probably has something to do with their harsh rural existence. Something like a dog burying a bone. From-away folks eat their tail first and often forget the big claws staring at them from the plate. This comes from eating crayfish, which, of course, do not have claws. A from-away southern crayfish eater thinks there is something phony about two big red claws attached to a Maine steamed lobster. Lobstermen and their families often crack the hot steaming lobster at all its joints as the first eating maneuver. This tradition allows the steam and heat to escape. Maine folks don't take too much time with eating, and the cracking allows them to eat rather rapidly without getting fingers or gullets burned.

For the unfortunate who do not have lobsters every Sunday, the above method is the best buy for your money. Granted, there are other ways to cook lobster. The boiling method is about the same except that the kettle is filled chock full of water. This method is inferior. Boiling water is not as hot as steam. The point is to cook the lobster, not bathe him.

There is baked stuffed lobster. Rich for the rich. Live lobsters are cleaved down the middle (talk about pain) with a sharp, broad chef's knife, and while the poor things are emitting death quivers, a stuffing of rich Ritz crackers, richer butter, a sprinkle of parsley, a splash of cream, and a slug of sherry is squished together. The whole thing is spooned into the cadaver's wounds, and all is baked for half an hour. Unless one is proficient in the bake, the lobsters come out burned on top and raw on the bottom. And dry and wet. Most Maine cooks who bake lobster ask themselves while they are eating them just why they did.

Lobster newburg. Well, you can make newburg out of chipped beef. Why blow $25 worth of lobsters to accommodate a couple of quarts of milk and cream and a few saucy spices?

Lobster stew ain't bad. Maine folks eat a lot of lobster stew. And there is a Maine way to make it. Figure at least a lobster a person. Steam by the Only Way Method, and when the lobsters are cool, shell 'em—shock 'em, the natives say. The tomalley and fat and coral are saved aside from the meat. The lobster shells are then put in a big kettle and smashed up. Cutting in small pieces with heavy kitchen scissors will do. Cover the shells with water and simmer for a couple of hours. Strain through a fine colander or sieve and set the broth aside. A goose egg of butter is melted to bubbles in a big iron spider, the tomalley, fat, and coral are added, and all is brought back to bubbles. The meat is then added and cooked until all is hot and the color is like the setting sun. Dump out all shells from the lobster kettle and dump in the spider full of lobster stew base. Let cool a bit so that the milk, when added, will not curdle. The liquid in lobster stew is up to the cook, but the general rule is one quart of whole milk and a half-pint of half-and-half for each half-pint of lobster broth. Vary the proportions for a thicker or thinner stew to suit. Lobster stew, like all stews, is better left a day. This is rarely possible, but do cook as far ahead of time as you can. When ready for serving, heat the stew to very hot (never boil it or it will curdle) and serve in thick-sided bowls. Salt and pepper should be on the table. And don't put any dumb crackers in the bowl and pour stew over them. Crackers go on the table with sour pickles. To each his own. There is one small, super-secret ingredient that can be added to a lobster stew before heating. A pinch of mint. Never mind the reason, just try it.

The only other lobster cookery worth mentioning, except a clambake, is lobster rolls. Lobster rolls, from the Maine point of view anyway, are made from leftovers. Their ingredients come from the lobster meat left in claws and bodies by guests of Mainers the previous evening. (There is a creeping, revolting practice invading Maine, whereby guests ask for a doggy bag and tuck their uneaten lobster supper in handbags to take home for the morrow's pickings.) The recipe for a Maine lobster roll is fairly simple. Mix the clear meat with just enough mayonnaise to skim the surface. Pile high on a hamburger bun and push the halves together. If no lobster meat squishes out the sides, put in more filling until it does. Serve with cold beer and pickle slivers.

Every cookbook in the world, and some that aren't, have every-which-way recipes on cooking lobster. Try them if you must, but remember that if lobsters were meant to be cooked in tomatoes and green peppers they would have vines growing from their ears.

A lobsterman does not eat that many lobsters. Perhaps he is like the farmer who cleans the hen coop every day and doesn't like omelets. What every lobsterman does love is: fish chowder.

Now, there's a right and wrong way to do anything. But in the case of making a fish chowder, the procedure is absolute and there is not one inch of middle ground. There are only a few people left who know how to make a haddock fish chowder. And damn few who possess the instruments to accomplish it. Anybody can put a skylab in space, but . . . .

The Maine haddock fish chowder is properly prepared on the surface of a Colonial Clarion, six-lid, woodburning kitchen stove blacker than the coal bins of hell. It takes years to learn how to run this five-dampered lady, so don't run out and buy one without including the purchase of a Maine grandmother in the contract.

The main and only ingredients are simple.

Fish. This must be a fresh-caught haddock, between five and eight pounds of it. "Fresh" does not mean shipped in ice to Boston and then back on the Greyhound bus. Take a walk down to the waterfront and do business with a fisherman. He's ornery, but honest. Buy the haddock with the guts out, but head on. This is fisherman style.

Salt Pork. Never, never buy salt pork at a store. It usually comes from Indiana or some strange place like that, where it's rumored that salt-pork pigs are raised. The entire pig is fat, no meat at all. The proper salt pork is found in crocks in farmhouse cellars. The salt pork comes from pigs fed on table scraps, McIntosh apples, acorn squash, and corn cobs. And hickory nuts when the pig does a little traveling. Finding a salt-pork source is like finding a bed of spring May flowers. Keep it to yourself.

Onions. Not from Bermuda or the New Jersey flatlands. No cowboy onions from Texas. The Maine fish chowder demands those small garden onions that bring tears to the eyes of goldfish. There are several thousand bushel in root cellars available for the asking.

Potatoes. Any good variety grown in downeast soil tempered with cow manure and seaweed, a tough act to follow.

Canned milk. What is there to say about canned milk? Except it's there.

Whole milk. It would be nice to intercept the milk on its way from the cow to the waterworks, but this may not be possible. Raw, whole milk from its source has been labeled contraband by the federal government, so about the only alternative is to buy the milk in paper cubes from the corner grocery.

Seasonings—salt, pepper, and bay leaf. The first two are standard offerings, but the bay leaf should be picked from seaside bushes in June, dried between pages of an old book for a couple of months, and then stored in a rubber-tight Mason jar.

That's all there is to it. Any outside persuasion to add or subtract from this formula is a con job.

Every noble Colonial Clarion is mulling along between October and May so it's

not necessary to outline cold-start procedures unless a summer chowder is wanted.

The first step is trying out the salt pork. The Clarion is fed small, split lengths of ash or beech and dampers are set at half-mast. While the stove is gulping wood and breathing tongues of fire, the salt pork is prepared by first cutting off the rind and throwing it to the dog. The neatly marbled pork is then diced into cubes about the size of sugar. The stove is ready when the stovepipe crackles.

It takes exactly three minutes to heat a #8 iron Griswold spider to salt-pork frying temperature. Dump the cubes in all at once. There is a big puff of smoke at first but this settles down to a sizzle when the spider is moved back to a middle lid.

Before cutting up the onions, which takes some courage, break out the chowder companion. Men cooks like beer or ale or a cheese glass of rum. Women cooks pour a healthy slug of sherry. One should never make a Maine fish chowder alone, which is the reason for the companion.

When the pork has reduced itself by a half and is the color of a May weasel, remove the scraps from the spider with a slotted wooden spoon and drain on a brown paper bag. Now is the time to slow down the Clarion with two large pieces of maple. Pour all the excess fat from the pork on top of the maple. Throw the onions in the spider and mix up with the small amount of fat.

While the onions are just glazing, cut the head from the haddock, cover it with water, and start it to boil on front-rear of friend Clarion. Follow through with the fish by cutting it in chunks to fit the pot, covering with cold water, and setting on front-front of stove.

Pour a little companion and peel three fist-and-a-half-size potatoes. Cut into irregular shapes the size of the thumb to the knuckle. Never, ever, make symmetrical or even cuts, as your chowder will look really dumb. Canned dumb.

Make the chowder pot of whatever you like. Blue agate is neat. Dutch ovens are cute but too greasy. Find one at an auction.

Refill your companion and check the fish. It is done when the water just comes to a scummy boil. Remove the fish and cool. Continue boiling the fish head. Boil the hell out of it. Adjust the Clarion's starboard quarter damper if more heat is necessary.

When the fish head stock is whitish and stringy, remove the fish head and give it to the cat. If you have a smart cat, he will not eat it right away, as it takes about two hours for a good haddock head to cool down. Dump the potatoes in the head stock and boil until the potato does not have a hard clunk against the side of the pot.

Now, dump the onions, potatoes, and head stock in your chowder kettle. Separate the haddock from its bones and skin and add to the kettle. Allow this ambrosian chowder base to cool slightly and marry into eternal bliss while you and your companion drink a toast to those who have gone down to the sea in ships, give me a star to steer her by, or whatever.

Canned milk is added to the cooled mixture by eye. The milk should just take up the water, which is a procedure impossible to describe in human language. You'll just know.

Whole milk is added according to your pleasure for thick or thin. You'll just know.

The pork scraps, which have been draining on the paper bag, are now crunchy little morsels and melt in your mouth like malted milk balls. Resist the urge to eat them like peanuts and instead dump them into the kettle with a goose egg of creamery butter. Batten down all the Clarion dampers and move the kettle amidships. When the butter has melted and spread across the kettle like a yellow sea dotted with pork scrap South Sea tropical islands, only then, is the Maine haddock fish chowder done.

Salt, pepper, and bay leaf are added. The chowder is removed from the Clarion and placed in the pantry on a maple trivet where it will cool and the honeymoon will continue for at least 12 hours.

With a glance at the exasperated cat stalking a tepid fish head, a nod to the dog chomping on a rubbery pork rind, a pat on the Colonial Clarion's bottom, and a final salute to your companion, there is nothing now left of the chowder ritual but agonizing anticipation for the arrival of tomorrow.

TEN

The Future

There are many who predict the near future demise of the lobster and the lobsterman. In fairness, only time will tell, but perhaps Mark Twain should be around today to say for the lobster that the report of his death was an exaggeration. The prediction by many biologists and fishery managers in the 1960s was that the lobster industry could not survive another decade under the increasing pressures of overfishing. And yet, in 1982 and 1983, the Maine landings remained a constant reported 22 million pounds.

True, new lobstermen enter the fishery but many also leave. There seems to be a leveling of effort in the past few years. For a fisherman to subsist on lobsterfishing alone, he must make a tremendous financial investment in this inflation-loaded, high-interest era unique in the history of this country.

It appears that the heritage of lobsterfishing will be passed along through families who have earned their namesakes and profession. And this is all well and good. They are the survivors, and they know how to make the lobster a survivor also. For the two coexist in and upon a sea of uncertainty.

Perhaps the greatest threat to the lobster fishery comes from over-regulation. A federal management plan for lobsters was born in 1983. And this year, and every year, self-interest and political groups assault the lobsterman and his prey with more and more laws, most of them having little to do with conservation. Sadly, some lobster scientists offer morbid theories only to perpetuate their tenures. Lobstermen use political jibes and tacks to foster special, provincial fishing regulations. Fishery managers and administrators attempt to appease the masses with rhetoric and grease for the squeaky davit.

Maine, this country's largest lobster producing state, and second in world production only to Maritime Canada, has offered only two legitimate lobster influencing facts in the last 50 years. One, that seawater temperatures affect abundance. And two, that the majority of lobsters are being caught before they mature and lay eggs. There is little that anybody can do about sea temperatures. And the biology of the lobster has been known for a century. That they are being caught before maturity is hardly a startling statistic.

The attempts at lobster management are almost exclusively aimed at what is going on, not what should go on. Scientific programs are redundant and aimed at popularity rather than meaningful probes. Maine, for instance, embarked on still another "tagging" study in 1984 despite the reams of printed documents from other tagging studies that showed unquestionably where and how and when lobsters migrate along the coast. But tagging is a popular project with lobstermen, and the scientists know this.

There are annual bills before the Maine legislature and other legislatures proposing to study lobster trap limits, to set fees for lobster trap tags, to pass special lobstering laws for specific sites, and to require mandatory courses and examinations for entering the fishery. There are initiatives to freeze licenses, set seasons, zone the coastline, close the summer season, restrict boat size, and institute four-day fishing weeks. The next legislature, and the next, will see more proposed restrictions on the fishery. Fishery administrators are asking for and receiving more authority to circumvent the legislative-bill route with its public hearing and instead promulgate rules with little or no advice or consent from the industry as a whole. The circumvention of the right-to-know-and-participate principle is perhaps the most dangerous bureaucratic design applied to the lobster fishery in the past quarter century.

And yet, and yet, the beautiful Maine lobster lives his secluded and mysterious life burrowed down in a rocky crevice or dark hole, paying no mind to the doomsayers and experts who presume to speak for him. He is a cool character—holding his own against incredible odds.

A Kittery Point lobsterman was asked once if lobstering was going to hell.

"Every day, every day, sonny, but we start afresh every morning."

Tough to destroy a philosophy like that.

Bibliography

Acheson, James M., Ann W. Acheson, John R. Bort, and James Lello. *The Fishing Ports of Maine and New Hampshire: 1978.* Orono, Maine: Maine Sea Grant Publications, 1980.

American Lobster Fishery Management Plan. Saugus, Massachusetts: New England Fishery Management Council, March 1983.

Anthony, V.C. and J.F. Caddy (editors). *Proceedings of the Canada-U.S. Workshop on the Status of Assessment Science for the N.W. Atlantic Lobster* (Homarus americanus) *Stocks, St. Andrews, N.B. October 24–26, 1978.* Canadian Technical Report of Fisheries and Aquatic Sciences No. 932. St. Andrews, New Brunswick: Department of Fisheries and Oceans Biological Station, March 1980.

Berrill, Michael. "Lobster Tales." *Natural History* magazine (American Museum of Natural History), Aug.–Sept. 1976.

Dow, Robert L., Frederick W. Bell, and Donald Harriman. *Bio-Economic Relationships for the Maine Lobster Fishery with Considerations of Alternative Management Schemes.* Seattle, Washington: NOAA Technical Report NMFS SSRF-683, March 1975.

Krouse, Jay S. *Movement, Growth and Mortality of American Lobsters,* Homarus americanus, *Tagged along the Coast of Maine.* NOAA Technical Report NMFS SSRF-747, September 1981.

Lunt, Richard K. "Lobsterboat Building on the Eastern Coast of Maine, a Comprehensive Study." Ph.D. diss., Indiana University, 1975.

Maine Marine Resources Laws. Hallowell, Maine: Maine Department of Marine Resources Biennial Publication, 1982.

Prudden, T.M. *About Lobsters.* Freeport, Maine: Cumberland Press, Inc., 1973.

Sheldon, William W. and Robert L. Dow. "Trap Contributions to Losses in the American Lobster Fishery." U.S. Fishery Bulletin 73(2):449–451. 1975.

Thomas, James C., Clarence Burke, Gary Robinson, and David Parkhurst, Jr. "Catch and Effort Information on the Maine Commercial Lobster *(Homarus americanus)* Fishery 1967 through 1981." West Boothbay Harbor, Maine: Maine Department of Marine Resources Lobster Informational Leaflet #12, July 1983.

Bangor

Belfast

Ellsworth

Islesboro

Penobscot Bay

Deer Isle

Isle Au Haut

Vinalhaven

Swans Island

Frenchboro

Bass Harbor

Tremont

Cranberry Isles

Winter Harbor

Prospect Harbor

Corea

Petit

Mi.
10   20

10   20   30
Km.